Voices on Word Matters

VOICES ON WORD MATTERS
Learning About Phonics and Spelling in the Literacy Classroom

edited by
Irene C. Fountas
Gay Su Pinnell

with chapters by
Billie J. Askew
David Booth
Diane E. DeFord
Dorothy P. Hall and Patricia M. Cunningham
Justina Henry
Susan Hundley and Diane Powell
Carol Brennan Jenkins
Carol A. Lyons
Andrea McCarrier and Ida Patacca
William Stokes
Sandra Wilde
Barbara Joan Wiley
Jerry Zutell

HEINEMANN
Portsmouth, NH

Heinemann
A division of Reed Elsevier Inc.
361 Hanover Street
Portsmouth, NH 03801–3912

Offices and agents throughout the world

The author and publisher thank those who generously gave permission to reprint borrowed material:

Figure 2-6 from *Word Matters: Teaching Phonics and Spelling in the Reading/Writing Classroom* by Gay Su Pinnell and Irene C. Fountas (Heinemann, A division of Reed Elsevier Inc., Portsmouth, NH, 1998).

Figure 7-7 from *Inside the Writing Portfolio: What We Need to Know to Assess Children's Writing* by Carol Brennan Jenkins (Heinemann, A division of Reed Elsevier Inc., Portsmouth, NH, 1996).

Excerpt from "A Pizza the Size of the Sun" by Jack Prelutsky. Text Copyright 1996 by Jack Prelutsky. By permission of Green Willow Books, a division of William Morrow & Co., Ltd.

Excerpt from *Pigs Aplenty, Pigs Galore!* by David McPhail. Copyright © 1993 by David McPhail. Used by permission of Dutton Children's Books, a division of Penguin Putnam Inc.

Library of Congress Cataloging-in-Publication Data

CIP is on file with the Library of Congress.
ISBN 0-325-00132-4

Editor: Lois Bridges
Production: Melissa L. Inglis
Cover design: Darci Mehall/Aureo Design
Manufacturing: Louise Richardson

Printed in the United States of America on acid-free paper

03   ML   6 7 8 9

We dedicate this book to our friends and colleagues

who joined with us in contributing their voices to word matters.

Contents

Acknowledgments

This book is the product of conversation and collaborative thinking. Its composition began when a group of academics met at the International Reading Association to share the responsibility for a symposium on spelling. That experience revealed common concerns and goals and provided a forum for sharing approaches and ideas for good classroom practice. We wish to acknowledge the members of that IRA symposium, many of whom co-authored this book, and we also thank colleagues who joined the conversation later by contributing chapters. This collection reflects a richness and diversity of perspectives and ideas, which we were privileged to compile and edit.

The collaboration included extensive work with the editorial team at Heinemann. This collaborative work included many late night conversations by both telephone and electronic mail. We express heartfelt thanks to Mike Gibbons and Lois Bridges who helped immeasurably in planning and making decisions about this book. Their guidance and good thinking are gratefully acknowledged. We also appreciate the work of Renee Le Verrier, director of production, Roberta Lew, permissions editor, and especially Melissa Inglis, whose attention to detail sustains the high quality of Heinemann's publications.

We also thank the teachers on whose work this volume is based. Every author speaks from experience in classrooms and from observation of and interaction with skilled and highly professional elementary teachers. We appreciate their work and its contributions to our collective knowledge. In particular, we wish to express our thanks to Kate Bartley, Mark Canner, Amy Davis, Florence

Metcalf, Irma Napoleon, Ida Patacca, Pat Prime, Stephanie Ripley, Kate Roth, Susan Sullivan, Kristen Thomas, Jean Westin, and Melissa Wilson, with whom we worked directly during the production of this book. A special note of appreciation is given to Bunny Meyer, who has always opened the doors of her school to enthusiastically support research and collaboration in the form of professional development that will benefit all children.

To colleagues at our two educational institutions, Lesley College and The Ohio State University, we express continuing appreciation for the brilliance of their work: Lisa Brandt, Diane DeFord, Rose Mary Estice, Mary Fried, Paige Furgerson, Peg Gwyther, Justina Henry, Sue Hundley, Alice Kearney, Sandra Lowry, Carol Lyons, Andrea McCarrier, Denise Morgan, Diane Powell, and Joan Wiley. We gratefully acknowledge the high quality teacher education that connects theory and practice and provides a backdrop for this book. We also acknowledge the contributions of Polly Taylor, Heather Kroll, and Jennifer Gleason for their communication and general support throughout this effort.

Our work at Lesley College and OSU has been supported over the years by philanthropic organizations interested in providing literacy opportunities for children. We express gratitude to the Charles A. Dana Foundation, the Martha Holden Jennings Foundation, the Noyce Foundation, and the John D. and Catherine T. MacArthur Foundation. Without their investment in the future, this work would not be possible.

Conceptualizing a book like this one, and working with the wonderful group of contributors, was made possible for us because we have had the opportunity to learn from great teachers and scholars, and we express appreciation to Martha L. King, Charlotte S. Huck, and Marie M. Clay for their wisdom. We also thank special friends Uri Treisman and Ken Wilson, both scholars who have shared with us a vision of the future. To Ann Bowers, Penny Noyce, and Joan Wylie of the Noyce Foundation, we express appreciation for the difference their work is making for children.

Finally, our families and friends, especially Catherine Fountas and Elfrieda Pinnell, as well as Ron Melhado and Ron Heath, continue to make their unlimited contributions of love and support and for this we are truly grateful. We also thank Madeleine Gifford, and her mother Beth Gifford, who gave us her writing as a window on her thinking about literacy.

I.C.F.
G.S.P.

Introduction

Every year, new teachers enter classrooms, ready to teach five-, six-, seven-, and eight-year-old children to read and write. Most of us during the first weeks of our early teaching careers were concerned about filling the days with activity—keeping children busy, orderly, and productive. We hoped that the children would like us, that they would find school pleasant, and that we could converse with them in friendly ways. But most of all, we hoped they would learn to read and write. It was not too hard to find activities to fill the day, but we soon learned that teaching was more than keeping children busy. We learned that our challenge was to help individual children learn literacy within a group setting. Finding powerful ways to support children's literacy learning has remained a challenge for teachers throughout the history of education.

Parents, educators, and policy makers search for the one best approach or even the one best activity that will ensure literacy. Yet studies continually remind us that reading and writing are complex processes and becoming literate is a multifaceted endeavor, unique for every young child. The curriculum that we create, the teaching and learning interactions that we foster in the classroom, the materials we choose—all must support this learning in all its complexity.

Voices on Word Matters is a volume of readings that range from detailed observations of individual children in reading and writing to analyses of classroom processes. The authors of this book focus on children's learning about letters, sounds, and words in the primary years. Letter and word learning is explored in a variety of reading, writing, and language contexts. This book has an important companion volume, *Word Matters: Teaching Phonics and Spelling in the Reading/Writing Classroom.* Together, the two volumes provide a wide range of practical ideas to use in classrooms, syntheses of research to help us conceptualize the classroom program, and close looks at children that extend our understandings of the reading and writing processes.

In Section 1, we provide two chapters focusing on word solving as a process. In Chapter 1, Pinnell discusses how we as teachers can observe reading and writing behavior for evidence of children's learning about letters, sounds, and words. In Chapter 2, Fountas presents a three-strand model for conceptualizing a curriculum that will provide for both breadth and depth in children's development of word-solving strategies.

The chapters in Section 2 focus on the context of writing. Wiley provides an introduction to a powerful instructional approach—interactive writing—that, along with other valuable learning opportunities, provides children with an explicit model of how a writer constructs words while writing an extended text. The procedures used in interactive writing are further extended by Henry, who describes the connections between what children learn in interactive writing and how they use those understandings independently in their own writing. McCarrier and Patacca take us into a kindergarten and describe three contexts that support children's learning about letters, sounds, and how words work. Lyons' chapter helps us to better understand the complexities of letter learning and provides a rationale for broad-based learning. Jenkins gives us a detailed picture of a child learning to spell and provides important principles for effective spelling assessment that informs teaching. Taken together, the chapters in Section 2 give direction and inspiration for creating a dynamic curriculum for teaching children about letters, words, and the writing process.

Section 3 focuses on learning about language. The writers describe ways to help children direct their attention to aspects of language from the language play that they enjoy so much and to discover important patterns in the way words are connected. Booth presents language and word play as a foundation for literacy learning. Zutell provides a definition, description, and examples of word sorting, an effective way of helping children derive knowledge of spelling patterns. Hall and Cunningham introduce the concept of multilevel learning so that teachers can effectively include all of the children in word learning, and they describe successful techniques such as using word charts, word walls, and word sorts. DeFord describes the vital connections that learners make in language and literacy learning. As the chapters in this section indicate, when children are engaged in word study, they are learning more than words. They are learning generative ways to work with words so they have the tools to expand their knowledge.

In Section 4, the authors focus on the ways in which children learn about letters and words as they read. Askew takes a close look at how young readers use problem-solving skills while reading text. Hundley and Powell describe how shared reading can help beginners develop important early reading behaviors such as word-by-word matching and noticing words within text. The emphasis in this section is on helping children develop a self-extending system for reading that improves and expands through use.

In Section 5, we examine research on spelling and reading over the past decades. Wilde reports evidence on how children learn to spell, and Stokes reports evidence on how children learn to read. If we do not have a sense of history, we are imprisoned in our own experience and, perhaps, the latest instructional fad. Our lack of historical perspective drives us to revisit the same tired arguments and failed programs again and again. If we are to design programs that serve all children successfully, we need to constructively build together over time, evaluating and reflecting as we go. Starting over year after year with the latest "instructional innovation" will not work—nor will "eclectic" approaches that provide some of this and some of that in a fragmented way. In this book, authors have shared many voices on word matters, with the goal of creating reading/writing classrooms in which all children become word solvers. To move forward toward this goal will require using our voices as teachers to move beyond debate to a coherent vision and sound practice.

Throughout this book, we emphasize the power of language as a tool for learning. And, learning applies not only to children but to ourselves as teachers. We believe that effective teaching of word solving begins with the foundation of our own professional understanding. No set of materials or prescription can precisely tailor a program that helps the children in your class to use what they know in the process of word solving. The sections of this book provide perspectives on various aspects of the curriculum suggested by the model—reading, writing, and word study—that will help children learn about language in connected ways. For every chapter, suggestions for professional development provide some ideas for the learning conversations that can take place among teachers to support the development of a dynamic and effective word-solving curriculum. We hope that teachers will use the suggestions as a support for their work and their collegiality. It is through talking with each other that we can strengthen our voices on important matters related to children's learning to read and write. There is no more important matter.

I.C.F.
G.S.P.

A High-Quality Literacy Program:
Make Way for Letters and Words

Word solving is the ability to take words apart while reading for meaning and to construct words while writing to communicate. Taking words apart while reading includes what is commonly called "phonics." Constructing words in writing is spelling. In both writing and reading, word solvers use a range of skills.

In Section 1 of this book, we explore word solving—how children learn word solving and how teachers can help them. Some key strategies are making connections between words—through letter-sound relationships, visual patterns, and meaning. As word solvers, children are active investigators of words and become interested in making those connections and learning how words work. In the process, they develop a powerful knowledge of principles and strategies they can use again in many other settings. Our observation of reading and writing behavior helps us discover what children know and what they nearly know as a basis for determining what they need to know next.

Phonics and spelling are important components of a rich literacy and language program that involves children in a wide range of literacy activities. In creating a literacy curriculum we must make matches between our knowledge of the reading and writing process, including word-solving strategies and their development, and our own observations and analyses of children's competencies and needs. As teachers, our knowledge of the linguistic system and how it works is key. We can help children develop word solving as we read aloud to them, engage them in guided reading, or enable them to read for themselves. Likewise, we can support word-solving strategies in writing as we involve children in language experience, interactive writing, and independent writing.

Finally, we propose a model that helps us think of the word-solving curriculum as a three-pronged approach: reading, writing, and word study. All three require attention to words and word elements. The overarching goal is to help children develop the knowledge of principles that they can use while reading and writing continuous text. And throughout the learning day in the literacy-rich classroom, oral language supports understanding so that children can make the connections they need. Learning conversations among children and the teacher foster literacy learning.

Word Solving

Investigating the Properties of Words

Gay Su Pinnell

Introduction

Word solving is a language process within reading and writing; that is, word solving involves taking words apart in reading and spelling words in writing. We find the roots of word solving in children's oral language experiences at home and at school. Their word-solving abilities are expanded as they develop phonological and orthographic awareness. Reading and writing provide contexts within which children use their growing knowledge of letters, sounds, and words. Observation of behavior within reading and writing is fundamental for learning what children know about word solving.

Achieving power over language and through language begins as infants learn that making sounds is connected to making things happen in their world. Very young children, even though they cannot talk as an adult would, nevertheless accomplish a wide range of purposes with language. They are gaining the power associated with words. As users of a language, we know hundreds of thousands of words and can use those words to construct oral and written texts that communicate meaning to others and accomplish our purposes.

Words are the building blocks of the larger stretches of meaningful oral and writ-

ten language. Alone, an individual word has meaning because it is part of the inventory of language knowledge that we have, but words are seldom used in isolation. When placed in a text—a political speech, a conversation among friends or family, a poem, a novel, the title of a piece of art—the word becomes powerful. Our history and customs are recorded in words. We use words when we talk and when we write and read. When children learn to talk, they become skillful users of words. As teachers of literacy, we have the opportunity to extend children's language learning by assisting them in discovering the processes of writing and reading. Along the way, they become users of written words and they become word solvers who can:

■ Recognize words.
■ Take words apart while reading for meaning.
■ Spell or construct words while writing to communicate.

Word solvers know the inner workings of words (how words work) and they can use that knowledge in the service of meaningful reading and writing.

To coin a phrase based on the title of this book, words do *matter*. It is essential for us as teachers to find ways to help children become word solvers. We define word solving as "a dynamic process in which the learner actively investigates how words work. Word solving is not just word learning. Its power lies in the discovery of the principles underlying the construction of the words that make up a written language" (Pinnell and Fountas 1998, 23). Along with the co-authors of this book, my concern is to discover how children *learn* how to be word solvers and how we can *teach* them to become word solvers.

A Foundation of Oral Language

Words make up language, which is primarily an oral system. Word solving as we define it in this book is built upon a rich foundation of oral language. It is sad when young children find themselves involved in drills and exercises with letters and sounds when they have never experienced a dynamic and meaningful connection between letters, sounds, and the language that they speak. Oral language expansion is a critical component of the good preschool, kindergarten, and elementary program. Children use language as a tool for learning across the curriculum, and they use language to tell about themselves.

One of our major goals as primary teachers is to support children's language development. Oral language is the foundation of literacy learning. Reading and writing are meaningful and purposeful because they represent and extend the oral language system.

Language is a gateway to new concepts, a means of sorting out confusions, a way to interact with people, a way to get help, a way to test out what one knows. Language enters into every activity we can envisage. It is the source of much pleasure for the child and the adult. It is a pervasive, persuasive, perpetual fountain of learning—and there is no equipment that will give the children the interactive experiences that will power their progress (Cazden 1988).

It is true that computer software and mechanical toys are achieving an interactive

quality that fascinates and delights both children and adults. Cazden (1988) notes, however, that our greatest technology is still the language we speak.

Oral language is the primary resource for children as they set out to learn about words. Their knowledge expands rapidly as they interact in conversation with adults. In addition, some of the first, most enjoyable, activities in sensitizing young children to oral language are the repeated experiences with songs and poems that they love to hear and say again and again. Parents and caregivers provide these early experiences and they are integral to good teaching in preschool and primary classrooms.

Using Phonological and Orthographic Information

Word solvers use letter-sound relationships as an important part of the processes involved in both reading and writing. The word *phonics* has traditionally been used to mean breaking the code that links spoken words—with their sequence of phonemes (sounds)—to the sequence of graphic symbols (letters) that appear on the page (see Stokes, Chapter 15). In writing, word solving means *spelling*. Writers, as they spell words, also make connections between the sequence of phonemes in spoken words and the graphic symbols that they write in sequence. In both reading and writing the relationships between oral and written words are much more complex than the letter and sound connections. Underlying graphic patterns in spelling, for example, signal meaning without being connected to sound. In reading, word analysis may take into account the same kinds of patterns. Phonological and orthographic awareness are considered basic bodies of knowledge that are keys to the process of solving words in both simple and complex ways.

Phonological Awareness
The phonological system of the language is the sound system. Oral language is conveyed

FIGURE 1-1 Children and Teacher Reading a Rhyme Together

by people's ability to make and understand sounds. Children become aware that words are made up of sounds—for example, when they can tell that one word "sounds" like another. We call that the development of phonological awareness. There is more to phonological awareness than identifying particular sounds in words, although that process is an important key to learning about words. Children also learn that words have more than one part (syllable) and that there are common clusters of sounds that tend to go together, such as at the beginning of words (like *street*). Phonological awareness means that children can connect words; can tell what sound comes first, next, and last; can tell when a word part sounds like another word in some way.

How do children develop awareness of sounds? Much is accomplished in the simple everyday kinds of activities that delight young children—like hearing and joining in on songs, rhymes, and chants; singing the alphabet song; and playing games (see Booth, Chapter 8). Knowing that words are made up of sequences of sounds is a big advantage to children entering the world of literacy; this "phonological awareness" or "awareness

of phonemes" refers to hearing and saying the words orally as part of language. Sometimes people talk about phonological awareness synonymously with "phonics," which is the relationship between letters and sounds. Phonological awareness actually refers only to oral language.

Orthographic Awareness

The orthographic system is the spelling system of the language. It is the way the symbols are arranged in patterns that can be connected to the words of the language. The graphic signs, or *graphemes*, are the letters that we use to construct words. Letters, by themselves, have no meaning (unless we are talking about a one-letter word like *a*). Grouped in patterns, according to the rules of the language, they make up the units of meaning in the language. We call the smallest unit of meaning a *morpheme*, and it may be a morpheme like *rain* that has meaning as it stands alone, or a morpheme like *ing* that does not stand alone but adds meaning to words. Morphemes are the building blocks of the words that form our lexical system—the words we know. Some words, such as nouns (*hat, coat*), have meaning; others, such as articles (*the, then*), have a function in the ways we put together sentences. The rules of *syntax* form the basis for mapping out our meanings onto words arranged in rule-governed ways into phrases and sentences and larger units of text.

Learning about words means learning how words work, how patterns of letters go together in complex ways. One of the skills young readers and writers develop is making connections between sounds and letters (see Wilde, Chapter 14). But two kinds of knowledge must be coordinated for this skill to be developed:

■ The child hears the sound.[1]
■ The child ascertains what makes a letter different from every other letter.

Orthographic awareness is the ability to notice and use critical features of the graphic symbols in the written language. In other words, children need to learn what makes a letter unique, and often these features are very finely drawn. How much difference, for example, is there between *m* and *n* or *h* and *n*? The differences are quite small and children need to learn what to look for when they are writing or reading words. The visual perception of letters is a challenge, but we are not just talking about letters in isolation. Letters are embedded in words and words are embedded in text. So, the real challenge for learners is to use phonological and orthographic information when they are reading and writing continuous text (see Lyons, Chapter 6).

Word Solving in Reading

Readers are processing written text, using many different sources of information simultaneously. For example, they are always bringing their prior knowledge, gained from life experience, to the understanding of a text. They are using the language systems that they have developed all of their lives. Their eyes are looking at words and capturing visual features (letters, letter clusters, word parts) that help them read the words with accuracy and check on their predictions. All of this information—language, experience, visual (print) features—is used together in a smooth and coordinated way.

Competent readers know most of the words that they read instantly; they give little attention to word solving or word recognition because the knowledge is there. Even competent readers, however, sometimes need to slow down and analyze an unfamiliar word. It is rare for us as adults to need to solve words, and then we do it rapidly and with only minimal attention. We are word solvers who can:

■ Recognize whole words without conscious attention.

■ Read a word without attending to every part of the word—using salient features picked up rapidly.

■ Connect new words to known words.

■ Use parts of words.

■ Use roots of words that have meaning (such as *phon*).

■ Connect spelling of words with meaning (signaling meaning by the way they are spelled—*there* and *their*).

All of these word-solving strategies are part of a reading process that we have developed. When young children learn to read, they must ultimately learn to read and solve words (see Askew, Chapter 12).

Using Running Records to Analyze Word Solving

A running record is a way of coding reading behavior, scoring the accuracy of reading,

---

[1]Deaf children, who cannot hear sounds, relate oral and written language by attending to orthographic features. They connect those features to signed words or to the vocal movement of the mouth, tongue, etc. Deaf children do learn to read, but the task is quite a challenge.

and analyzing the way a reader processes a text.[2] The analysis provides a way to gather information about a reader, building a portrait of growth and change over time through periodic collections of running records of reading behavior. The teacher observes the reader in a way that both can see the text, and the teacher makes "shorthand" notes using a coding system on a form or blank piece of paper. Running records are quick and convenient because they provide a great deal of information without having the teacher tape the reading to listen to later or type out the text prior to assessment. In the examples here we have provided the words below the coded reading behavior so that you can interpret the examples, but in actual practice you take running records by simply looking at the text the child is reading and recording behavior on a form or blank piece of paper. Running records would not be used to record and analyze the reading of lists of individual words.

To code the reading behavior, the teacher makes a mark for each word in the text. For example, the symbol (✓) indicates an accurately read word. The coding system also allows for marking behavior such as substitutions, omissions, insertions, and repetitions. Although the teacher codes by marking each word, the whole record shows reading of continuous text. The analysis enables you to look at word solving in relation to the child's use of language and meaning. We are looking at the way the reader processes all the information *together* while reading words in a text.

Figure 1-2 shows Antoine's reading of *The Hole in Harry's Pocket* (Bloksberg 1995). This story is about a little boy who loses and then finds the money his mother has given him. It is a Level I[3] text, approximately the end of first-grade reading as defined on a gradient of text difficulty. The reading is shown here in a running record.

Even this short segment of Antoine's reading provides ample evidence that he is becoming a word solver. He was reading with a high level of accuracy, keeping his attention on the meaning of the story. Accurate reading is an indication that readers are self-monitoring, or checking on themselves while reading, to be sure that what they are reading makes sense, looks right, and sounds right.

Antoine immediately recognized most of the words in the story, which indicates that he has been building a large body of words that he knows. He substituted *curve* for *curb*, using print information as indicated by his consistency with the first three letters of the word. He also used language structure and meaning. His substitution made sense. There is only a small phonological difference between *curve* and *curb*. In his oral language, he may have actually called the curb a *curve*, or he may simply have been using a word he had heard before and that sounded like it might fit visually as well as make sense.

Although we cannot know for sure what is happening in the child's head, running records provide ongoing information that enables teachers to hypothesize about the kinds of word solving going on. The important evidence is that the reader is actively searching for and using what he knows in

---

[2]Three sources for learning more about running records are (1) *An Observation Survey of Early Literacy Achievement* (Clay 1993a). Marie Clay is the developer of the technique known as the running record. In this comprehensive book, she provides the research base for running records as well as thorough directions for coding, scoring, and analyzing records of reading behavior. (2) *Knowing Literacy: Constructive Literacy Assessment* (Johnston 1997). Peter Johnston provides valuable information about the running record, including many examples and directions. (3) *Guided Reading: Good First Teaching for All Children* (Fountas and Pinnell 1996). In this book we provide directions for taking running records and using them in guided reading.

[3]This level indicates that the book is part of a guided reading collection organized into a gradient. Levels begin with A, very simple texts that we might expect kindergarten children to begin reading, and cover the range of reading levels in the primary grades (see Fountas and Pinnell 1996).

Antoine's Reading of *The Hole in Harry's Pocket*

				Error	SC

√ √ √ √ √
Harry   liked   to   walk   to

√ √ √ √ √
the   store.   He   liked   to

√ √ √ curve
hop   on   the   curb.   Ⓜ Ⓢ Ⓥ

√ √ √ √ √ √ √ √
He   liked   to   look   in   all   the   windows

√ √ √ √ √ side- √
and   count   cracks   in   the   sidewalk.

√ √ √ √ √ √ √
Harry   got   the   milk.   But   when   he

√ √ √ √ √ √ √
looked   for   his   money,   it   was   gone!

Where | SC   can | SC   √   √ R   Ⓜ Ⓢ Ⓥ   M Ⓢ V
What   could   he   do?   Ⓜ Ⓢ Ⓥ   M S Ⓥ

Key
√ = accurate reading
Errors: child's attempts, including substitutions and parts of words, indicated above the line
R = repeated as indicated by arrow
M = used meaning as a source of information
S = used language structure (syntax) as a source of information
V = used visual information (print features) as a source of information
SC = Self Correction

FIGURE 1-2   Example of Reading Behavior: Antoine's Reading of *The Hole in Harry's Pocket*

the reading process. That searching behavior is essential to becoming a word solver.

We see another example of word solving when Antoine was working out the word *sidewalk*. He first said *side* and then immediately said *sidewalk*. My guess is that he noticed the first part of this multisyllable word and then the last part, putting it all together. Antoine was learning what word solvers do.

Word solvers take words apart while reading; they notice how new words are connected to the words they already know and find parts that will help them.

Finally, we see an example of Antoine's ability to solve words using his knowledge of language structure. He started the sentence by reading *where* for *what* and following that substitution used *can* for *could*. During his first attempt, *where*, he was using visual information—noticing the first letter cluster is evident. Reading the word *can* following the word *where* certainly reflected knowledge of language syntax. It may be that Antoine did not fully attend to visual features of either *what* or *could* but was using some visual information along with language knowledge. He then repeated from the end of the line, reading accurately. He used all sources of information as he proceeded to the next sentence. When he got to the end of the sentence, he probably noticed that what he had read didn't sound right. It didn't fit with his sense of the syntax of language, and that triggered him to look more closely at the sentence. Going back and reading accurately, Antoine was using print information—his words were accurate—as well as language knowledge in a coordinated way.

Word solving while reading continuous text is a complex, coordinated process. It is similar to but different from simply reading a word in isolation. Most teachers have worked with children who read words correctly in isolation on word cards and then miss them while reading a text. It is possible to learn about letters, sounds, and words and still not be able to work that knowledge into the efficient reading of a text. Being a good reader does mean having the skills to identify words in isolation, but it is much more. Word solving serves the reader in constructing meaning from the text.

Word Solving in Writing

Writers, too, use word-solving skills. Writers compose and construct messages on a base of oral language. Their task is to compose messages using both oral and written language, making sure that they match the right form and function of written language to the meaning and purpose of their message. Written language, writers know, is different from oral language in qualitative ways. There are differences in sentence structure and even in words (such as the use of the words *said* or *exclaimed* to produce dialogue). Writers have to keep all of that in mind as they simultaneously compose meaning and write the graphic representation letter by letter, word by word, arranged in order in space on a writing surface. They construct or spell words while mentally constructing meaning as they go. All of these behaviors are smoothly coordinated.

Competent writers have a large body of words that they can quickly and automatically write or type on a computer screen. They appear to be giving most attention to the meaning of the message and little attention to the construction of words; yet, they are constantly monitoring for accuracy. One of the ways they monitor is by reading and rereading what they have written while they are still composing and writing. Of course, after writing, competent writers proofread, checking for accurate spelling and punctuation, as they make sure the message conveys what they want to say.

There are times when writers slow down to consider aspects of words. Even competent writers have to think how to spell words with particular features that they do not have completely under control (such as whether to drop the *e* when moving from *acknowledge* to *acknowledgment* or *judge* to *judgment*). Word solvers in writing sometimes write a word down on paper so they can look at it, asking, "does it look right?" Good spellers have a sense of when a word isn't quite right. They are comparing the word to internally held patterns and checking whether what they have produced matches that pattern.

Of course, nowadays we use spelling checks on the computer, but it's pretty obvious that you have to know a great deal about spelling to be an efficient user of such checking systems. When word solvers in writing want to use a word that they do not know how to spell, they can make good attempts because they are able to use sophisticated skills, such as:

■ Using known words as a base.

■ Thinking about what the word means and connecting to word parts or words that mean the same thing.

▮ Using letter-sound relationships to represent the parts of words.

▮ Remembering patterns and detecting the presence of patterns in the word when they think about it or say it aloud.

▮ Drawing from a large core of words that they automatically can write with little conscious attention.

As young children learn to write, they learn that writing has purpose and form. They learn that writing can be used to express their thoughts and that putting down one's language in written form means making some adjustments in the way that it is produced. Additionally, they learn to solve words. Solving words in writing refers to spelling them. In the example in Figure 1-3, Madeleine, age six, demonstrated her ability to compose a meaningful text and to construct the text by writing the words.

The message is indeed amusing. But if we analyze it carefully we can see that Madeleine is demonstrating some important understandings about the writing process, including a growing ability to solve words.

Madeleine had a clear *purpose* for her message—a special and meaningful communication to her dad. You can tell just by reading this message what a priority Margaret's toilet training was in that household at the time. She also chose a particular *format* for the writing, relating purpose to *genre*. Notice that this piece of writing is nothing less than an office memo! Madeleine's writing comes from her particular experiences. She has noticed that you use different formats for different kinds of writing. She also included the salutation *Dear Dad*, not conforming exactly to office memo format but indicating that she understood something important about a letter. She used punctuation in the piece—a comma after *Dad*, an exclamation point, a question mark, and an ampersand, again reflecting her experiences with written language. Only by looking at print in various contexts could Madeleine

have built this level of knowledge of these conventions.

Word-solving strategies are also evident in the piece. First, there are quite a few words that are spelled in a standard way. Madeleine was obviously building up a collection of known words that were useful to her as a writer. Writing would be tedious indeed if one had to figure out the spelling of every word. She could even spell long words such as *Margaret* and her own name, *Madeleine*. Of course, Madeleine was highly motivated to learn these family names; nevertheless, both names represented a challenge for a young writer.

There were three words in the piece that Madeleine almost knew, and she made good attempts. She was using letter-sound analysis very well but did not know all of the rules and patterns. For *toilet*, she wrote *toylit*. For the first part of the word, Madeleine probably used a known word based on taking apart the word *toilet* to consider the first syllable. For the last part, she was using regular letter-sound patterns to construct the syllable. Apparently, Madeleine considered *beyem* (standing for the commonly used abbreviation BM for *bowel movement*) to be a word, possibly one that she had heard frequently but had never seen written (a good example of the differences between oral and written language). She used letter-sound relationships to construct the word; notice the prominent *y*. If you say *BM*, you will hear it too. Finally, she wrote *Momy*, which is almost right, but she missed the conventional pattern of doubling the *m*.

Madeleine's writing reveals growing competence in word solving in writing and active searching for the information needed to produce her text. She found examples in her own experience with written language. She was making important connections between phonemes and graphemes, and she was noticing overall patterns in words that would help her. Word solving in writing means learning how to analyze the patterns in words—sound patterns and letter patterns

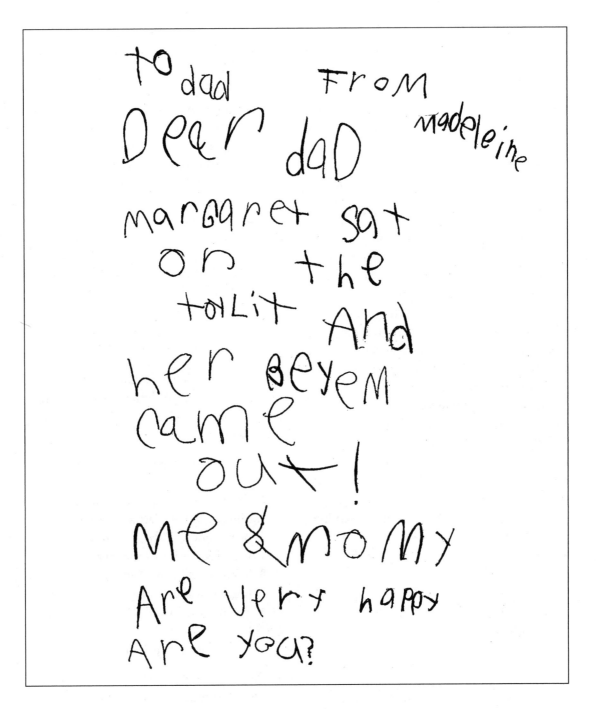

FIGURE 1-3 Madeleine's Writing

and how they represent meaning. At the time of this writing, Madeleine was a beginning word solver.

Word Solving Across Reading and Writing

You probably noticed that both Madeleine and Antoine demonstrated evidence of strategies and understandings that could be useful in either reading or writing. For example, Madeleine's sound-to-letter analyses that served her so well in writing could also help her do a letter-to-sound analysis in reading either to figure out new words or to check on herself as a reader. We do not know the extent to which Madeleine was transferring knowledge from one setting to use in another, but we do know that if we could teach her, we could build on that knowledge.

Reading and writing are complementary and similar processes. What is learned in one area supports learning in the other. Reading offers a way to help writers see how other writers use language and communicate meaning. It provides models for written language and gives the young writer a perception of how certain words look. Writing slows down the process so that young literacy learners can examine the details of print. Sometimes children, because of more extended experience in one area, show much more progress in one area or the other. And, progress often looks different in that the skill areas are disparate—children can write words that they don't necessarily notice while involved in reading continuous text, and they can read words that are too complex for them to write. You can assist the learning process by helping children make connections across reading and writing, and, as we will see in the next chapter, there is a place, through word study, for directing children's attention to specific aspects of word solving. Observing for evidence of word solving across writing and reading contexts will provide a dynamic starting point for instruction.

Suggestions for Professional Development

1. Organize a cross-grade-level meeting to examine evidence of word solving at several different levels.

2. Kindergarten, first-, second-, and third-grade teachers can collect the following:

❚ Samples of children's writing.
❚ Records or tapes of observed reading behavior. (Use running records if you know the procedures, or bring informal reading inventories or other observational records. As an alternative, simply observe several readers, noting important word solving, or bring a short videotape of a reader.)
❚ Pieces of interactive writing or other group writing.

3. Share samples of student work first in grade-level teams or pairs.

4. Then, look at samples in cross-grade-level teams, in order from younger to older children.

5. For each grade level, make a chart of the understandings about letters and words that children are revealing in their writing and reading.

6. Now, compare evidence across the grade levels.

❚ What do children control at the different levels? What do they know or nearly know? What differences can you observe across the levels?
❚ What kinds of strategies do children use across the levels?
❚ What do you think children at each level need to know? How does that change across the levels?

7. As a follow-up to the meeting, read and discuss Chapter 1, "Eight Principles of Literacy Learning," from the companion volume *Word Matters: Teaching Phonics and Spelling in the Reading/Writing Classroom.*

Word Matters

A Curriculum for Helping Children Become Word Solvers

Irene C. Fountas

Introduction

Word solving is not developed through a single lesson or series of lessons on a topic. In spite of the many claims of success that direct, systematic teaching garners, it must be coupled with independent application of skills across a wide range of literacy contexts. This chapter provides a model to help educators conceptualize a curriculum that will support children's learning of critical word-solving strategies through reading, writing, and word study. Each type of activity across a wide range of reading and writing activities enables children to learn word-solving strategies. And every instructional context described in this chapter enables teachers to demonstrate these powerful processes to children. Moreover, reading and writing activities are connected and build on each other. Word study involves direct attention to aspects of words and is explicitly related to the ways we work with children while they are reading and writing continuous text.

It is exciting to examine children's reading and writing behavior because it always reveals much about children's growing knowledge of written language. Observations of children at work, such as the examples provided by Antoine and Madeleine in Chapter 1, prompt this question: How can I help all children in my classroom become active word solvers in reading and writing? In this book and in its companion volume, *Word Matters: Teaching Phonics and Spelling in the Reading/Writing Classroom*, we and our colleagues describe how word-solving strategies are developed across a wide range of language and literacy activities in the classroom.

Observation: An Integrated Part of Instruction

Observation and analysis of children's literacy behaviors are the foundation for designing a dynamic and exciting curriculum for helping children become good word solvers. But observation does not take place on the one hand and instructional design on the other. Observation is an ongoing process that is integral to teaching. Throughout every activity mentioned in this book, the teacher is constantly observing and interpreting the children's behaviors. With young children, observation is the basis for assessment; when observation is systematically applied, it is synonymous with assessment. Teachers may assess in formal and structured ways, gaining information on a whole group of students. The information from formal observation helps teachers recognize and plan instruction in the larger sense. But observation is also informal and ongoing. Both kinds of observation are systematic; both are needed (see Jenkins, Chapter 7). Observation of student behavior provides teachers with the evidence of what children know and what they almost know.

A Range of Language/Literacy Experiences

No single lesson or kind of lesson will build the complex kinds of strategies good readers and spellers use. Just consider the implications of the diagram in Figure 2-1, with the reader/writer at the center.

This diagram represents a rich set of experiences that support the development of competent readers and writers. We stress that these experiences are very much interrelated in the literacy curriculum. For example, children may be writing stories related to those that they encounter in reading. Or, they may be discussing literature related to an overarching theme study such as space or growing. But we present them here to illustrate the varied contexts within which children learn and use word-solving skills.

Reading Contexts
We will briefly describe each of the reading contexts in our framework.

Interactive Read Aloud
The teacher reads to children from a wide selection of children's literature that includes a variety of genres. Children expand their language knowledge and knowledge of the world through hearing literature and participating in discussions of language, content, and illustrations.

We have called this instructional context *interactive* to emphasize that children are not passive listeners. Reading aloud to children is permeated by meaningful conversation as the teacher and children talk about the ideas in the book, comment on action and characters, and anticipate events. Teachers of young children find it especially effective to read favorite stories aloud again and again. Children begin to learn the text of favorite stories and soon join in on refrains and favorite parts of the text, gaining power over the meaning, the story, and the language so that they can produce it themselves.

As they encounter a piece of text like a nursery rhyme or a folktale again and again, children notice more about the plot, the characters, the text structure, and the words. In a way, they make it theirs—a linguistic resource that can be tapped again and again in many ways. If we think about our own reservoirs of linguistic knowledge, we would include folktales, fairytales, fables, texts from the Bible, and so on, that just seem part of us. Knowing these texts helps us understand the metaphors and literary references in our society (such as a "good Samaritan" or a "princess").

Rereading is enjoyable in itself, but it also helps children develop an inner sense of the structure and characteristics of written language. They learn to use syntactic patterns like "'Not I!' said the pig." This activity places children in the position of orally producing the kind of language encountered in written texts rather than in oral language.

In terms of word learning, through reading children hear words aloud that would not ordinarily appear in oral language, thus increasing their vocabularies. When a reader, adult or child, encounters a word in reading, it helps very much to have heard the word aloud in multiple contexts. It also helps for readers to actually say the word aloud to themselves many times.

Shared Reading
The teacher and children read together from an enlarged text (see Hundley and

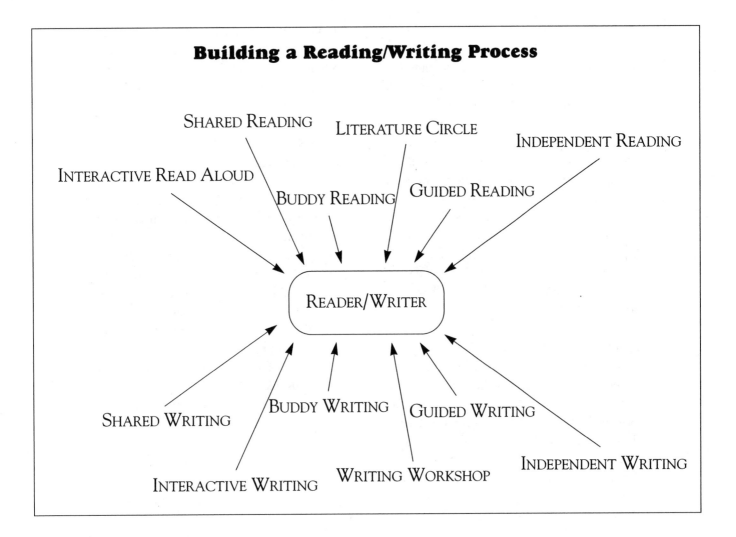

FIGURE 2-1   Building a Reading/Writing Process

Powell, Chapter 13). Typically, texts are read again and again. Like the interactive read aloud, shared reading prompts children to make texts their own. This activity is not the same as "memorizing," although some memory is obviously involved. The objective is not for children to recite texts. In shared reading, children have a text in mind that they have heard and participated in reading. This text is more complex than the children could read alone at this time, but, with support, they are able to produce the story, poem, or song when cued by the print. To understand how this support works, we might reflect on some of the "shared experiences" that we have. For example, singing a song with a group allows us to keep up and sing along when, alone, we might not remember all of the words or the tune. In a similar way, shared reading supports the young reader in "behaving like a reader."

With each reading, the children have more expertise in reading the text and are able to notice more about it. For example, children typically begin to notice words within the text. The teacher fosters this behavior by prompting children to search for particular words or to use word knowledge to check on their reading. Shared reading is a good context for developing some knowledge of high-frequency words, an important advantage for beginning readers and writers. It also provides a powerful context for helping children learn to read with good phrasing and fluency.

Literature Discussion

Through literature discussion, also known as literature circles (see Figure 2-2), literature study, or book clubs, the teacher helps children learn to talk with each other about books. The topic of discussion can be anything—favorite characters, the way the author uses language, or new words the children notice and try to puzzle out the meaning of. Literature discussion extends the encounters with text provided by reading aloud; here, children are using their own language to talk to their peers and the teacher about a text, revisiting the words or illustrations to deepen their understandings of how authors and artists communicate meaning.

Guided Reading

In guided reading, the teacher brings together a small group of children who are similar in their reading development (see Askew, Chapter 12; Fountas and Pinnell 1996). Based on observation, the teacher forms the group, and for a small period of the language arts block (perhaps fifteen to thirty minutes), children are reading with a group of peers who are displaying similar reading behaviors and are reading at just about the same level. Note that grouping for guided reading is a dynamic process. As children change and grow, there will be variations in their rate of progress and in the nature of the understandings they develop, so the groupings need to change. Children are grouped and regrouped through the use of systematic observation as an integral part of the process.

The teacher's role here is to select a text for the group that is "just right"; it is within the control of members of the group. The text contains ideas and words that the children either know or can figure out given the strategies and skills that they currently possess. There will be just a few problems to solve. The problems are important, however, because they prompt children to become active solvers of words within the reading of continuous text.

In guided reading, each child in the group reads the whole text or a meaningful part of it after the teacher has provided an introduction. During reading, the teacher may interact with individuals to prompt and encourage the use of effective strategies, but in general the emphasis is on keeping the reading going

FIGURE 2-2   Children Having a Literature Circle

and processing a whole text. After the reading, the teacher and children will revisit the text for teaching opportunities. The teacher usually provides some explicit examples of thinking about the meaning of the text, analyzing it, or solving words. Throughout the guided reading lesson, there are opportunities for the teacher to draw children's attention to any aspect of the text that will help in reading, including ways to solve words.

Buddy Reading

Buddy reading (Figure 2-3) places children in a supportive context that will help them become independent at word solving. Some optional routines for buddy reading are:

▌ Two readers reading together in unison.
▌ One reader reading the whole book and then the other doing the same.
▌ Readers taking turns reading the pages of a book.
▌ Readers taking turns reading a different whole book.

Independent Reading

In independent reading, the reader is alone with the task of reading a book. Word-solving strategies here are applied independently. Everything we do in the supportive context of the classroom is directed toward children's being able to use skills and strate-

gies in an independent reading process. We don't want readers to use word-solving strategies only when prompted; we want them to know how to search and check on their own (Askew, Chapter 12). Spending time reading independently is essential for developing readers.

Writing Contexts

Like reading, writing contexts range from the teacher's writing *for* children to children writing *by themselves*.

Language Experience

A traditionally used technique for helping young children develop voice in writing and learn about the process of writing is for the teacher to act as scribe while children compose the text. Through this process, they learn that what can be said can be written down. After all, sentences have to be composed in certain ways to make good written text, and there is opportunity within language experience to talk about that.

Language experience also provides many opportunities for the teacher to demonstrate how to write, use writing conventions, and construct words. The texts produced are usually more complex than those in the next two settings described—shared writing and interactive writing—because they are based on

FIGURE 2-3 Buddy Reading

children's oral language. Some children will be able to read the language experience charts, but many will not be able to do so without a great deal of coaching. We believe that language experience charts serve the purpose of demonstrating the writing process and helping children use language in sophisticated ways; it is not necessary to spend a great deal of time teaching them to read the charts.

Shared Writing

Shared writing is similar to language experience in that the teacher is the scribe for a group of children, but in this case much more attention is given to cooperative composition. The teacher guides the composing process so that the text produced is highly readable for the group of children. Within the process, there are many opportunities to give attention to the conventions of print (such as using space, creating lines, using capitalization and punctuation, and spelling words).

Interactive Writing

Interactive writing is similar to shared writing in the composing process, but an additional action makes it possible to help children attend closely to print. The teacher and children share the pen in the construction of the text, word by word. As they make their own contributions to the construction of words, children learn important techniques, such as saying words slowly to help in thinking about letter-sound relationships, using known words to construct new words, and using resources such as word walls and charts (see McCarrier and Patacca, Chapter 5; Wiley, Chapter 3).

Group writing experiences are particularly effective when the teacher combines language experience with shared writing and interactive writing. Sometimes, in the same chart (for example, as a record of a scientific experiment), the teacher will act as scribe and recorder for the children some of the time, which is language experience; the children will compose with the teacher some of the text (shared writing); and the teacher and children will share the composing and

writing of some of the text (interactive writing). This combination of techniques is evident in Figure 2-4 and Figure 2-5, writing produced by Kate Roth and her first graders.

Buddy Writing

Also called "partner writing," buddy writing involves two children planning and working together to create a cooperative text. One might produce the illustrations while the other writes the text. Or, both may compose and take turns writing. It is a supported setting that enables children to help each other become more independent in writing.

Writing Workshop

Writing workshop can actually involve several different kinds of writing. The structure of writing workshop provides for a combination of intentional or direct teaching and demonstration of some aspect of the writing process that the teacher wants to help children learn. The "minilesson" may focus on anything—choosing a topic, composing a title, using paragraphs, or spelling words. In fact, a spelling curriculum may be extended through the writing workshop minilesson as the teacher prompts children to actually use spelling principles in their own writing. The minilesson may involve some interactive writing or teacher demonstration; the goal is for children to become independent writers. In writing workshop, teachers also have individual conferences with children, and children share their work with others in the class for feedback.

Guided Writing

Guided writing involves working with a small group of children who are similar in their strengths and needs in the writing process. For example, during writing workshop you might pull together children with similar instructional needs and have a "group conference." Minilessons and sharing of their work are integral to the process.

Independent Writing

When we refer to independent writing we mean all of the writing that an individual

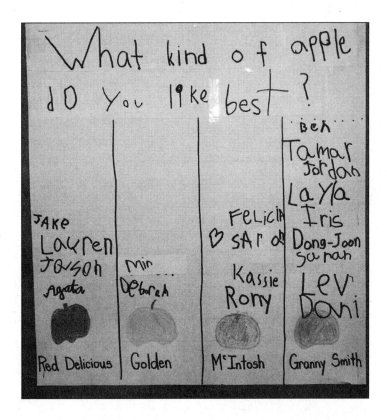

FIGURE 2-4 Interactive Writing, Shared Writing, and Independent Writing

engages in with minimal teacher support. The support has been provided through previous teaching. This process might involve the child's writing independently during writing workshop time, writing in science or social studies, or composing sentences to go with an illustration. It might be the children's writing in journals as a regular part of the day. Whatever the setting, the emphasis is on independence (see Henry, Chapter 4). Children who are becoming word solvers know what to do when they want to write a word they do not know. They use a flexible range of strategies, such as thinking how the word sounds and saying it slowly, thinking how the word looks, thinking of words they know that are like that word, or referring to a word wall or personal dictionary for support.

All of the approaches listed here for reading and writing involve important opportunities for learning how to solve words. Word solving cannot be accomplished solely through isolated experiences with words. Readers and writers need to use the informa-

tion as they process continuous text. Aspects of word solving are brought to children's attention in many ways and in many contexts. In the next section we propose a way of thinking about the development of word solving across the curriculum.

A Model for Teaching Children to Become Word Solvers

The wide range of instructional contexts we've listed may be categorized into reading and writing activities. Oral language flows through all activities, weaving meaning together. In all of those reading and writing activities, children also learn about word solving. What about learning activities that focus children's attention on words? Is there a time in the curriculum when it is appropriate and effective to investigate words to learn more about them? We think so, but we also caution that the curriculum is not composed of a patched-together series of isolated activities. All learning contexts work

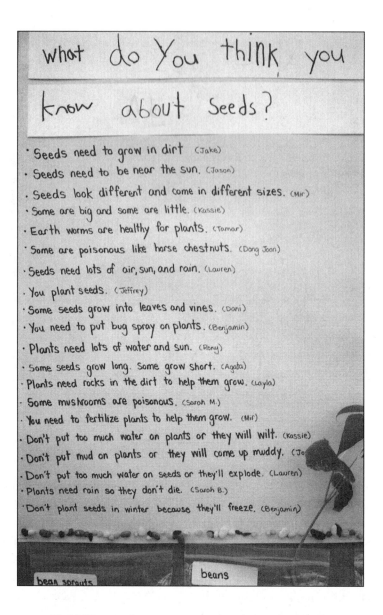

what do you think you know about Seeds?

• Seeds need to grow in dirt (Jake)
• Seeds need to be near the sun. (Jason)
• Seeds look different and come in different sizes. (Mir)
• Some are big and some are little. (Kassie)
• Earth worms are healthy for plants. (Tomar)
• Some are poisonous like horse chestnuts. (Dong Joon)
• Seeds need lots of air, sun, and rain. (Lauren)
• You plant seeds. (Jeffrey)
• Some seeds grow into leaves and vines. (Doni)
• You need to put bug spray on plants. (Benjamin)
• Plants need lots of water and sun. (Rory)
• Some seeds grow long. Some grow short. (Agata)
• Plants need rocks in the dirt to help them grow. (Layla)
• Some mushrooms are poisonous. (Sarah M.)
• You need to fertilize plants to help them grow. (Mir)
• Don't put too much water on plants or they will wilt. (Kassie)
• Don't put mud on plants or they will come up muddy. (Jo
• Don't put too much water on seeds or they'll explode. (Lauren)
• Plants need rain so they don't die. (Sarah B.)
• Don't plant seeds in winter because they'll freeze. (Benjamin)

bean sprouts   beans

FIGURE 2-5   Interactive Writing and Shared Writing

together to support children's individual processing skills. When words are investigated in one context, the understandings will be useful in another context. For example, if children are noticing *ing* words in shared reading, those kinds of words might surface in interactive writing, and they might also be learning how to add *ing* to a word to make another word in an activity that we call *word study*.

Word study is defined as learning about words through "focused attention to words and word elements, with the goal of helping children become excellent readers and writers" (Pinnell and Fountas 1998, 31). A curriculum to teach word solving involves the investigation of words and how they work in reading, in writing, and in word study— three interrelated areas.

The instructional model presented in Figure 2-6 is a conceptual tool for helping teachers design curricula that provide for breadth and depth in learning. As children engage in many different kinds of reading and writing activities, you can support word solving as part of the process. While you pro-

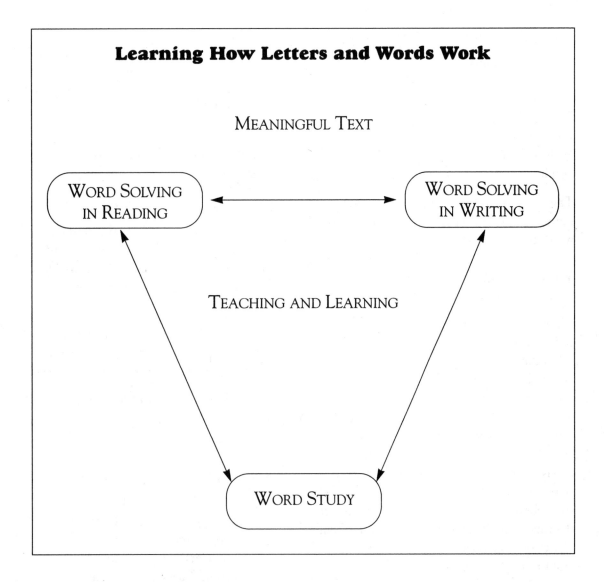

FIGURE 2-6   Learning How Letters and Words Work

vide opportunities for children to hear written language read aloud and to read for themselves, you can draw children's attention to words and how they work. Within writing contexts—language experience, shared writing, interactive writing, writing workshop, and independent writing—you will find many different opportunities to help children work with words.

The third area in the instructional model, word study, provides still more opportunities to focus children's attention on aspects of words. Word study experiences involve direct attention to words through minilessons, independent application of strategies, principles and concepts, explo-

ration and discovery regarding words, and summary and sharing of new learning. Word study is based on your ongoing observation of what children are demonstrating they know. Additionally, it stems from your basic knowledge of the language system and what children need to know about how words work.

Word study actively involves students in investigation of words (DeFord, Chapter 11; Hall and Cunningham, Chapter 10; Zutell, Chapter 9). It might include contexts such as:

▮ Letter sorting.

▮ Word sorting.

▮ Making word webs.

▌ Using letter books and alphabet books.

▌ Making or building words from letters or word parts.

▌ Letter or word games.

▌ Creating and using word charts and word walls, which form the first references for children to use in writing and reading.

The chapters in this book provide a rich array of examples to help you design effective word study activities.

Word Solving Across the Curriculum

Three contexts are represented in the diagram in Figure 2-6 but the three areas are not separate from each other. As we conceptualize a curriculum, we are always moving back and forth among the contexts of reading, writing, and word study. What is learned in one area assists learning and/or is applied in another area. There are meaningful connections (analogous to "echoes") in the learning conversation and in the way attention is directed throughout the school day. For example, about the time a group of children were making wall charts of compound words in word study, a child in guided reading commented, "There's one of those words that have two words joined together!" Teachers guide such "noticing" through their own examples, and soon children are searching for connections.

The model presented provides a framework for thinking about a word study program that is comprehensive. Word study, as presented in this chapter and in this book, is an active process in which children investigate how words work. They learn specific principles and, in the process, discover more. Word solving also takes place across many literacy contexts in which children are involved in reading or writing continuous text. Word solving cannot be compartmentalized in a curriculum. As teachers, it is our responsibility not only to be sure we have organized and planned to support children's word solving,

but to be sure that we provide for connections so that children can actively use what they know about words. It is through this active language use that they become competent and skillful word solvers.

Suggestions for Professional Development

1. Use the observations of children's reading and writing behavior that you have analyzed by grade level (see "Suggestions for Professional Development" in Chapter 1). Think about what the children know, nearly know, and need to know.

2. For the children at your grade level, design one important instructional goal in reading and one in writing.

3. For each goal, think of how to support children in:
   ▌ Reading activities.
   ▌ Writing activities.
   ▌ Word study activities.

4. Ask:
   ▌ How can I support the children's learning of the same concept or principle across contexts?
   ▌ What language can I use that will be specific in letting children know what is expected of them?
   ▌ What examples will be most powerful in helping children learn a strategy that they can use in their independent reading or writing?
   ▌ Are there explicit connections across the reading, writing, and word study contexts?

5. As a follow-up to the meeting, read and discuss two chapters from the companion volume to this book, *Word Matters: Teaching Phonics and Spelling in the Reading/Writing Classroom*:
   ▌ Chapter 2, "Designing a Quality Literacy Program."
   ▌ Chapter 3, "Becoming a Word Solver."

Writing: Constructing
Letters and Words

What does word solving in writing look like? Competent word solvers use a range of strategies for constructing words or spelling while at the same time composing messages. Effective writers know many words that they can write easily and quickly, but their knowledge is not a simple collection of remembered words. Word solvers know how the system works; they know what to look for in words and the connections to make. They know some powerful principles that help them hypothesize about words and make close attempts even when they are not completely sure how to spell a word.

Competent word solvers in writing have a good grasp of the mechanics of the writing process; they can form letters easily and quickly and write a large number of known words. They are good at monitoring their efforts, checking on what they write. They use space between words and between lines of print. When they approach words that they do not know how to spell, they actively seek to solve them. They can write words left to right, letter by letter, checking on their efforts by using knowledge of relationships between letters and sounds and the visual patterns. They have specialized knowledge about words, such as the fact that every word has at least one vowel and that words can be divided into syllables, each of which has at least one vowel. Sophisticated word solvers use knowledge of word roots, reflecting their awareness of some of the historical development of language. Also, every good speller has some individual ways to remember tricky words that do not follow common patterns.

We summarize word solving in writing by thinking about several broad strategies. Learners think about how words sound and the relationships between letters and letter clusters (*hat, same*). They think about how words look—that is, they use visual strategies, including the clusters and patterns of the letters in words (*night, learn*). They also think about the meaning of words. We call these *morphemic strategies* because word solvers are looking for and combining significant parts of words that have meaning (*sing, singing, singer; hop, hops, hopped*). Finally, if writers are to achieve independence in word solving, they must learn ways of using references and resources (such as dictionaries, computer spell checking, thesauruses, etc.) to learn more about words. From the very beginning, we want children to inquire into words, discovering their properties as they work with them and learning more about the words that they want to write.

The chapters in Section 2 provide descriptions of children's behavior and of instructional settings designed to support the development of word solving in writing. Wiley introduces us to interactive writing, a powerful way of demonstrating the process of writing to young writers. An authentic writing experience that involves a group of children, interactive writing provides a way for the teacher to explicitly demonstrate writing processes.

Henry provides another example of interactive writing instruction but goes on to give us a portrait of how a young writer applies understandings, developed in group instruction, to his own independent writing. McCarrier and Patacca provide an extended description of learning in one kindergarten classroom. They describe a range of experiences, including interactive writing, that help children learn to look at print, and they describe some ways of looking at evidence of children's learning in this important area.

Lyons writes about what it means to learn letters. The complexities of learning are illustrated by a case study of a child who is building a network of understandings around words and letters. In the last chapter of Section 2, Jenkins provides a close look at a second-grade child, describing him as a reader and writer and discussing how he is developing a variety of flexible spelling strategies. Jenkins' chapter is particularly helpful for designing systematic spelling assessment.

Interactive Writing[1,2]

The How and Why of Teaching and Learning Letters, Sounds, and Words

Barbara Joan Wiley

Introduction

Interactive writing, a powerful tool that eases the transition to literacy for beginning writers, was developed by a group of researchers and teachers who were looking for ways to maintain the complexity of the authentic act of writing while at the same time help children develop a range of strategies for encoding the messages. They wanted, in the process, to develop phonemic and orthographic awareness and help children use that growing knowledge while composing and constructing continuous text. Interactive writing, as described in this chapter by Wiley, helps children learn about letters, sounds, and words within purposeful, enjoyable use of language.

Wiley provides a thorough description of the processes involved in interactive writing, with suggestions for getting started and trying it out in your own classroom. She suggests that interactive writing helps children work "on the edge" of their knowledge, taking on new learning with the teacher's carefully planned support. In interactive writing, the children are producing a written product that they can read and enjoy; but they are also learning critical concepts related to becoming word solvers in writing and reading.

Interactive writing is a teaching procedure that helps children learn how to write and to spell in a supported way. Interactive writing has been defined as a transition tool that helps young children attend to the message and the details of written language (Pinnell and McCarrier 1994). It is a form of shared writing in which the teacher scaffolds not only the craft of writing but also the

---

[1]This chapter is based on a presentation entitled, "The HOW and WHY of Interactive Writing" that was given by Barbara Joan Wiley and Justina Henry at the February 1997 Reading Recovery Conference, Columbus, Ohio.
[2]Interactive writing is a term coined by a research group composed of faculty members from The Ohio State University and teachers from Columbus, Ohio, Public Schools. All members of the group were Reading Recovery teachers who were accustomed to using the close observation of children as a guide for teaching moves. Also, they were concerned about helping young children, especially those who had limited experiences in literacy, to understand how words work. The group examined Moira McKenzie's (1985) work in shared writing and enthusiastically adopted the approach as having power in helping children understand the writing process. They varied the approach with a "share the pen" technique that involved children in contributing individual letters and words and later phrases to the group writing. Interactive writing is described in Button, Johnson, and Furgerson (1996); Fountas and Pinnell (1996); McCarrier and Patacca (1994), and Pinnell and McCarrier (1994).

process of writing by sharing the pen with students (Button, Johnson, and Furgerson 1996).

The strength of the interactive writing procedure demands two levels of expertise. First, teachers need to know how to use the technique at a procedural level. Next, teachers needs to refine the technique by making on-the-spot teaching decisions that are based on the immediate needs of the students with whom they are working.

The first level of expertise is the *how* of interactive writing. The second level of expertise is one of refinement and is the *why* of interactive writing which refers to the understandings underlying teacher decision making—the theory. Together practice and theory support young children's learning about how written language works and why words are spelled the way they are.

The How of Interactive Writing

Interactive writing is a process in which teachers and students work together. Before they write they compose a message together. During the writing of that message they share the pen as the words are written on a large piece of paper. After the text has been written they reread the message together. For example, a typical early sequence of interactions might sound something like the following:

Before Writing
The students offer from five to ten suggestions as to what they'd like to write.

During Writing

Teacher: Good, let's write, *The hen was red.* Clap it with me.

Teacher and Children: The hen was red.

Teacher: Let's count the words.

Teacher and Children: The hen was red. Four words.

Teacher: Dave, you know *The*, write it for us.

Dave: (writes the word *The*)

Teacher and Children: The hen—

Teacher: hen. What do you hear?

Children: h, n

Teacher: Yes, I hear those sounds. Helen, come and write the *h* for us. It's like the *h* in your name. (Teacher points to Helen's name on the name chart.) I'll put in an *e* that comes next. Nathan, come write the last letter in this word.

And so it continues.

After Writing
Often one child will point to the words as the students reread what has been written. The teacher reads with the group or hangs back, depending on the students' abilities.

Responsibility for deciding what to write, the actual writing of the words, and the rereading of the text are shared between the students and the teacher. The goal is for the students to do as much of the work as they are able to do with the teacher stepping in only as needed. Figure 3-1 lists possible teaching actions and the reasons for each during interactive writing.

Thinking in terms of a "before, during, and after" the writing of the text helps to plan and guide teaching decisions. In the following sections, I present some more detailed suggestions for initiating interactive writing for the first time. Many of the "nuts and bolts" procedures outlined here will become routine as the teacher and students engage in interactive writing on a daily basis.[3]

Creating an Intimate Environment
Effective use of interactive writing requires a setting in which the teacher and children can have the conversation they need to

---

[3]The following sections were developed by Justina Henry and Barbara Joan Wiley for The Ohio State Early Literacy Learning Initiative.

TEACHER ACTIONS	RATIONALE
Before writing:	
Have an authentic reason for writing.	Children have a real reason to use written language. Word construction and word learning are undertaken for a purpose.
Use children's words.	The children in the group compose the message. The mechanics of writing are related to the words they want to write. If they've said it, it will be easier for them to reread it later.
Repeat the message out loud.	The teacher helps the children remember the composed message so that it readily comes to mind while they are engaged in the mechanics of writing. This frees their minds to think of other things.
Clap, snap, or count words.[2]	Children become aware that the message is composed of individual words in sequence.
During the writing of a message:	
Have children say words slowly before writing them.	Children realize that words are made up of sequences of sounds and become more sensitive to the sounds in words.
Link words to names and/or to known words.	Children make connections between the sounds and letters in words they know and the words they want to write.
Comment on known words.	The teacher explicitly demonstrates a way of thinking that seeks to solidify what is known and to make connections between known and unknown words.
Reread the sentence.	Rereading helps children to keep the message in mind while they focus on the details of print; rereading gives practice in early reading behaviors and also assists the reader to keep the message in mind.
Engage in word construction that helps children see how words work.	The teacher shows children how the relationships between sounds, letters, and letter clusters help in learning how words work; common spelling patterns will be explored and internalized as words are related and generated.
After writing:	
Guide children to point and read the message.	The message, story, or other form of writing provide support for rereading, practicing early reading behaviors, and learning some high-frequency words.
Display the writing for children to reread.	Rereading independently provides practice in processing written text, reading words, practicing early reading behaviors, connecting writing and reading, and learning some high-frequency words.
Comment on the authentic reason for writing.	The children understand that the message was written for a purpose and that it is meant to be read and used.
May use the writing for extension.	The conversation surrounding the writing as well as the product itself may be extended through art, other media, or the creation of more text; children may produce their own pieces of writing, learning that one piece of text is connected to others.

[1]Adapted from a checklist for interactive writing created by Linda Mudre in 1994 (workshop materials).
[2]A variation is to place blank white cards, one for each word, on a board or in a pocket chart, ready to write words.

FIGURE 3-1 Interactive Writing[1]: Teacher Actions and Rationale

plan, compose, and reread the piece of writing, as well as discuss the construction of words. With an intimate environment, children will feel real ownership in the piece and the teacher can easily elicit and recognize their contributions.

Work in Small Groups

All participants should be able to see and hear each other as well as see the piece of writing on the easel. Interactive writing is often used in whole class settings, but at times, it might be wise to work in a small group for one or more of the following reasons:

■ You are just beginning to use the procedures of interactive writing.

■ You want to focus the attention of a small group of children who are at about the same place in reading and writing progress.

■ You want to give extra, intensive help to a small group of children who are just beginning to work with print while the rest of the class is more advanced.

■ A small group of children are working on a special project.

When the group of children is smaller it is easier for them to focus on the task at hand. They can sit closer to the chart. They may even be able to sit in chairs in a tight semicircle close to you and the easel. Working with a smaller group on chairs:

■ Allows you to lean forward close to them more at eye level as you interact with them.

■ Has the effect of eliminating much of their movement on the floor that distracts them from the task.

■ Enables children to see the text easier and more quickly make their way up to the easel to contribute a word or letter or point for rereading, thus helping to keep the pace of the lesson moving with less chance for attention to wander.

Create a Supportive Environment

It is important to have the necessary materials close at hand to allow for the quick pacing of the lesson that helps to keep the students engaged. In preparing a supportive environment you may want to think about the need to have:

■ "Fix-it" tape ready (Post-it Correction or Cover-up Tape).

■ Magna Doodle ready. The Magna Doodle (white board, small chart paper, or small chalkboard) is essential in helping children focus on your teaching points (i.e., letter formation, links with other words, etc.). Many children miss the links *talked* about; they need to be *shown*.

■ The children sit so that everyone can see.

■ The children sit so that there is walking space or a path to the easel. It is helpful to leave a "walkway" down the middle of the group as they are sitting on the floor. This arrangement allows easy access for children coming to the easel and helps maintain their interest and participation in the task.

■ Name chart nearby so that it can be seen and used.

■ Name chart on your right so that it is within your easy reach.

■ Pointers of multiple lengths ready.

■ A pointed marker ready. These markers are especially made to be used on chart paper. They are pointed and fat and easy for children to see and use. They are called Poster Markers. Also, when the children draw on the chart paper, they may prefer using fat watercolor pointed markers rather than the thin ones.

■ Unlined chart paper.

■ A large easel that can hold 36" x 24" chart paper.

■ A word wall nearby so that you know what words the students can write quickly.

Recognize Achievement

Recognition is important in keeping children engaged in the writing process. Additionally, recognition gives students feedback on their learning so that they move forward in their understanding of literacy. Recognition is appropriate when children offer what they know, partially know, make a link on their own, detect errors, and self-correct. The effectiveness of your recognition is determined by the focus of the lesson. The focus needs to be clear in your mind, otherwise how will you know what to celebrate? You celebrate with the children their small steps toward controlling what they need to learn next.

Making the Task Authentic

Generating the text and discussing how to spell the words makes sense to children when they are writing a meaningful message to a real audience. This understanding will support their taking on of new knowledge about written language.

Establish a Reason to Write

The teacher and students need to collaborate in establishing a reason to write. The opening conversation of the interactive writing lesson sets the stage for writing and informs the children about the authentic form of writing (i.e., list, log, letter, survey, retelling, etc.) Once the purpose and form are determined (this can be done quickly), the rest of the work on generating the text and thinking about letters and words makes sense to the children because they are creating a meaningful message. When the task makes sense, it will be easier for children to attend to the visual features of the print. The meaningfulness supports their attention to the details. Also, it is easier to involve students and maintain their attention if there is an authentic reason for writing.

Establish an Audience

Helping children visualize an audience for their writing sparks an enthusiasm for the task. If you make clear, explicit statements about why they are writing and who will read the created text, it will help children to understand that writers write for specific purposes. Writing to inform others and writing to remember are two functions of writing. There are many others.

Individualize the Text

It is easier to individualize texts to the students' interests when working with a small group of children. There is a greater chance that a child's actual words will be the ones that are chosen to be written. Children's names can actually be used in the text that is written. When children are writing something that is important to them, that is interesting to them, or that is personalized to them, they become highly engaged in the task. When children are engaged they are more focused and there are fewer management concerns, and they work harder to learn more.

Establishing Routines

To make the interactive writing experiences effective, be sure to create established routines and clear management guidelines. Children need to know what is expected of them. Routines allow an activity to move along smoothly and quickly, which keeps children engaged. For example, routines help people to know what kind of dialogue to expect, what kinds of risks will need to be taken, etc. Bruner (1983) argues that the establishment of routines frees participants' minds to think on higher levels (they don't have to worry about the mundane).

Be Consistent

▮ Use specific phrases over and over again (i.e., "Say it, think it, and hear it"; "Read it fast"; "Say the word slowly"; "That's a fast word"; etc.). Repetition helps to establish routines.

▮ Work in the same location each day.

▮ Follow a set sequence of events (i.e., generate text together, say the sentence two or three times, clap or snap the words, say the first word slowly, generate sounds that are heard, link sounds to the name chart, write the first word, reread what has been written so far, etc.).

Set Expectations

Take time to discuss appropriate behavior with the group and create a feeling of community as much as possible. Establish guidelines for behavior with the group. Have them help you decide on these. Reflect on what your expectations are for them and make these clear to the children by stopping any inappropriate behavior—like walking away from the group, not listening to each other, etc. Be explicit and firm in setting limits. Use external mediators when necessary. For instance, have the child who has a difficult time attending sit on a carpet square, hold a stuffed animal named Listening Bear, etc. (Bodrova and Leong 1996).

Keep Children Engaged

Young children prefer to participate rather than just observe. They also like to display their knowledge. So, devise interaction routines that will keep them involved while a classmate is writing on the chart. This requires practice on your part, because your attention is divided, but it may be necessary until they learn to attend without your direction. For instance, when one student is writing *t* on the chart, say to the others, "Let's make a *t* in the air. Ready, let's all say it—down and across—*t*. Down and across— *t*. Now you know how to make a *t*." Another way to keep them engaged while someone else is writing is to enthusiastically acknowledge those other students who also heard or said the word slowly. Experiment with different tones of voice to see if the children's attention is captivated by more or less animation and expression.

When learning how to use interactive writing, be sure to monitor and act on the children's interests. Remember to keep it short. Think about pacing. Read the group. Many teachers use the motto, "Less is best."

Stop the lesson when the children's interest wanes. Tell the children that you will quickly finish writing the sentence and that the group will return to the project the next day. Or, rekindle the children's attention by a slight change in the activity. For example, you might take time out from writing to have the children come up to the chart and illustrate the text, refocus the group by pointing and rereading all of the text that has been written so far, lower your voice, etc. There is an art to knowing when to pull back or move on to another activity. Finely-tuned group management will keep the children eager to return to interactive writing another day.

The Why of Interactive Writing

Teachers implement interactive writing as a transition tool to help children learn how to write. But, for interactive writing lessons to be truly powerful, teachers must move beyond procedural knowledge. They must refine their lessons to meet the needs of the group of children they are teaching as well as for the individual students within the group. The teachers' knowledge of students is what enables them to make just the right instructional decisions at just the right moment. The power of the "teachable moment" is that when children are working at the "cutting edge" of their abilities they are more engaged, there are fewer management concerns, and learning occurs.

When children work with very easy, known material they may be "spinning their wheels" and not learning because they have lost interest. If children work with material that is over their heads they may become frustrated and escape by tuning out. Either way, children will not continue to make progress as writers.

Vygotsky (1986) defined the "zone of proximal development" as the distance between what children can do unassisted and what they can do with an adult's help. Interactive writing is an assisted learning situation. Children's abilities are stretched. They can do more and experience greater success with teacher assistance than they could writing alone. Thus, they are working in the "zone" in which learning occurs. With detailed, sensitive observations of children's writing behavior, teachers can help them successfully use existing knowledge but also "push the limits" for more learning.

Following the Children

Interactive writing lessons become more powerful when they are based on observation and analysis of the behavior of the children at a particular point in time. Teachers need to also think about a continuum of progress students tend to make in writing so that they can focus their teaching on what typically comes next for a group of children (Henderson 1981). Think about decision making in three areas. For the children in the class, ask:

1. What do these children KNOW?
2. What do these children NEED to know next?
3. How can I TEACH these children what they need to know?

For example, early in the year a kindergarten teacher, during an interactive writing lesson, may be helping the children understand that what they know about their own names can help them when they are writing. The teacher will have a name chart close by the easel and will frequently use it as a resource. For instance, when Brenda Greene and her students were writing about *Humpty Dumpty*, she noted that Danyelle's name started just like Dumpty as she pointed to Danyelle's name on the name chart (Figure 3-2).

Later in the year as the children gain knowledge, Brenda uses the name chart less for initial and final consonants. Instead, the children are asked to slowly say the word they want to spell and listen for the sounds they hear. The name chart might be visited for letter clusters such as *ch* or endings such as *y*.

Later still, you may ask the children to listen for sounds in the order in which they come in words. As the children build a core of known words, help them to use these words to make and solve new ones through the use of analogy. For example, during a lesson you may say, "Since you know both how to write *cat* and what sound Roger's name begins with then you can figure out how to write the word *rat*." In addition to the name chart you may begin a chart entitled, "Words We Have in Our Heads" (Figure 3-3).

Later still, the class may construct a word wall (Cunningham 1995) that has known words displayed alphabetically (Figure 3-4).

Interactive writing will look "similar but different" in a first- or a second-grade classroom. We can think of shifts over time as a continuum of progress (Figure 3-5).

Following the Child

Children do not always progress sequentially through developmental stages as a group. Children learn in fits and spurts, as well as recursively (Clay 1991c). Therefore, it is important for us as teachers to use our knowledge of individual children as a basis for teaching in interactive writing lessons. This type of teacher decision-making "on the run" is highly refined and addresses individual students' current needs on a day-by-day basis. For example, when Francee Eldredge, a kindergarten teacher (see Figure 3-5 on page 35), acknowledged her children's responses when they were writing about the Gingerbread Man, she praised their responses at multiple levels. After asking them to say the word *man* slowly so that they could hear the sounds in the word, she said, "Good, some of you knew the first letter right away and were saying *m*, others were saying the whole word in order to hear more sounds, and others noticed that *man* was like *and*, a word we know." In this short transaction, Francee was supporting and valuing the individual children's abilities to:

■ Hear beginning sounds.
■ Say words slowly and listen for sounds in sequence.
■ Know word-ending chunks.

FIGURE 3-2   The children in Brenda Greene's kindergarten class use the name chart as a resource throughout the day, not only during interactive writing lessons.

Even though all of these children were kindergartners, they had individual strengths and needs and consequently needed to be taught differently.

Another kindergarten teacher, Sharon Esswein, in reflecting on an interactive writing lesson she had just completed with her class, was able to describe how her teaching moves were based on individual children's needs. Sharon's comments were:

I chose Brian to point to the previously written text as the class read it together with him in a shared reading activity.

1. *First make a big ball.*
2. *Then you make a medium ball.*
3. *Make a small ball for the head.*

I picked Brandon because I knew he would be a good model. He could easily point to the words as we read them. I also knew that it was important for us to remember what we had written so far so we could think about what might logically be the next step in making a snowman.

Then the children and I negotiated to write, *"Put two sticks for the arms."*

For the first word *put*, I chose Wayne to come up to write the *t*. Wayne was working really hard on letter identification and during his guided reading lesson the previous day we had worked on the letter *t*. We had read *Huggle's Breakfast* and we had worked on the *t* in telephone. I said, "Wayne, come on up. We're going to make that *t* we worked on

Words we have in our heads! ☺

ThE	STOP	See	At
No	go	He	
CAT	She	Mommy	
Yes	Dog	in	
is	to	This	
A	Zoo	AND	
MOM	me	off	
DAD	We	on	
		will	

FIGURE 3-3   The children in Tracy Michalak's kindergarten class wrote this chart entitled, "Words we have in our heads!" during interactive writing lessons.

yesterday." I tried to make that link for him. I asked him, "Wayne do you remember when we made that word that started with a *t*? Remember what Huggle ate?" He said, "The telephone." "You remember the *t* ?" I asked. He thought he did. He put the first stick down and then went on to make something that looked more like an *E*, so we used the correction tape. At this point, I knew that he needed a little more support so I said, "Wayne you already have the stick down, good job. Now all we need to do is put a cross on it." He was able to do that. I told him, "You made a *t*." Then I asked, "Wayne, what did you just make?" He said, "A *t*." What's important here is that I was getting him to say the letter as well as to write it.

As the lesson continued, I picked individual children to come up to the easel to write depending on what they knew and what they needed to know next.

In this statement, Sharon reflected on how she used her knowledge of individual students' strengths and needs to make powerful teach-

ing decisions. She had designed a task for the group as a whole, but within that, she was thinking about individual learners. Sharon's story illustrates the multilevel learning that is possible in the interactive writing context.

Effective teachers use both general knowledge of how children typically grow and particular knowledge of individual students' understandings to refine their teaching (Bredekamp and Copple 1997). Teachers' knowledge of their students can be gleaned from both formal and informal assessments. Using this knowledge, teachers can act on what they know about their students and refine their interactive writing lessons to help their students learn easily. As Clay writes,

The teacher has a general theory in her head about children's responding. This is a theory she should check against what she is able to observe and infer from the individual child's responding, and which she should be prepared to change if the two are in conflict. (Clay 1991a, 233)

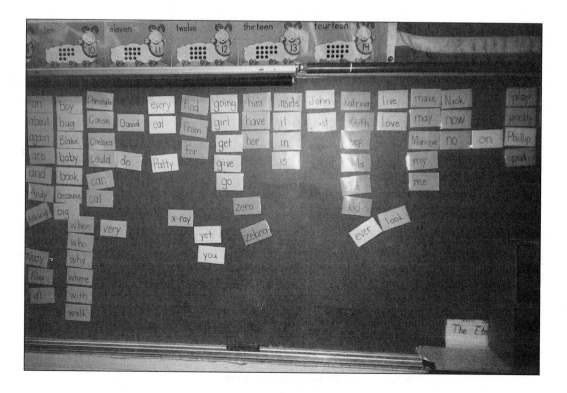

FIGURE 3-4   The words on this word wall in Shelly Schaub's class are backed with magnetic tape so that they can be moved around, sorted, and used as a resource at tables, as needed.

When involved in interactive writing lessons, teachers and students work together as they put theory into practice. Their joint journey in education becomes an adventure in learning where theoretical views regarding how children think and learn become practical views regarding spelling and writing. In local classrooms these theories and practices are shaped and become more effective by noting and acting on both the entire group's developmental level and the individual students' knowledge level. The key is that as children shift in their ability, teachers shift in their teaching. As Clay has said:

Sensitive and systematic observation of young children's reading and writing behaviors provides teachers with feedback which can shape their next teaching moves. Teaching then can be likened to a conversation in which you listen to the speaker carefully before you reply. (Clay 1979, 6)

When teachers' decisions regarding educational practice depend on the interest and abilities of their students, the theory regarding why children learn and the practice regarding how teachers teach become mutually facilitating forces that extend learning on a day-to-day basis.

Suggestions for Professional Development

Participate in a two-step process for supporting individual children's learning in group situations.

Step One

1. Analyze one or two children in your class. You might want to use Clay's observation instruments, especially the Letter Identification, Writing Vocabulary, and Hearing and Recording Sounds in Words assessments. (See Clay 1993a for directions and material.) Administer the assessments and bring the results to a meeting with grade-level colleagues. If Clay's assessments are not accessible, have

Emergent/Early Writers: Kindergarten

The teacher and children will make the name chart using children's first names. Use the name chart frequently as a resource for learning about initial and final consonants in words and letter formation.

The teacher encourages children to slowly say the word they want to write and make connections to letters and sounds, as words are written. Use the name chart as a check or reference.

The teacher and children create a word chart and later a word wall of high-frequency known words and use word walls interactively.

Emergent/Early/Transitional Writers: Grade One

The children will be linking to clusters and patterns in the name chart (which now has first and last names) rather than only the beginning and ending sounds in their names.

Once concepts about print like spacing, punctuation, capitalization, directionality, etc., are learned they no longer need to be referred to during interactive writing lessons. For example, many children space first with their hands, then with their eyes, and eventually unconsciously in their writing.

The children are able to hear sounds in sequence as they say words slowly and they can represent more and more vowels conventionally.

The teacher may quickly write in the words that the children can easily write automatically in order to save time and to pace the lesson so that more text can be written at one session.

The children correctly write words with unusual spelling patterns because they are visually connecting words they know to words they don't know.

The children begin to quickly write in phrases rather than single letters or words. As the children grow in their knowledge of the writing process, they write a larger percentage of the text.

The children are learning strategies that help them deal with multisyllabic words that include first clapping the segments and then analyzing the segments by: articulating slowly, linking to known, and using visual memory of word chunks and patterns.

Early/Transitional Writers: Grade Two

Interactive writing is done less frequently and often for a particular purpose. For example, when the children are facing a new challenge in their writing (i.e., note taking, complex punctuation, new genre, etc.) or when the teacher wants to establish a community of writers (i.e., writing a group thank you letter, making a request, writing a list of things to do, etc.) The lessons may begin to look more like shared writing where the teacher writes the text, possibly on an overhead projector, while collaborating with the children regarding the message.

As the children become more and more adept at writing they will spend less and less of their language block time involved in the activity of interactive writing and more time in elements such as writing workshop.

[1]Interactive writing lessons move from short (5-10 minute) lessons to longer (10-20 minute) sessions as routines, interests, and a knowledge base are established. Length of any lesson will depend on the children's interest and engagement, the difficulty level of the task, the purpose, and the time available. In general, lessons for kindergarten students are shorter and those for first graders are longer; however, as children grow more advanced, interactive writing may become a short "minilesson" for a particular teaching purpose.

FIGURE 3-5   Following the Children: Shifts Over Time in Interactive Writing[1]

What does the child know? Look at the evidence from the assessments and writing samples.	What does the child *need* to know? Think about what the child needs to know next to be a better writer.	How can I teach what the child needs to know through interactive writing? Generate specific language and/or actions.
Name:		
Name:		

FIGURE 3-6   Assessing Children's Strengths for Interactive Writing Lessons

each member of the group bring four to five writing samples from one child.

2. Place children's names on the grid shown in Figure 3-6 and generate responses in each category. It's a good idea to take one child at a time and fill out the grid together with a grade-level colleague. Mutual support will help in seeing children's strengths and thinking about priorities for teaching. At the end of the session, each of you will have one or two children in mind but will have analyzed several more.

3. Discuss each child and think about what to teach for in interactive writing.

4. Plan a common writing event, perhaps in response to a piece of literature. It is a good idea to use the same book in each classroom because it makes it easier to compare the range and variety of children's responses; however, different ideas and selections can also be used.

Step Two

1. For one or two weeks, develop the interactive writing idea, involving the whole class or a small group of children in your classroom. At the same time, notice how the child you assessed responds. Try to make opportunities for that child each time the interactive writing group meets.

2. Meet again with grade-level colleagues to discuss how:
   ❙ The individual child responded to instruction.
   ❙ You used the individual child's knowledge and strengths in the lesson and extended learning further.

3. As a follow-up, read and discuss Chapter 15, "Interactive Writing: Developing Word-Solving Strategies," from the companion volume *Word Matters: Teaching Phonics and Spelling in the Reading/Writing Classroom.*

Becoming a Writer
Learning Through Interactive Writing

Justina Henry

Introduction

Whenever we involve children in group instruction, we are always concerned about its impact on student learning. To what extent are children able to apply what they have learned to their independent work? In interactive writing, we bring children together to produce a common text. Individuals contribute some of the writing of letters and words, but the purpose of the "share the pen" quality of interactive writing is to bring powerful examples to the attention of the entire group of children through teacher-student interaction. Simultaneously, we involve children in composing a message for a real purpose and examining words within that process.

Observing children within the group setting provides one way of determining how they are responding and how much they are learning. Another way of assessing the power of our interactive writing lessons is to closely observe children while they are in the process of writing independently. In this chapter, Henry follows one child, Paul, from the group setting to independent writing, presenting a detailed example of his behavior. The example provides a model for describing how children are connecting these two important settings for writing—interactive and independent writing.

During interactive writing experiences, teacher and students gather near chart paper placed on an easel to jointly compose and write a message. During these daily lessons in kindergarten and first grade, students learn concepts about print, functions of written language, and how words work.

Terry has engaged her kindergarten students in interactive writing since the first day of school. The students have explored written language by writing, reading, and rereading their texts. They have written invitations to other kindergarten classes in the building inviting them to visit their room for a storytelling party, made signs to advertise the primary book sale, and composed a list of classroom rules. These activities, and numerous others, have enabled them to learn about the hierarchical relationship between the letters, words, sentences, and the whole message. They have learned about letters (letter formation, letter-sound relationships, etc.), words (the concept of *word* and left-to-right serial order of letters within words), and sentence structure—all within the context of writing meaningful messages.

These lessons have helped the students learn early strategies: one-to-one matching, left-to-right directional movement, and locating known and unknown words.

Through instructional conversations, the teacher assists the children by teaching, prompting, demonstrating, and confirming. Each day, the children also write independently, selecting topics of personal interest. Terry observes the children as they write in their journals. She confers with each student individually about their writing. These brief conferences enable her to assess their progress and make one or two teaching points. These interactions with each student inform her teaching decisions for subsequent interactive writing lessons.

What Terry has discovered is that the students have become more independent in analyzing the words they want to write. These young writers have developed many strategies for spelling and consequently are doing more for themselves.

In this chapter, I describe one interactive writing lesson and then explore the spelling strategies of Paul, an emergent writer in Terry's kindergarten classroom. My purpose is to show how a sequence of literacy classroom events—reading aloud, shared reading, interactive writing, and independent writing—supported Paul's learning about written language, particularly spelling. I will also talk about the implications for supporting the development of spelling strategies during interactive writing.

Reading Aloud and the Interactive Writing Lesson

On this day in January, Terry and the children gathered on the carpet to revisit different versions of *The Three Little Pigs*. Terry asked the children if they want to hear Paul Galdone's *The Three Little Pigs* (1979) or James Marshall's *The Three Little Pigs* (1989).

Terry: Raise your hand if you want Paul Galdone's. Raise your hand if you like James Marshall. What are you thinking about? Katy, why do you think you want James Marshall's?

Katy: I like the pictures.

Terry: You like the pictures. Zachary, why do you like James Marshall's?

Zachary: He puts all the characters in clothes.

Kevin: I like the stick houses.

Terry: Let's listen to James Marshall's *The Three Little Pigs*.

Terry read the story to the children and then they participated in a shared reading of a teacher-made big book of *The Three Little Pigs*. The print was written on sentence strips with words large enough for all to see while reading the story together. One child pointed to the print with a pointer while another helped turn the pages. All read the text with expression while the child pointed to the words one by one. Terry helped them develop their understanding of the characters:

Terry: Are you ready to be the wolf?

Terry and the children [reading with feeling]: Little pig, little pig, let me come in.

Revisiting a familiar story like this one enables children to learn more about concepts about print and the features of letters and words. It also prepares them to write their own version during the interactive writing lesson. Retelling and writing a favorite story helps them think about the sequence of events, characters, and features of letters and words.

Then Terry and the children decided to retell the story of the three little pigs by making a story chart, a large mural with pictures, and text made by the children.

Terry: If someone came here and they read our story chart with pictures, it would be like the book of *The Three Little Pigs*.

Cory: That would be cool!

Terry restated the task: "We're going to write our own story of *The Three Little Pigs*. It won't say *The Three Little Pigs by Paul Galdone* or *The Three Little Pigs by James*

Marshall. It will say *The Three Little Pigs by Room 9.*"

In the following example, the conversation supported the children's thinking in solving the problem of finding the right words to retell one of their favorite stories.

Terry: Should we write the title first?

Zachary: The three little pigs . . . by

Terry: Zachary says we should write by . . . by Room 9. Now we have to think in our heads how we are going to start our story of the three little pigs. How does a story start?

Amanda: Once upon a time.

Terry: Some stories start "Once upon a time . . ." Should we start our story of the three little pigs like that? Who else has an idea about how this story should start? Zachary, what's your idea of how it would start?

Zachary: There once . . .

Terry: There once . . . what?

Zachary: Lived a pig with three little pigs.

Terry: There once was a pig with three little pigs . . .

Marcus: Mother pig . . .

Terry: There once was a mother pig . . . That's a pretty good start. We can put that word mother in there. Let's count the words.

Terry held her fingers up one by one while the children said the words they wanted to write.

Terry: There are ten words.

Terry led the children in writing the title of their story, *The Three Little Pigs by Room 9.* Then they repeated the first sentence of their story and decided the first word they needed to write was *There.* Terry said the word slowly and invited the children to say it with her. They decided that they could hear *th* and *r.* Rebecca came up to write *th.*

Terry: She heard the *th* sound. [Terry writes the rest of *there.*]

Kevin: That's *There.*

Terry: You're exactly right.

Ronald: *There* has *the.*

They reread *There* and predicted the next word to be written, *once.* The children said *once* slowly and Amanda offered *w,* a logical choice.

Terry: *Once* sounds like it should start with a *w,* but it is spelled like this. [She writes *once* on the chart next to *there.*]

Marcus: The word *on* is in it.

With Marcus pointing to the words, they reread what they had written and predicted the next word in their sentence: *was.* Terry invited Patrick to write the word *was.*

Terry: He wrote the word *was* for us. Write the next word, Patrick, *a.* [Patrick wrote the word on the chart.] He wrote the words *was a* for us. Let's read it!

Terry's words carried the message that writers know how to spell many words. The next word was *mother.* Terry modeled how to say the word slowly in segments and then the children said the word slowly the same way.

Terry: Katy thinks she remembers *mother* from when she drew the character yesterday and she wrote *the mother pig.*

Katy wrote MO. When Katy hesitated, Terry prompted her to say the word slowly, and then Katy wrote *th.* Then Terry prompted her to recall what comes before the *r.* When Katy wrote the *e* and then the *r,* Terry said *er* in a positive tone of confirmation. "Very good, Katy." In this way, Katy learned that it was good to remember the spelling of words the class had written before. The children were learning to closely observe how words look. They were becoming aware that a direct letter-sound link in the English language does not always exist.

They were relying on their visual memory as well as auditory analysis to spell words.

During the writing of this one word, *mother*, Terry didn't explain where to put the letters on the chart paper, proper spacing between words, or letter formation because the children already knew these concepts from other writing experiences.

Opportunities for new learning emerged from what the children controlled. Terry facilitated their developing spelling strategies: articulating the word slowly, segmenting the word, listening for known parts, analyzing the segments in serial order, and using visual memory of previously written words.

Terry expected the children to make links to known words (e.g., *the* and *mother*). She highlighted their verbal links while the word they were discussing was written on the chart paper. Either Terry or one of the children covered part of the word to show the known chunk within the new word. This procedure made the link more explicit because the children could connect and confirm the oral explanation with the print.

Throughout the process, Terry continued to use the name chart hanging adjacent to the easel to point out important connections from known words to the words the children wanted to spell.

Terry called on the children to deliberately remember an item, focus their attention, and think. These children were learning to attend to the features of words and were anxious to show Terry their discoveries. Her goal was to help the children use the known words and word chunks to write the words of their messages. For instance, she wanted them to learn that they could use the known word *me* to write something new, like *meat*, or *mean*, or *meet*. Learning to look for known letter patterns within a written word is an important visual task to learn.

When they were almost finished with their writing, Terry said, "Here we go. Let's see what word is next." She took the pointer and they reread the sentence to predict *pig*, a known word. The next word was *with*, and Terry helped them articulate the word slowly. They heard the *w*, and then after repeating the word they heard the final *th*. Terry asked, "What else?" Terry repeated the word slowly, stressing the middle of the word. She said, "I hear Amanda say *i*. W-*i*-th . . . w-*i* th . . . the tricky sound is . . . ?" Terry realized that analyzing a word in sequence and attending to the middle would be new learning for the group. She led them in saying it again slowly a few more times to hear the middle sound: w-*i*-th. She said, "It's an *i*," and wrote it on the chart. Although they were not able to hear and record the *i*, they had experienced a new strategy for analyzing the words they wanted to write.

Then as a group, they reread the text and decided to write 3. They wrote it quickly and then they predicted that the next word was *little*. Paul came up to the easel and wrote *tl*. Terry noticed this action and said, "Let me see what you have so far." She covered his letters with the correction tape and prompted him to say the word slowly. "What's the first sound you hear for *little*?" They said the word together: *little*. Terry enunciated the parts clearly and, with the prompting of the other students, Paul wrote the word on the chart paper.

The group reread the sentence again. So far they had written *Once there was a mother pig with 3 little . . .* They were excited about knowing how to spell *pigs*—a known word! Terry said, "I hear you say p-i-g, but the word is *pigs*. . . ." The children called out "s," and Terry confirmed, "Yes, *pigs* has an *s*." Katy came up to write *pigs*.

Terry: Here we go—she is going to write *pigs*. Give her a chance to make those letters. What goes at the end of that story? [Katy put in a period.]

The lesson ended with everyone reading the sentence again while Katy pointed to the words one by one.

Independent Writing

As the group lesson finished, the children left the carpet to write independently in their journals. The routine had long been established and the children were accustomed to writing their own stories.

Influenced by the morning's activities, Paul decided to write about the three pigs (Figure 4-1). An analysis of his writing shows that Paul had internalized ways to help himself write the words of his message. Paul composed his message and analyzed each word aloud. His message reads, *And the mom was sad because the three little pigs were lost because the mom did not have no money to keep the pigs*.

His process of analyzing the words he wanted to write in his journal is presented in Figure 4-2. The analysis begins with the word *because*, after he had written *And the mom was sad*. The analysis indicates that Paul had learned to control a number of important strategies for spelling the words of his message. He remembered the words of the sentences he wanted to write and analyzed each word differently.

■ Paul knew how to separate his message into individual words. He wrote his message left to right, with a return sweep, and top-to-bottom. He used his finger to mark the space between the words. His knowing the boundaries of each word helped him separate the segments and analyze them one by one. Each time he attempted to analyze the segments, he learned more about hearing the phonemes and matching them with letters.

■ He could segment words and analyze the segments in left-to-right serial order. Saying the word aloud helped Paul hear whether the word had one, two, or more segments.

■ He could isolate and stress sounds within segments. He separated the segments into sounds by saying each sound with emphasis to hear the sound better and match it to a letter.

■ Paul knew to repeat words and parts of words. He repeated the words or segments he was analyzing. Perhaps this helped him focus his attention on the sounds and link them to something he knew about letters and/or sounds that letters represent.

Paul efficiently wrote known words without articulating them slowly. He was able to write the words of his message independently, although not entirely in conventional spelling, using several strategies that reduced the memory requirements of the learning process. In addition, noticing the discrepancies between his expectations of word spelling and conventional spelling may have enabled Paul to learn new spellings more effectively. Eventually Paul will internalize the strategies, and learn more about words, and he will rely less on simple letter-sound correspondences.

Paul is becoming skilled at phonological processing. He can recognize and is able to manipulate speech sounds. He has learned how to listen and divide words into segments. Paul used his knowledge of letter-sound relationships to sequence sounds and syllables in the words he wanted to write. He will soon learn that it is possible to construct spellings of unfamiliar words by using orthographic patterns of known words. Paul can be helped to understand that rhyming words often have similar word spellings (e.g., if he knows *pig*, then he can spell *jig*, etc.).

Like the other kindergartners in his classroom, Paul is a language user. Becoming a language user means choosing one's own topics, writing and reading every day, and sharing stories. In the process, the students learn more about writing each time they write. Teachers can design a classroom structure that will support students as developing writers by including a daily schedule of reading aloud, shared reading, interactive writing, and independent writing experiences. The following list includes ways teachers can facilitate children's development of spelling strategies during interactive writing.

■ Teach the students to articulate the words slowly (rather than isolating the sounds). Invite them to try on their own and observe their control of analyzing the sounds they hear in the words they want to write.

■ Help the students move beyond analyzing words at the letter level. Teach them to hear

FIGURE 4-1   Paul's Writing

known chunks. Write words on a white board or chart paper and point out the similarities and differences between words. Discuss how they can hear and see the known and unfamiliar parts. For instance, write and analyze *go* and *going*; *the* and *there*; *cat* and *mat*, and so forth.

❚ Expand on any chunks the children notice as they articulate words they are trying to spell. Acknowledge their cleverness and write the chunk on chart paper for all to see. Show them how this chunk is in one or two other words. List the words and point out their similarities and differences. For instance, if they hear the *br* in *brushes*, the word they are analyzing, link it to known words, perhaps *bread* and *brown*, or *Brian*, a classmate's name. Point out to them that if they know

brown, they can figure out how to begin to write *brushes*. In this way, they can learn that analogies are useful in thinking about how words work.

❚ Notice the students' confusions and address them in one or two immediate teaching points. Help the children develop visual perception strategies by making clear the links between what they know and what they want to write.

❚ Begin a collection of high-frequency and interesting words on a word wall for word study. Add to and refer to these lists of words over the weeks.

❚ Follow up these discussions by providing time for independent exploration activities at centers. The students can engage in word-sorting activities using and extending

Description of Paul's Writing Process

He wanted to write *because.*

Says	Writes	Behaviors indicating use of strategies
Be	B	Says the first segment and writes what he hears.
cuz	c	Says the second segment and writes the first letter of the second segment.
second segment		
cu	o	Says the consonant and vowel of the second segment and writes *o* (the position of the mouth when saying the letters *o* and *cu* is similar).
cuz		Says the second segment, stressing the last sound.
cuz	z	Says the second segment and writes the letter of the last sound heard.
because		Says the word he has just analyzed and written.

Paul continued to write the words *the, did, not have, no, money,* and *to.* Consistently, he said the word aloud, stressing each segment of the word as it became necessary to write it. He also tended to repeat the word after writing it, as if to check the letter sequence. On more complex words, such as *money,* he divided the word by syllables as he pronounced it. For familiar words such as *to,* Paul was able to say and write the word all at once.

He wanted to write *keep.*

Says	Writes	Behaviors indicating use of strategies
keep		Says the word.
ke	c	Says the initial consonant and vowel and writes the initial consonant sound.
ke		Says the initial consonant and vowel (repeated).
k		Says and stresses the initial consonant (onset).
ke	ep	Says and stresses the initial consonant and writes the vowel and final sound.
keep		Says the word just analyzed.

Paul continued to write his message, working out *the* and then spelling *pigs*—P-I-G-S, much as the group had done in the interactive writing lesson.
When finished he announced, "I'm done!"

FIGURE 4-2   Description of Paul's Writing Process

the words that were discussed during interactive writing lessons. Observe the students working independently or with partners participating in a word-sort activity.

❙ Make specific links to the students' names by using a name chart. Be sure the chart is close to the easel and in clear view so that it's possible to make links during the writing of the words of the message. For example, say "Oh, the beginning sound in *shoe* is like the beginning sound in your name,

Shannon." Touch the letters in the name on the name chart.

❙ Try asking the students to respond to these questions when they are attempting to write an unfamiliar word: "What do you know about?" "What does this remind you of?" or "What is this like?" These questions prompt the students to make their own connections as well as convey the nature of the task: to make links independently. The idea is to create a metalinguistic dialogue about letters, words, sentences, and language and how it all works together in reading and writing.

❚ Teach for independence and encourage changes over time as the children become more competent. Comments should convey that the students are expected to remember without prompts.

❚ Provide feedback to the students in the form of explicit praise for problem solving new words independently. Encouragement and praise from a teacher creates enthusiasm that maintains students' attention to the writing task.

Giving children strategies for spelling can help them understand the underlying alphabetic link between spoken and written words. They may have learned sound-letter rules but need explicit instruction to understand how this knowledge can help them spell words. Teachers of emergent and early learners observe the students during everyday reading and writing activities to determine what instructional steps to take next:

❚ What do they control in writing? In reading?
❚ Are they developing control of strategies for spelling?

Teachers will find it beneficial to analyze the students' independent writing to determine their control of word analysis and the extent of their writing vocabularies. The children's responses to the tasks of the *Observation Survey* (Clay 1993a) provide baseline data and a starting point for instructional decision making. Knowing the students' strengths and instructional needs will enable teachers to determine an emphasis for each lesson.

Suggestions for Professional Development

1. This chapter provided a detailed description of an interactive writing session as well as a follow-up description of one child's independent writing. Of course, you won't conduct every interactive session exactly this way. Your decisions depend on the children and what they know and need to know. Look at Paul's writing and the description of his writing process. With colleagues, consider the following:

❚ What behaviors does it seem that he learned from participating in interactive writing lessons?
❚ What does he control and use independently?
❚ What does he need to learn now?

2. Conduct an interactive writing session with your whole class or a small group of your students. Then, direct the students to produce their own writing on a similar topic.

3. Follow one student in independent writing. Observe for about fifteen minutes, noting the writing process in as much descriptive detail as you can.

4. Bring the student's written product and your observational notes to a follow-up session with colleagues. Use the questions that guided Terry's work with her own students for your student.

5. Think about the next interactive writing session in which this student will participate.

❚ What should be the focus of the lesson?
❚ What learning opportunities would you like to provide for this student?

6. Discuss with your colleagues some specific interactions that you think would help your student develop his or her spelling ability.

7. As a follow-up, review and discuss Chapter 16, "The Writing Workshop: Support for Word Learning," from the companion volume to this book, *Word Matters: Teaching Phonics and Spelling in the Reading/Writing Classroom*.

Kindergarten Explorations of Letters, Sounds, and Words

Andrea McCarrier and Ida Patacca

Introduction

As young children become word solvers in writing, they increase their sensitivity to the sounds and signs of language through their many experiences with meaningful print. Children develop phonological and orthographic awareness through group processes such as interactive writing, but there are other ways of focusing on print that are particularly helpful to young children, especially those children who have not had extensive preschool experiences with written language. McCarrier and Patacca, who have worked together as a classroom research team for several years, help us understand the very personal nature of those first experiences with print as well as how teachers can use personal connections to support learning. For example, powerful networks of learning can be built around children's own names. The authors report their year-long documentation of children's learning about letters and words. The instruction in this classroom is multifaceted. The teacher, Ida Patacca, engages children in looking at their own names, encouraging them to use their knowledge to write continuous text. Interactive writing is an important instructional tool in the process. Explicit modeling and linking to what children know are hallmarks of this instructional process. The authors also provide important evidence of children's literacy achievement as a check on whether instructional goals have been met.

Rayshawn, his teacher, and the members of his kindergarten class were working together to write labels on their story map of *The Great Big Enormous Turnip* (Domanska 1969). The group wanted to write *grandmother*. Ida, the teacher, invited them to say the word *grandmother* together. The children said that they heard *g*, and then Ida wrote *g*, followed by the *r*.

When Rayshawn saw the *r* go up on the chart, he said, "Hey, what's my *r* doing up there?" It is not an accident that Rayshawn recognized the *r*; it's the most important letter in his name.

Ida said, "Rayshawn, the *r* is in a lot of words, just like your name. Mr. Rader, the principal, has a name that starts with *r*, too."

Rayshawn thought that was a pretty good idea. He liked sharing his *r* with the principal, and he was also pleased to find that the gym teacher's name began with an *r*.

Then Mrs. Law, the classroom assistant, announced that her middle name, *Rose*, began with an *r*. This presented a dilemma to

Rayshawn, who said, "It can't be in a girl's name!"

Even from this short observation, it is obvious that Rayshawn was building a network of understandings around something that he knew—his name. In this chapter, we describe how children use their names as a valuable resource in becoming literate. At first, literacy knowledge is highly personal, but through classroom experiences such as Rayshawn's, it can become public and systematized. The key is to start with what children know, what they connect to themselves, and find interesting.

Rayshawn identified with the print version of his name because it represented him in a very personal way. Indeed, for most children, recognizing letters in a name is a significant first step in literacy, followed closely by the realization that letters are used to represent all kinds of things in our world—people, objects, places, and so forth. This personal literacy soon encompasses the names of other people in the class, their friends, their teacher, and their families. According to Clay (1991a), "A child's name has singular importance as he embarks on learning about literacy." Clay's theory suggests that a child's name may be the first "program for action" that the child can use. For example, it's possible to write one's name in many places and for many purposes; it is always the same program for action. Soon, though, children begin to build networks of understanding around this program.

In another situation, the group was writing "*Eat lots of great food*" as part of a study on healthy foods. They were making a list of what they need to do to stay healthy. The sentence was generated by the group and written on a large piece of chart paper by the teacher and the children. When they got to the word *great*, Ida asked them to say the word slowly and to think about the sounds they heard. Many children in the group responded by saying, "*R*, just like in Roy's name."

The group of children were building a common set of knowledge about sounds and letters. They shared this body of knowledge because they had worked together in many experiences and their teacher had encouraged them to make links. Assisted by group conversations, each child was gathering a set of understandings about literacy that was both personal and shared across peers.

Teachers help children build a network of information that they can then use to learn more. This network of information is built through working with print in many different ways. This body of knowledge includes:

- Names of people in the group.
- Letter names.
- Sound-letter relationships.
- Some individual, high-frequency words.

Many of these items of knowledge are connected to the children because they are loaded with meaning; they have emotional appeal. This process is different from learning an alphabet chart with pictures such as a dog for *d*. What is happening here is a personal connection—*d* is for *Dejohn*—and it has a powerful impact. Not every letter is explicitly taught as an item, but letters are explicitly taught and learned through these personal connections.

Why is this body of knowledge important? Knowing the letters in one's name, putting them together to make one's name, and using names to make new words in interactive writing not only helps children learn the particular items. The process also helps them become strategic in their learning so they can use what they know to get to what they need to know. They learn what letters are and how they are used. They learn that letters with the same name have different forms—uppercase and lowercase, different sizes, different fonts, and so on. They learn to put letters together to make words and/or identify letters in words. They learn to connect letters and letter clusters with sounds. They learn how to use a known word in many ways as a resource. If we can help children understand that principle, the knowledge can be used in many different ways. It becomes a tool for further learning.

Important networks of understanding can be built around children's names, and that knowledge is broadened and systematized through the first year of schooling. Here's a brief example:

1. Roy entered kindergarten knowing that the oral name "Roy" is his and represents him.

2. He began to learn that a visual rendition of "Roy" also represents him.

3. He learned that his name is made up of the letters R, o, y, and that they must be in a particular order.

4. He learned that the written symbols that make up Roy have names themselves—the names of the letters.

5. He learned that the written symbols are connected to the oral rendition of Roy and individual letters or letter clusters are related to sounds.

6. He learned that we can hear those sounds in many other words; and we see those letters in many other words.

7. The same process occurred with Roy's last name and with his knowledge of the names of his classmates and teacher.

Children who learn that the letters have names and connections to sounds that they can find in many places in printed language have taken a big step in literacy learning. It is a step that creates networks of knowledge that they can use in many ways.

In Roy's kindergarten class, he experienced a series of literacy activities designed to actively foster the creation of networks of understanding. In this chapter we describe three contexts for literacy learning, each based on using children's names as a foundation for systematizing knowledge, and we provide examples of children and their

teachers working together. Finally, we discuss the achievement of this class as a whole. For purposes of this chapter, we will focus only on the measurement of letter knowledge and sound-letter correspondence, two elements that are strong indicators of success in later grades. We also note, however, that children in this classroom learned to write their own messages and to read simple storybooks.

Three Contexts for Literacy Learning

As an experienced kindergarten teacher, Ida uses a combination of reading and writing experiences as well as letter and word study. She designs these study sessions to help her young students learn about letters, sounds, and how they are used to create written messages. Her classroom is a rich learning environment that invites children to use literacy in many ways. For example, she reads aloud to children several times a day, relying on a fine collection of children's literature. She involves them in shared reading, and they have opportunities to read for themselves from Ida's well-developed classroom library. She brings children together for guided reading lessons, and she uses writing workshops to guide them in producing their own writing. She teaches her students about words and how they work in every classroom literacy activity.

By the end of the year, Ida expects that the students in her kindergarten class will:

■ Recognize and name the uppercase and lowercase letters of the alphabet.
■ Know the sound-symbol relationships of most consonants.
■ Have a beginning awareness of the sound-symbol relationships of vowels.
■ Know how to form the uppercase and lowercase letters of the alphabet.
■ Use visual information to monitor while reading.
■ Know some words in every detail and be able to write and/or read them.

How can these high expectations be achieved? Ida organizes instruction into three contexts.

Focused Letter and Word Study Using a Name Chart

The name chart (Figure 5-1) is a powerful tool for introducing children to the way letters are used to record oral language. To create the name chart, the teacher places the names of all children on the chart, grouping together the names that begin with the same first letter.

As Ida directs her students to focus on a word that is extremely important to them—in this instance, their own names—she helps her students learn some important ideas about written language. For example, they learn that:

■ Their name is always the same sequence of characters/letters.
■ There is white space around their name.
■ Several letters cluster together in their name.

■ The beginning letter of their name is connected to words that sound the same.
■ The last letter of their name is connected to words that sound the same.

Teachers use the name chart as a way to build item knowledge. This is especially true when teachers are working with children who enter kindergarten with limited knowledge of letters. Here are some suggestions for using the name chart to develop specific knowledge.

■ Point to each name on the chart as the children read the names aloud, demonstrating the relationships between written and oral language.

■ Have children locate names on the chart after saying them slowly.

■ Use the name chart as shared reading, pointing to each name.

■ Draw children's attention to names that are alike in any way (first letter or letters, last letter or letters, etc.).

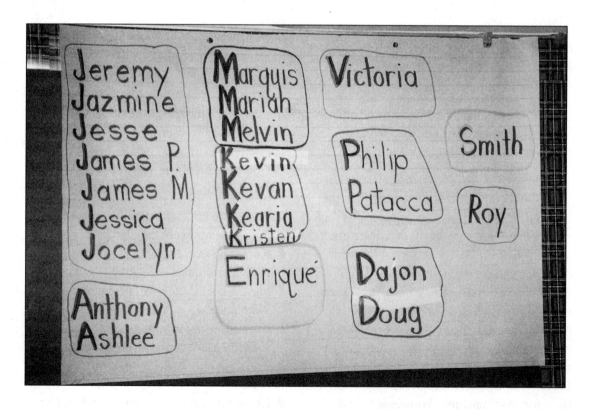

FIGURE 5-1 Name Chart

■ Be clear and explicit when linking names to words that are written in interactive writing. (Point to the name or have a child point.)

Kindergarten teachers also use the name chart as a resource for writing. In fact, the name chart is one of the first references that children learn to use. This action teaches children to use what they know to figure out something they do not know. During interactive writing, we often use the name chart to draw children's attention to letters—their names, form, and sound. For example, if the children in the class are labeling the items they want to put in "Old Mother Hubbard's cupboard," and they want to write the word *raisins*, the teacher can point to Roy's name on the name chart and say, "*Raisins* starts with an *r* just like *Roy*—*Roy, raisins*. Say it with me: *Roy, raisins*."

The teacher might then ask Roy (or another child) to come up to the chart and write the letter *r* while the other children practice making an *r* in the air or on the carpet. If many children do not know how to form the letter *r*, the teacher can demonstrate on the Magna Doodle or a white board, hold up a magnetic letter, or point to the *r* in Roy's name. If children are more advanced and it seems especially important to use a lowercase letter, the teacher can find lowercase *r*s in the names of Kearia, Jeremy, and Mariah.

During this brief interaction, the teacher will have focused children's attention on the letter-sound relationship of *r*, the name of the letter, and coordination of visual and motor skills they need to form the letter. This kind of explicit teaching helps children develop better control over all the ways of knowing a letter, and at the same time it teaches them how to use this knowledge in generative ways.

Gaining Access to Words Through a Name Puzzle

The name puzzle (Figure 5-2) is a focused word study experience that helps the young children gain access to an important item of knowledge—their name as a word—as well as the individual letters in the name. The task for the children is to place the letters of their name, written on individual tagboard squares, in the correct sequence, from left to right. When the children have assembled their name, they point to each letter and tell the teacher the name of each letter.

This focused experience is especially useful for children who enter school with limited knowledge of letters. Every time children search for the letters they need to assemble their name puzzles and identify the letters in their name in a left-to-right sequence, children learn more about the distinctive features, proper orientation, and names of the letters in their names. They are learning how to look at print with a set of letters that have special importance to them.

Introduction to the Name Puzzle

Each year, most children entering Ida's kindergarten classroom have a limited knowledge of print and how it works. Most children cannot write their first names. Ida uses the name puzzle as one way to help children begin to look at print. She uses names as a vehicle for building an understanding of letters, words, and how they work because she wants to begin with print that has special significance and is of high utility for that child.

As children assemble their name puzzles, they start to understand that:

■ Their spoken names can be represented by a series of symbols called letters.

■ Letters, themselves, have names.

■ Letters are used to build words.

■ Each letter looks different from every other letter, and letters must be oriented in a particular way.

A few weeks after school has started, Ida introduces the name puzzle to small groups of children. As soon as a child is able to assemble her own first name and identify each

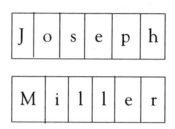

FIGURE 5-2 **Name Puzzle**

letter, Ida adds the last name. By the time the children are able to assemble the first and last name and to name all of the letters included, they have become familiar with the letter names, distinctive features, and correct orientation for the letters. They have also learned that the letters within a word have a specific sequence—a sequence that cannot be altered.

Learning About Letters, Sounds, and Print Through Interactive Writing

Emergent readers and writers need to know more than the names of letters, their distinctive features, and their correct orientation in order to become proficient readers and writers. They must learn the function that letters play in written language. For example, children need to learn that, with two exceptions (*I, a*), words are formed with groups of letters, and that the sequence of letters used to write a word never changes.

Developing control over sound-symbol relationships in both reading and writing is essential if children are to become proficient readers and writers. The sound-symbol relationships are not taught during the name puzzle activity. Teachers explicitly teach sound-symbol relationships as they confer with children during independent writing, during shared and guided reading lessons, and during interactive writing lessons, which we will focus on here. Teachers teach children how to say words slowly and then write down the letter or cluster of letters they need to represent what they hear in

written language. This is the process that Clay (1993a) refers to as hearing and recording sounds in words.

Interactive writing is a tool for teaching young children how to use the conventions of written language in order to record messages. During the lesson, the teacher and students collaborate on the negotiation and writing of the text. They share the pen; the teacher contributes only what children are unable to write alone or without assistance.

There is always an authentic purpose for writing because the writing is linked in some way to what children are studying. For example, children who are listening to several versions of a folktale may decide to write their own version. If the children are cooking, they may use interactive writing to create a shopping list or write a set of directions for their parents to follow (Pinnell and Mc-Carrier 1994).

Once the purpose for writing is identified and the form and content of the message are established, the teacher helps children record the message using the conventions of written language. For example, children learn that messages are written from left to right and top to bottom, the function of space to denote word boundaries, and the use of punctuation to indicate units of thought.

All words in the message are written conventionally. Most words are constructed with the help of the teacher, using the process of saying words slowly to hear and record sounds in words. Children are explicitly taught to use this process as an aid for writing many words.

The only time the teacher may not require students to adhere to the conventions of written language is when young writers use uppercase letters in nonconventional ways. The rationale for this exception is related to teaching children to learn how to use what they know about written language to write a word that they do not know. The distinctive features of uppercase letters seem to be easier for young children to notice than the distinctive features of lowercase letters. Consequently emergent writers may feel more confident in using the form over which they have greater control—an uppercase *B, D, Q,* or *M* instead of a lowercase *b, d, q,* or *m*. (In fact, for several of the lowercase letters, the distinctive features of the letter must be combined with the proper orientation; *d* becomes *p* or *b* if it is not oriented in the conventional manner.)

Interactive writing is an instructional context in which teachers help children attend to the details of written language as they write for authentic purposes. During interactive writing lessons, teacher and children attend to all levels of written language: the message, sentences, words, and letters. After the children have decided on the message they want to write, the teacher helps them select the proper format for that kind of text (e.g., a list, a letter, a story).

The teacher then assists them in using the conventions of written language that are appropriate for that piece of writing. In almost all pieces of interactive writing, children will learn the conventions regarding the format of texts: left-to-right and top-to-bottom directionality and spacing between words. They will also learn when, why, and how writers use punctuation to communicate messages to their readers.

Teachers also help children learn strategies for learning how to write words. They teach children the process of hearing and recording sounds in words, how to use what they know about the way to write one word (*gruff*) to write another word (*great*). They teach children to check their writing to be sure the word looks right. Finally, they teach children to use the resources around them—words on the word wall or other pieces of interactive writing—in order to write words.

This close attention to letters, words, and sounds is a key feature because it helps young writers understand how to encode the messages they want to write in a very supported context. At the same time, good teachers know that is important for children to rehearse what they are learning about the writing process during interactive writing as they compose and record their own messages during independent writing.

A Sample Interactive Writing Lesson

Ida integrates the language arts with content-area teaching whenever possible. About mid-September the children had started talking about good health habits, and the children were making a list (see Figure 5-3). During the negotiation of the text, each child had an opportunity to contribute an item for the list. Because several children said something about eating good food, Ida suggested that they add a sentence about being healthy.

Melvyn: Eat good food.

Ida: Eat good food. You know what? You all have such wonderful ideas. Here's what we're going to do. We're going to take this sentence strip and we are going to write one of those good ideas on this sentence strip.

Child: How come you said one?

Ida: Well, we can't do all of them. Maybe we'll have time to do two today. A lot of you said, "*Eat lots of great food.*" That's a really good one. If we try to write that one, I wonder how many words we will have to write. I am going to see if I can count how many words. And you help me count by counting on your fingers.

Children: 1, 2, 3 . . .

Ida: No, don't count out loud. Say the words of the sentence.

Ida and Children: Eat lots of great food.

Child: Five.

Ida: That's five words. I am going to say it again to make sure. You check on your hand.

Ida and Children: Eat lots of great food.

Ida: That was five words. What's the first word?

At this point the lesson moved from establishing the message to recording it on the sentence strip. The following interaction illustrates the construction of the word *eat*.

Ida: Phillip, come on up here [to the easel used for interactive writing]. Let's get a nice dark marker—black would be fine—so that it shows up here. Now. Phillip, I have a question for you. If we are going to write the word *eat,* where are we going to start to write? [Phillip pointed to the left-hand side of the sentence strip.] Well, why do you want to start there? [Phillip pointed to the sentence strip again.] But how come there? You're right. But how come there?

Phillip [joined by a few other children]: Because we always start on the left.

Ida: That's exactly right. We always have to start on the left. And you are going to start on the left and you are going to write *eat.* But, hang on a minute. [Ida turned to the class and said the word slowly with the children—*eat.*]

Children: E!

Ida: E. We can hear it. You know what? We need to make an *E* just like Enrique's *E.* All the way on the left. [As Ida talked, she walked over to the name chart and pointed to the letter *E* at the beginning of Enrique's name.]

Enrique: I can do that.

Ida: I know that you can do that too, Enrique. You are good at your *Es.* [Ida continued to point to Enrique's *E.*] Oh, look how carefully he is doing this. And he has started all the way over on the left. Wonderful.

The lesson continued and the children collaborated as they shared the pen with the teacher to create the text in Figure 5-3.

Later in the year, the children had become much more sophisticated in their knowledge about letters, words, and how they work. Children in the class wrote many words quickly, knowing every detail. They spontaneously made links to the names of children in the class and used the name chart to check words. Members of the class were using important concepts in producing their own independent writing. The piece of interactive writing in Figure 5-4 is an example. Ida and the children were providing directions for making "stone soup."

By mid-April, many children had become quite proficient writers. They could write stories with two or three lines of text and use many of the basic conventions of written language such as left-to-right directionality and spacing between words. Most could write many high-frequency words and analyze words to identify the first and last letters.

Documentation of Progress

We have described three instructional contexts for helping children learn about letters and words:

■ The name chart.
■ The name puzzle.
■ Interactive writing.

The first two contexts represent focused study of letters around children's names to develop beginning understandings of words. The third context is much more complex, but it is tightly connected to the first two. It is through interactive writing that kindergarten children begin to understand how to

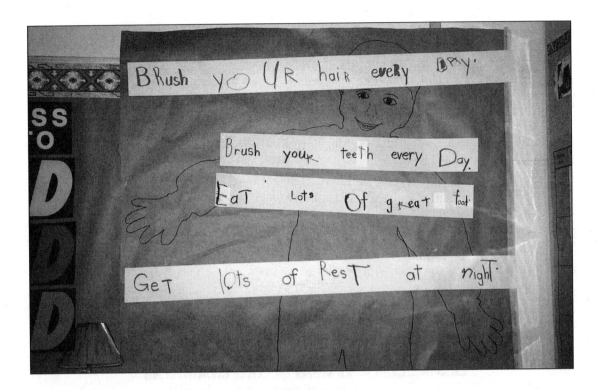

FIGURE 5-3 Interactive Writing (Good Health Habits)

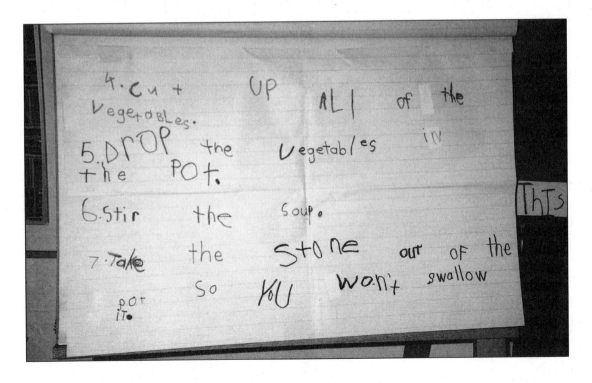

FIGURE 5-4 Interactive Writing (Stone Soup)

use their knowledge in the construction of something they want to write.

Did Ida achieve her goals? The tables in Figures 5-5 and 5-6 show the progress of each one of her students throughout the year. Two measures are represented: Letter Identification and Hearing and Recording Sounds in Words (Clay 1993a). In the letter identification task the teacher asks children to name the letters of the alphabet, to say the related sound, or to produce a word that begins with the letter. Typically, in the United States, children simply name the letters. The high score is 54 (to include 26 upper- and lowercase letters and the print characters for g and a). Results of the letter identification assessment are presented in Figure 5-5.

The average score just prior to school entry was 6.59, with a range of 0 to 44 letters. Most children were just beginning to look at print. By spring, almost all children had learned the letters. Kevin and Jessica will need extra help.

In the Hearing and Recording Sounds in Words task the teacher asks children to try to record the sounds in words that are presented in the form of a brief "story." The student receives one point for every sound recorded with an acceptable letter, with a high score of 37. This assessment requires that children hear the sounds that are embedded in words

---

Individual and Mean Scores on Letter Identification
Fall '96 and Spring '97

Student Name	LID Fall	LID Spring
Syha	-*	54
Roy	2	54
Douglas	0	39
Jocelyn	3	51
Katelynn	-	54
Nichole	-	54
Kearia	7	52
Jazmine	7	54
Brittany	-	22
Camaron	-	52
Enrique	12	53
Markus	-	49
Dajon	9	54
Kevan	44	54
Sobenie	-	54
Ashlee	0	54
Marquis	2	54
James	8	54
Mariah	4	54
Kevin	0	-
Anthony	13	54
Jessica	0	11
Melvin	1	54
Mean	6.59	49.32

*- indicates the child was not enrolled in the class when the task was administered

FIGURE 5-5   Letter Identification Assessment Results

**Individual and Mean Scores on Hearing and Recording Sounds in Words
Fall '96 and Spring '97**

Student Name	HRSIW Fall	HRSIW Spring
Syha	-*	18
Roy	0	31
Douglas	0	17
Jocelyn	1	26
Katelynn	-	33
Nichole	-	22
Kearia	2	32
Jazmine	1	22
Brittany	-	6
Camaron	-	26
Enrique	0	31
Markus	-	6
Dajon	0	29
Kevan	8	32
Sobenie	-	34
Ashlee	0	18
Marquis	0	27
James	0	27
Mariah	0	33
Kevin	0	-
Anthony	1	30
Jessica	0	6
Melvin	0	29
Mean	0.81	24.32

*- indicates the child was not enrolled in the class when the task was administered

FIGURE 5-6   Hearing and Recording Sounds in Words

rather than stressed in isolation. Results of the Hearing and Recording Sounds in Words assessment are presented in Figure 5-6.

It is obvious that skills for hearing and recording sounds were slower to develop than skills for letter identification. That makes sense. Children were learning the concept that words are made up of sequences of sounds, and then were also learning the visual features of letters. As those understandings became clearer, it became easier to make connections between letters and sounds in words. Nevertheless, the average score in May was 24.3 of the possible 37, with a range of 6 to 34. Most of the children

were demonstrating a good beginning understanding of the alphabetic principle and how to apply it in writing.

These documented results indicate that almost all of the children in this kindergarten class learned items of knowledge (such as words and letter-sound relationships). They built up a repertoire of useful information that will help them as they enter first grade.

Suggestions for Professional Development

1. Organize a team in your school to document the results of using the three

contexts for teaching about letters and words. Note that these three contexts combine:

- ∎ Direct teaching of sound-letter relationships.
- ∎ Examination of words.
- ∎ Using knowledge of letters and words to write, and then read, a simple text.

2. Administer Clay's (1993a) Letter Identification task and Hearing and Recording Sounds in Words task to the children in a kindergarten class[1]. You may want to work with the whole class or a small group.

3. Alternatively, you may want to administer any letter identification or phonics test you know and typically use.

4. Work intensively using the three instructional approaches presented in this chapter. Try to work for at least one month, every day. Ideally, if you have your own class or small group, work for about three months for a short time each day.

5. While instruction is progressing, make informal notes of behaviors that indicate children are beginning to notice aspects of print and to connect letters and sounds.

6. At the end of the period, assess the children again. What learning is evident? What would you predict if you continued the instruction for several more weeks or months?

7. Share experiences with using the name chart, name puzzle, and interactive writing. What did you learn from the experience? What are the implications for the curriculum?

8. As a follow-up, read and discuss Chapter 5, "Interactive Word Walls and Charts," Chapter 7, "Building on Early Learning," and Chapter 9, "What Children Need to Know About Letters and Words," from the companion volume to this book, *Word Matters: Teaching Phonics and Spelling in the Reading/Writing Classroom.*

---

[1] If letter and word knowledge is typically low for entering first graders, you can use a first-grade class. Or, you may consider working with a group of very inexperienced first graders for a short time. First-grade children, and even second-grade children who have had limited experience with print, may need the instructional approaches included in this chapter.

Letter Learning in the Early Literacy Classroom

Carol A. Lyons

Introduction

Letter learning alone is not sufficient to assure competent reading and writing; it is, however, foundational in literacy learning. As children learn letters, they learn to discern the distinctive features that distinguish one letter from another. When they can distinguish letters they can attach names to them and relate sounds to these written symbols. The challenge to the young reader or writer is not only to learn letters and make connections between letters, sounds, and letter names, but to use this information to work with letters that are embedded in words, sentences, and longer texts. Our goal is to help children use their knowledge as a tool in the complex processes of reading and writing. We should not assume that alphabet learning is simple or easy.

In this chapter Lyons helps us understand how many different kinds of complex knowledge go into recognizing and forming the letters of the alphabet, and she helps us understand that preschool, kindergarten, and first-grade environments must be rich in opportunities for children to explore the network of information associated with letters. Letter learning, with all the complex understanding implied, is critical in the first years of schooling. In addition to excellent classroom practice, teachers must be pre-

pared to offer as much individualized, explicit instruction as children might need in order to help them tell one letter from another and categorize letters.

Learning the ABCs is part of childhood. We now know that many different factors contribute to the early learning of literacy, but alphabet learning is still a critical factor. In fact, learning the letters and their corresponding sounds has been identified as a *necessary factor* (Adams 1990).

What Does It Mean to Learn Letters?

Knowing a letter means knowing it as a distinct entity, not just being able to name or sing the letters of the alphabet and give their sounds. It means acquiring the ability to compare and contrast each letter in the alphabet with every other letter. According to Clay (1991a), "what we have overlooked for too long is the fact that before a child can attach a sound to a letter symbol he must first of all be able to *see* the letter symbol as an individual entity different from other symbols" (266). In this chapter, I will discuss *what* a child must learn how to do in order to see a letter symbol as an individual entity, *how* a young child acquires this ability, and *why* acquiring this ability is critical to becoming literate.

Seeing a Letter Symbol as a Distinct Entity

The eyes look at a letter, collect the visual information, and direct this information to the brain. The information that the brain receives from print is visual information. However, this act is not sufficient to explain reading. For example, six-year-old David looked at a beautifully illustrated book with many words on the page. Using good oral language skills and pretending to read, he told a meaningful story that corresponded to what he saw in the pictures on each page, but he did not read one word of the printed text. David had access to the visual information because his eyes could see the print, but he was unable to notice or use it effectively.

Our eyes look at and perceive information that make up individual letters (the circles, curves, tails, squiggles, etc.), but it is the brain that determines what we really see and how we see it. Perceptual decisions are based only partly on information received from the eyes, and they are greatly influenced by the knowledge we already possess.

This knowledge enables us to:

■ Search for and detect distinctive visual features of the letter (for example, the placement of dots, lines, circles, and tails that make up components of a particular letter).

■ Distinguish relevant features of one letter from those of another letter (such as to distinguish relevant features and components needed to form a lowercase *b* from essential features and components needed to form a lowercase *d*.

■ Identify the relevant features of a letter and search for that particular information in print.

Some young children come to reading and writing ready to use the visual information they see. They have acquired the ability to recognize the distinctive features by which various letter configurations are categorized. Another first-grade student, Mary, said that the only difference between the letters *b* and *d* is that "when writing the letter *b*, you put the stick on the left side of the circle, and to write a *d* the stick goes on the right side of the circle." Mary had developed a complex category system for organizing letters. As Clay (1991a) notes:

> . . . each letter must be contrasted with every other letter so that thousands of discriminations are made initially on some basis that works for a particular child and probably not like any of the systems adults think of. At the earliest stage this is not phonetic learning or alphabet learning, or even key word learning. It is something inarticulate and unsystematic that works for an individual child. (266)

Mary was able to recognize, categorize, and label the essential features of the *b* and *d* that make them similar and yet different enough to have different names.

David, on the other hand, could not name or write any letters, including the letters needed to write his name. He had not acquired the category system for classifying distinctive features of letters. He needed to now learn to pay close attention to the lines, circles, tails, squiggles, dots, and so on that make up the features of individual letters. He needed to learn to tell what makes one letter different from every other and how making a *t*, for example, is similar to but differs slightly from making an *f* or an *i*.

Learning how to see a letter symbol as a distinct entity and how to discriminate one letter from another is a very important skill that requires the child to grasp a great number of abstractions. For example, when learning how to write the lowercase *h*, the child is expected to remember that:

■ A straight line that looks like this [|] and a line that looks like this [∩], placed together in just the right relationship like this [h] and not like this [ɗ].

■ Together these lines have a name that people call by the nonsense sound "aich" (/ aich /).

■ An "aich" has another form consisting of three different lines that look like this: **H**.

■ These three lines must also be put together in just the right relationship, like this: **H**, to form an uppercase "aich."

■ Furthermore, even though the uppercase *H* looks different from the lowercase *h*, it is still the same nonsense sound, "aich."

Letter Learning and the Demands on Memory

Learning how to discriminate among letters—to attach lines, circles, dots, and tails in just the right way and then attach nonsense names to these different squiggles—requires much abstract thinking and places a high demand on five different aspects of memory. Each aspect performs a different function (Smith 1994).

Sensory Store

The first aspect, *sensory store*, refers to the eye's perceiving visual information in print, such as individual letters and combinations of letters that form words. This perceptual information is stored for one to two seconds while the brain makes some decisions about the distinctive features of specific letters. For example, the child notices that *b*, *d*, and *p* are comprised of the same two features—a stick (or line) and a circle.

Short-Term Memory

The second aspect, called *short-term memory* or *working memory*, includes the brief time that an individual can maintain attention to something immediately after its identification. Everyday examples of working memory include holding a person's address in mind while listening to instructions about how to get there, or remembering an unfamiliar telephone number while dialing it. Children learning to write their names must remember how the specific features of a letter are connected while they attempt to write the word in the right order of letters.

Long-Term Memory

The third aspect of memory, referred to as *long-term memory*, includes information transferred from short-term memory by associating it with previously stored information. The following example illustrates this process.

When asked how to write the first letter in her name, Mary said, "First you make a straight line down. Then you pick up your pencil and put it at the top of the line you just made and make a slanted line down, and then at the bottom of that line you make a slanted line up, and then at the top of that third line you make another straight line down that is the same as the first line you made." Mary was then asked how to write her grandmother's name. "I call her *Nanny* and I think you make a big *N*, almost like writing a big *M* except to make a big *N* you only use one slanted line." Mary had noticed that the distinctive features needed to write *N* were the same as the distinctive features needed to write *M*.

This example suggests that the information needed to write *M* has been stored in long-term memory, and Mary had accessed this perceptual information to write *N*. It is important to note that many children, without being able to articulate the process as readily as Mary, successfully store the information in long-term memory and use it to make letters. Smith (1994) cautions that there is no movement in just one direction from short-term to long-term memory; there is always individual selectivity about how much is remembered and the manner in which remembering takes place.

In learning letters, individuals have idiosyncratic ways of selecting how to locate and recognize certain patterns and sequences of the stimuli (lines, tails, curves, etc.). The child's visual scanning of letter forms, and the idiosyncratic way of labeling or categorizing each one to establish its identity as different from all others, are critical learning that involves strengthening and refining the associative links among the features of a pattern that is stored for a brief time in sensory memory. Through repeated experiences with the single bundle of associated features that comprise a single letter, the letter is stored in short-term and eventually long-term memory (Adams 1990). However, this single bundle of associated features that comprise one lowercase letter may also be used to make up parts of other lowercase letters (*h*, *r*, *n*). It is no wonder that sometimes children who are just learning to store and use this kind of information mix up similar-looking letters. For efficiency in our alphabet, these letters are composed of many of the same patterns. The child must perceive the patterns (which includes how the features are precisely put together for any given letter), store them briefly in sensory memory, categorize and label them in association with already established knowledge, and use the information in the various ways required by literacy. Achieving this goal requires tremendous and complex learning.

How a Young Child Learns Letters

Learning letters means:

❚ Identifying a letter by noticing the particular features that make it up.
❚ Visually discriminating one letter from another by comparing the patterns.
❚ Using this information to form the letter.

Prior to entering first grade, many children develop one or more systems for identifying a letter and distinguishing among letters. A system can be any way of knowing about a letter. A child might know the name of the letter, might know the associated sound but not the name, or might connect the letter with a particular object or name of a person. At first this knowledge is very personal; children find their own ways of weaving understandings around a letter to help them remember it and produce it.

Often, children have several kinds of knowledge that they connect with a single letter. They acquire this kind of ability through home, preschool, and/or kindergarten experiences that include being read to frequently, participating in storytelling or book-sharing activities, and having many opportunities to write down messages and stories.

But some children, for a variety of reasons, have more difficulty developing these systems for identifying letters and distinguishing among them. Even though David attended kindergarten on a regular basis, he entered first grade unable to name or identify any letters. A teacher can provide the child with many opportunities to learn how to recognize the distinguishing features of a letter and use this information to form the letter, but the child must develop a personal basis to visually discriminate one letter from another. Through successful practice, most children will gradually learn how to systematize this knowledge and begin to search for and detect features of a specific letter that distinguish it from another.

The most powerful and effective way for children to begin learning this complex process is by writing their own names. In the following example, David, who paid little attention to the details of print and relied on strong language skills to "read," was learning how to attend to and break up the relevant features needed to write the first letter in his name.[1] This example shows the kind of explicit teaching that may be necessary for some children to understand what to look at and how to move in letter learning. The teacher began by saying, "David, let me show you how to make the first letter in your

---

[1]The process exemplified here is similar to that described by Clay (1993a).

name." Taking David's hand, she demonstrated the movements in the air while saying, "down, up, and around. That is how you make the first letter in your name, David. This is a capital letter *D*."

David's teacher identified the first letter of David's name by movement, and she provided a verbal description of the movement while forming the letter. As she said "down," her hand and her visual focus moved together in the air to represent a straight line from top to bottom. When she said "up," she retraced the imaginary line upward. While saying "around," she made a semicircle movement, joining the top line to the bottom imaginary line. The teacher used language to guide, direct, and regulate the child's and her own behavior while forming the letter.

The teacher used language and movement together. Why would that process be effective to help a child like David recall how to make a specific letter? We can find a theoretical explanation in the work of Luria (1980), who discovered that individuals were more likely to remember information when three parts of the brain were processing the same information simultaneously in different ways:

❚ The eyes (occipital lobe) are focusing on making the lines, curves, and so forth needed to form a particular letter.

❚ The ears (temporal lobe) are simultaneously hearing the verbal direction.

❚ The hand (parietal lobe) is simultaneously making the necessary movement to form the letter.

Thus, language becomes a tool for focusing the individual's attention on the task at hand and regulating the child's behavior so that three parts of the brain are processing the same information at the same time in an integrated, coordinated way.

The teacher was helping David develop an appropriate scanning sequence for forming the letter *D*. With fast, fluent practice, this scanning pattern became more automatic. While David engaged in the formation of a *D*, he simultaneously learned about the detailed patterns of print. When the teacher observed that David was able to coordinate the verbal description and movements vertically in the air, she asked him to write the letter on paper.

Teacher: David, now it is time to make the capital letter *D* on paper. [While holding David's hand, she provided a verbal description of the movement to form a *D*, just as she had done in the air.]

Teacher: What letter did you make, David?

David: A *D*. It's the first letter in my name.

Teacher: That's right. Try to make the capital letter *D* by yourself.

David: [Closing his eyes, David orally directed his hand to form the letter *D* vertically in the air. Then, he wrote the letter on paper.] First you make a stick and then go over the stick like this and then around like this.

Teacher: That's right, David. I especially liked how you said exactly what you were doing while you were making the letter. Let me show you how to write the rest of your name.

David was learning how to visually scan the letter *D* and how to attend to the features of the letter. The teacher finished writing David's name. She was providing a visual model so he could learn what his name looks like in print.

For several days David, with occasional support from the teacher, provided a verbal direction of the movement while writing the letter *D*. He wrote the letter using vertical (in the air) surfaces and horizontal (in a salt tray) surfaces. He also used different media—chalk, water pen on a blackboard, felt pen, and pencil—to write the letter *D*. He was gaining speed and accuracy every time he wrote the letter. He was also learning how to put the features of the letter in a set sequence, and he was becoming flexible in the use of different media and surfaces while analyzing the letter's features and components. David's highly practiced verbal responding skills guided his visual responding for eye-voice matching. As Vygotsky (1978) has claimed, "children solve practical tasks with the help of their speech, as well as their eyes and hands" (26).

After five days of practice, David did not need a verbal direction to guide the formation of the letter *D*; nor did he need help from the teacher. He had gained control of the action sequence needed to form the letter. He had acquired the ability to relay perceptual information perceived by the eye (sensory memory) to short-term memory and transform this information to long-term memory, which enabled him to recall how to form and name the letter *D*. More important, he had learned an associated bundle of features to form a capital letter *D* (a stick and curved line) that could be used to form other letters.

Occasionally, however, when shown the letter *D* and asked for a letter name, David resorted to verbally describing the movement needed to form the letter. He had the representation of the letter in his mind, but in order to remember the letter name, he had to verbally describe the action needed to form the letter. David was learning how to use language to regulate, organize, and direct mental processes, and he was providing structure for analyzing information previously learned. He learned how to form the rest of the letters in his name using the same procedures. The teacher, holding David's hand, modeled the movements needed to form the *a, v, i, d* vertically in the air while providing a verbal description of the movements. Then she guided David's hand as he practiced this process on vertical and horizontal surfaces with a variety of media. She provided a verbal description of the movement to form each letter while David wrote each letter on paper.

David developed a specific program of action for learning the letters in his name—identifying the letters by movement, providing a verbal description of the movement, and then providing a visual model of the letter by writing it on paper. Writing in the air and verbally describing the movement pattern seemed to make it easier for this child, who had previously given very little attention to the features of print, to write letters on paper. Within three weeks of daily practice, David learned how to write his first name on paper without progressing through this sequence of action. He also learned those five letter names.

Learning a name for each letter and how to recognize the letter in print were important new understandings that prompted David to acquire additional understandings. Once he had learned to write his own name, David wanted to learn to write his brothers' names.

David: How do I make the first letter in Mike's name?

Teacher: The first letter in Mike's name is M. We make it this way. [She modeled it in the air.]

David: Say the words to make the letter.

Teacher: [Providing a verbal description of the movement.] Down, retrace the line up, slanted line down, slanted line up, straight line down.

David: Show me!

Teacher: [Holding the child's hand, she verbally described the movement to form M while making it vertically in the air.] Now you try to write the capital letter M in the air.

David: Down, up, slanted line down, slanted line up, down. I see a V in the middle of the M just like in my name.

Teacher: That is right. You are seeing how parts of a letter V in your name can be used to make other letters.

David: I can write the first letter in Mike's name by myself. [David wrote the letter M on paper while verbally describing his movement.]

After several weeks of daily practice, using the same procedures, David learned how to write *Mike* and *Bobby*. He noticed similarities and differences between letters and several features of a known letter, usable in other letters.

It took many other experiences for David to truly "know" the *D* and other letters in his name. But he did not always need this kind of detail and explicit teaching on every letter. He was learning how to learn letters, what to look at, and how to write them. Eventually, he was able to apply this learning process more quickly to other letters. Most children will not need so much time and so much explicit help to learn letters, but for all children, using movement and language will support the process.

Using a Personal Alphabet Book to Help in Letter Learning

In order to learn how to read, David needed to learn to recognize letters as rapidly as possible without receiving any prompts or relating specifically to previous learning (for example, without verbally describing the movements to form a letter). For many children who are have difficulty learning letters, a personalized alphabet book is an effective way to help systematize learning.

A personal alphabet book (Figure 6-1) is a paper book that presents the letters of the alphabet in sequence, with a drawing of an object for each letter. When a child has learned a good number of letters (ten to fifteen), write only these letters in the book, leaving empty pages for letters to be learned (see Clay 1993b; Pinnell and Fountas 1997). The alphabet book provides an organized frame that will help a child associate a specific letter form to a letter name and develop letter-sound relationships. The child can read the known letters and identify the objects that begin with those letters daily as a way of firming up letter knowledge. Then teachers can introduce and add new letters over time until the child has learned all the alphabet letters.

According to Clay (1993b), a personalized alphabet book has been more useful than commercial alphabet books for children who are having difficulty learning letters. For children who are learning letters quickly, however, a beautifully illustrated alphabet book is an enriching experience. Many kindergarten teachers offer a variety of experiences with the alphabet, including personal ABC books, alphabet charts, name charts organized according to the alphabet, and children's literature focusing on alphabet concepts. A print-rich environment will give children many opportunities to attend to the visual features that distinguish letters from each other.

FIGURE 6-1   A B C Book

Learning to Differentiate Letters

As they enter first grade, many children can identify a large percentage of the letters by name. But identifying letters by name in isolation is not the difficult part of learning to read. "It is extracting information from embedded letters while reading for meaning that is the challenge, and the real learning goal" (Clay 1991a, 239).

In order to engage in this complex process, children must learn that letters are actually conglomerates of features, of which there are a dozen different kinds. Additionally, the only way letters look different from each other is the presence or absence of these features. Letters that have several features in common need to be regarded as similar, and letters that are constructed with different feature combinations need to be regarded as dissimilar.

Learning letters is a necessary skill in learning to read because:

■ It helps children reference small units of print called *letters* when talking about printed forms they are reading and/or writing.

■ Learning letter names of the whole alphabet provides children with a record, an inventory of what they know and what they need to learn.

■ Children need to learn letters so they can use this visual information to monitor and check on themselves while reading and writing sentences.

Being able to effectively and efficiently use the visual information perceived involves learning how to correctly process several sources of sensory input and many stimulus interactions at any one time. Successful readers begin very early to attend to visual information as well as language and messages while reading and writing continuous text. As they progress, visual processing occurs without much conscious attention. Learning a few letters is the necessary first step in gaining control of this complex process. Although children do not need to learn all or even half of the letters before they can begin to read texts for meaning, they do need to learn more letters as they gain more experience in reading and writing. Acquiring this ability is critical to becoming literate.

To help children learn about letters, we teach them to say the letters of the alphabet, and we teach them to recognize the letters and use the visual features. This learning involves:

■ Finding out what exactly are the distinctive features by which various configurations should be categorized as different from each other.

■ Identifying a set or combination of features that are critical for particular categories (that is, what makes a "letter" what it is).

■ Associating a name (A, B, C, etc.) with each category.

In order to help beginning readers acquire these complex sets of understandings, teachers provide many opportunities for children to:

■ See the letter symbol as an individual entity.

■ Attend to the sequence or order of letters.

■ Identify as distinct entities letter forms commonly used in English orthography.

■ Categorize, recognize, and classify distinguishable features of one letter from another letter.

■ Identify letters embedded in text.

■ Discover names and sounds for most letters so they can use several different means to identify letters.

■ Develop speed, fluency, and ease in remembering letter names.

■ Develop speed, fluency, and ease in forming letters.

■ Gain speed and fluency in developing letter-sound and sound-letter correspondence.

Speed and accuracy in forming, naming, and recognizing letters is an index of the thoroughness and confidence with which the children have learned the letters' identities. Children's knowledge of the alphabetic principle—which includes a conscious awareness and conceptual understanding that (1) printed words are made up of letters that have the same sound values in many words and that (2) printed letters or combinations of letters represent sounds—is a necessary factor in becoming literate. Accumulated research (Adams 1990; Clay 1993a) suggests that it is not simply the accuracy with which beginning readers can name letters that helps them learn to read. It is the fluency, speed, and ease with which they can do so that facilitates the building of a reading process. The speed with which children can name and recognize individual letters is both a strong predictor of success for pre-readers and strongly associated with reading achievement among beginning readers. All of this research suggests the need for a strong letter learning program in kindergarten—one that involves children in noticing, making, and using letters in many different ways.

Suggestions for Professional Development

1. Select three children to explore letter learning. You might want to select a variety of children, none of whom have full control of alphabetic knowledge. One might be a child who is like David and cannot recognize or write even one letter, and the two others might have some knowledge.

2. Assess each child's knowledge of the letters (upper- and lowercase).[2] In order to discover the child's "way in" to a letter, gather three types of information.

   ■ Can the child name the letter?
   ■ Can the child make a sound associated with the letter?
   ■ Can the child connect the letter with a word? If so, what?

Some of the children will have one way into a letter; others will have several. This knowledge will vary according to individual letters. For example, children might have several ways into letters associated with their names.

3. For each child assessed, ask yourself:
   ■ How many letters does the child know?
   ■ How many capital letters?
   ■ How many lowercase letters?
   ■ Does the child know the *same* capital and lowercase letters? What are the differences?
   ■ Does the child have any letter confusions?

Make some hypotheses about why the children might know the letters they do. Consider:
   ■ What is the child's "way in" to letters in general?
   ■ Does the "way in" differ for different letters?
   ■ For letters that the child connects to words, what kinds of words are used?

4. Compare the three children on letter learning at this point in time.
   ■ How are they approaching the task in different ways?
   ■ What personal experiences might have contributed to their learning?
   ■ What do they need to know now?

5. Assess these three children again in four to six weeks. Ask the same questions again

---

[2] Clay's *Observation Survey of Literacy Achievement* (1993a) is a good source for directions and forms to use. The forms in this book are reproducible.

and discuss and compare their progress with colleagues.

6. Work with a group of teachers to follow a small group of children (or even a whole class) from the beginnings of letter learning to their achievement of full control of the alphabet. This kind of study can be undertaken over a six- to nine-month period.

7. Take two steps toward strengthening the letter learning program in the kindergarten and first-grade classrooms in your school. Analyze the classroom learning environment and the program for teaching about letters. Think about Luria's (1980) notion about engaging the three parts of the brain at the same time—using the ears, eyes, and hand to help in learning. Consider:

- What are the opportunities children have to say and hear letters of the alphabet (for example, alphabet rhymes, charts, and books read aloud)?
- What are the opportunities for children to see, notice, and touch letters in different contexts?
- What are the opportunities for children to write letters in different contexts?

Think about how these three areas of learning can be expanded and also coordinated to enhance learning, and create a plan for achieving these goals.

8. As a follow-up, read and discuss Chapter 8, "What's in a Word? Phonological and Orthographic Awareness" in the companion volume to this book, *Word Matters: Teaching Phonics and Spelling in the Reading/Writing Classroom.*

Assessing Spelling Knowledge

The Child as a Reader and Writer

Carol Brennan Jenkins

Introduction

We become effective teachers of word solving as we learn to select and bring to children's attention clear examples that illustrate key principles. Our decision making during reading and writing is basic to fostering the teaching conversations that enable children to learn the principles and strategies they need to develop as effective readers and writers. We must also carefully plan word study opportunities to meet children's specific needs. Otherwise, we run the risk of wasting valuable teaching and learning time.

We waste time when we go over something in a rote way that children already know. We also waste time and risk confusing children by focusing on ideas and concepts that are beyond their current experience. In either case, the learner cannot be active and word study becomes tedious. The key to making good instructional decisions is learning about children through careful observation of their daily reading and writing behavior. The child's developing word knowledge is evident in book reading (as we record behaviors in running records) and in a variety of literacy events, such as journal writing and conversations about reading and writing.

In this chapter Jenkins describes the rich assessment data from one child's literacy experiences to show the specific information available to document understandings and to inform subsequent teaching. She provides a detailed description of the strategies a child has learned how to use as a writer and the influences of his reading, demonstrating the reciprocal aspects of literacy. In addition, the author presents a series of guidelines for the assessment of word knowledge that link the extensive collection of data with effective teaching.

It's snack time in Christopher's second-grade classroom. While his peers chat or play with games, Christopher pulls out his juice box, raisins, and the story he has been writing. As I pull up a chair, Christopher explains that he's written "an awesome story about a magic train, and it's twelve pages long." He adds emphatically, "And it's not done yet." I tell Christopher that I'd love to hear his story. With an impish grin, he reads "The Magic Train," the first two pages of which are presented in Figure 7-1. Without taking a breath, he then explains his plans for the next episode:

Christopher: He [Edward] meets the wizard, Billy, and then they take the ship called the

The magic train by Christopher

Once there was a boy named Edward. He had a sister called Lindcy. Edward loved castles. One night he woke up he herd a train. He looked out the window and saw it. On the train there was

a sign. This what it said on it. castle express. Edward got dressed and went down stairs. The conductor said all abord. Edward ran out the door. The conductor said are you coming. or not. Edward said yes. Soon they were on there way.

FIGURE 7-1   Christopher's Story "The Magic Train"

Titanic to the North Pole and meet Mrs. Claus who is—her first name is Jessica in the story—and they meet the elves, Joseph and Samantha.

Carol: Christopher, you're a wonderful storyteller.

Christopher: I take my favorite things and put them into stories. This is based on *The Polar Express* by Chris Van Allsburg [1985].

Carol: Oh, I was going to ask you where you got your idea for this story. Which parts are like *The Polar Express*?

Christopher: When they go to the North Pole and they take a train and it's during the night. But there aren't any castles or knights in *The Polar Express*. I just put them in because I like knights and castles and the Titanic. I know a lot about the Titanic. It's in my journal. Wanna see?

Carol: Oh, yes.

Christopher: Reader and Writer

Assessment of Christopher's knowledge about how words work begins with an assessment of Christopher as a reader and a writer. In addition to examining the spelling strategies he uses, his knowledge of sound-symbol relationships, and of spelling patterns, it is important to know what Christopher thinks about himself as a reader and as a writer. How extensively does he read, and with what degree of proficiency? What is his interest in and pursuit of writing? The stronger the child's profile as a reader, the greater the likelihood that the child will intuit knowledge about the orthographic features of words and will use the knowledge during the act of writing.

My brief interlude with Christopher provided evidence that he is a strong reader and writer. He chose to write while his peers played. He offered to read his story, and he did so with impressive fluency. He interjected comments throughout ("Why didn't I number all the pages?"). He offered his up-

coming plot episodes, without prompting, as if to satisfy my need as a reader for story closure. He acknowledged the intertextual influence of Chris Van Allsburg's work on his piece. It is clear that Christopher did what all storytellers do, in the words of Jane Yolen (1991), "We thieve (or more politely) borrow and then we make it our own" (147). Enter the knights, kings, queens, ship masters, and the Titanic.

My hunch about the extent of Christopher's literate activity was confirmed with the arrival of his journal and subsequent conversation. Eager to resume our conversation about the Titanic, Christopher flipped through his journal, read the excerpt in Figure 7-2, and gave a biographical sketch of Molly Brown. He then explained that he had "a very big book on the Titanic at home" that his father read to him. I asked him if he read at home, and he replied, "Yes, all the time." His journal entries corroborated his response. In a September entry, he wrote, "I like to read after school." In October, he wrote, "I can't wait to home becuse. I have some good books I am reading . . ." In January, he wrote, "I can not wait until we have d.e.a.r" (Drop Everything and Read). In his journal, he frequently mentioned books he was reading and included global responses such as "It is good." and "I like it." His reading log of books read during DEAR time showed a preference for fiction. He shuttled back and forth between picture storybooks such as De Paola's *Fin M'Coul* (1981) and Seeger's *Abiyoyo* (1986), and chapter books such as Rylant's *Henry and Mudge* (1987) and Dahl's *Matilda* (1988). In his journal he noted, "One of my favorite authors is Roald Dahl. He wrote alot of books. I like all of the ones I read by him so far."

A conversation with Christopher's mother confirmed the extent of his passion for books:

One summer, while he was a preschooler, we went to the library and brought home thirty or more books a week and read them all; some

going to do in
gym today. I can
not wait until
Friday. My mother
is going to tape
the second part
of the Titanic
movie tonight. It is
a good movie. I
know the name
of one of the
people on the
56 ship that served
the dasaster. Her
name is Molly
Brown. I have a

FIGURE 7-2   Christopher's Journal Entry About the Titanic/Molly Brown

of them over and over again. I took out over three hundred books that summer. Now my biggest problem is getting him to do something other than read. He's up at 6:00 in the morning with the TV on and a book in hand. When I call him for breakfast, he'll say, "But I'm just at the good part." Would you believe that when I have a dentist's appointment, Christopher won't leave the office until he has finished the chapter he's on.

Christopher was the most prolific writer in this second-grade classroom. While many of his peers were only halfway through their journal notebooks, Christopher was on his second notebook. Most days he averaged two pages of text. Christopher used his journal not only to chronicle past experiences but also to catalog his interests ("I have a pencil colection."), to record his knowledge ("Did you know inscets have six legs. And three body parts."), and to self-reflect ("I finshist my skeleton. I labed the bones. It was hard work."). His journal sparkled with a joie de vivre; sentences such as "I had fun." or "I can't wait to . . ." populated his journal. In December, he wrote, "I like writing in my journal. It is a lot of fun." The ultimate confirmation of Christopher's affinity for writing occurred at the end of our conversation about "The Magic Train." I remarked that I thought he was a talented writer. He replied, "Yup, that's what I want to be when I grow up—an author." His mother was delighted to hear this because Christopher did not write at home. Moreover, her attempt the previous summer to persuade him to keep a journal had failed. Alternating intense spurts of reading and writing activity are characteristic of the literacy development of many youngsters (Bissex 1980; Durkin 1966). Christopher's writing spurt probably kicked in during second grade because of daily writing workshop.

Indeed, Christopher's engagement with literate activity was intricately tied to the print-rich environments of home and school. Christopher's second-grade teacher, Becky Shepard, saturated her curriculum with books, drama, and author studies. With respect to writing and spelling, she implemented a curriculum in which there was extensive daily reading and writing, children were taught to use spelling strategies, and proofreading was valued.

Assessing Christopher's Spelling

Let's look at an analysis of Christopher's spelling knowledge and usage. To learn about his word knowledge, we'll use writing samples in Christopher's portfolio in conjunction with other critical corroborating data (observations, conversations, interviews, and parental input). We'll note his use of spelling strategies, the developmental nature of his hypotheses about the orthography, his skill knowledge and usage, and his attitude about writing and spelling.

Spelling Strategies

Take a moment to read the following sentences and to fill in the missing word:

> The car accident caused blood to burst from her blood vessels. The doctors worked frantically to stop the h_____.

Now, identify the strategy you used to spell this word:

a) *Phonemic Strategy:* I sounded out the word and arrived at one of the following approximations: *hemorijing, hemmoridging, hemoriging.*

b) *Visual Strategy:* I knew the word could not be spelled phonemically so I tried to visualize the word in books I have read in order to recall the sequence of letters. I arrived at one of the following: *hemorraging, hemmohraging, hemorrhaging* (If curiosity already hasn't sent you to the dictionary, the correct spelling is shown below.)[1]

---

[1]hemorrhaging

c) *Morphemic Strategy*: I used my knowledge of Latin/Greek roots (e.g., *rrhagia*, which means discharge, or *hem* or *hemo* which means blood) to arrive one of the following: hemmorrhage, hemorrhage.

This activity illustrates the degree of cognitive activity that undergirds spelling as well as the three primary spelling strategies that writers, including Christopher, have at their disposal. Using Christopher's writing samples, the Spelling Strategy Inventory in Figure 7-3, and the Spelling Survey in Figure 7-4, let's examine his use of these strategies. Adapted from Powell and Hornsby (1993), the Spelling Strategy Inventory requires writers to spell three groups of words; each group of words taps one of the primary spelling strategies. Since an analysis of any writer's spelling isn't complete without the writer's thoughts on the subject, Christopher's insights on the Spelling Survey, adapted from Wilde's (1992) Spelling Interview, also are integrated.

Phonemic (Sound) Strategy

Emergent spellers in kindergarten and first grade rely almost exclusively on the phonemic strategy. They sketch out the sounds in words and write the corresponding letters. Older spellers, like Christopher, also often rely on the sound strategy during their initial attempt at an unfamiliar word. Christopher's writing samples in Figures 7-1 and 7-2 reveal his use of this strategy and his awareness of certain spelling generalizations. He correctly encoded the words such as *Titanic, Brown, woke, sister*. He had similar success with the words in Group A of the inventory (Figure 7-3) because of their phonemic regularity. When I asked how he arrived at the spelling of *scrub*, he said, "I sounded out *sc* but sometimes a *c* can sound like a *k*. Is this right? It looks right." Here, we see that his phonics knowledge and his attention to the visual aspect of words came into play. When asked about *fantastic*, he said, "I sounded it out like this—the word, *fan*, then *tast*, *t-a-st*, then *ic*. I wasn't sure about *i-c* or *i-c-k* but I think it's *i-*

c." This example illustrates what Christopher means in Item 2 of Figure 7-4. He approached unfamiliar words by sounding words out by syllables and writing them down. His speculation about whether the syllable was spelled *ic* or *ick* again reveals his attention to the visual aspect of the word. He used the visual strategy to make his decision. Of course, Christopher's writing samples also contained spelling approximations that show reliance on the phonemic strategy, such as *abord* in Figure 7-1 and *dasaster* in Figure 7-2. (Other approximations in his journal included *favoret, eysoftagus, forteen, tipes, chese*.)

My hypothesis is that Christopher had minimal exposure to words such as *aboard* and *disaster* in the books he read. In such cases (similar to our effort at *hemorrhage*) the visual strategy had limited applicability. At best, he could ask a friend or consult a dictionary. His approximations *servied* (survived) and *dasaster* (disaster) alert us to the relationship of pronunciation and spelling. These and other examples throughout his journal (*eysoftagus, niney, difrent, digestum*) show the importance of demonstrating to children the technique of alternate pronunciations. We need to show children how we call upon the alternate pronunciations of "*Wed-nes-day*" or "*nine-ty*" while spelling these words. When we introduce children to new vocabulary words as part of a curricular study, such as *digestion* and *esophagus*, it is helpful to take the time to write these words on the board, to pronounce them, to ask the children to pronounce them, and to use them as often as possible.

Visual Strategy

While the phonemic strategy has a strong influence on all spellers, good spellers understand intuitively that only about 50 percent of the words they spell are phonemically regular (Hanna, Hodges, and Hanna 1971). Consequently, they override the urge to spell words solely on the basis of sound-symbol relationships and work actively to attend to visual images—exact letter sequences—of

Name _Christopher_

Spelling Strategy Inventory

Group A Words

What did you do to spell this group of words?

1. _flash_

2. _scrub_

3. _fantastic_

Group B Words

What did you do to spell this group of words?

1. _because_

2. _laghter_

3. _Picure_

Group C Words

What did you do to spell this group of words?

1. _Skiped_

2. _burned_

3. _action_

moshtion

FIGURE 7-3   Christopher's Spelling Strategy Inventory

Name *Christopher A. Magliozzi*

Spelling Survey

1. Do you think you are a good speller? How do you know?

No   I do not know but I think in my mind that I am not it helps me to work better

2. What do you do when you come to a word you don't know how to spell?

I sound it out. write it down. I make it into smaller words. And I strech it out.

3. How do you know if you've spelled a hard word right?

I read the word.

4. Suppose your friend spells the word, night, like this—nit. What would you tell your friend?

If it was a test I would not say anything. If not a test I would tell him or her how to spell it if I new.

5. Is it important to spell words correctly? Why or why not?

It is importand to spell words correctly to me. Because If I write a awsome story or something else I want them to be able to read it.

FIGURE 7-4   Christopher's Spelling Survey

words they have seen in print. Christopher, indeed, is one of these good spellers. Even when he was fairly certain that he could rely on the alphabetic principle for words such as *scrub*, he went the next step and asked, "Does it look right?" Christopher attended to the visual demands of the Group B words. When I asked him to tell me how he figured out this group of words, he pointed to *laghter* and *picure* and replied, "These two are the hardest. I still don't think I got that one right [pointing to *laghter*]. I don't think it looks like I normally see that word spelled." Interestingly, when Christopher first attempted this word, he wrote, *laf*, and erased it. Then he asked if he could try it on the back of the sheet, and he proceeded to write three versions of the word (Figure 7-5). Then he transferred his final choice to the Group B section. Discussion about his problem-solving efforts follow:

Christopher [pointing to *laghter*]: Well, normally *ght* can sound like certain things and I knew *laughter* had *ght*. I've seen it in my books.

Carol [pointing to *lafter*]: What were you thinking about when you tried this spelling?

Christopher: What I was seeing was if it looked better with an *f* there but I didn't think so.

Carol: But when I say the word, *laughter*, I hear an *f*.

Christopher: I don't only stretch it out, like, I look to see if it looks good and I proofread it and stuff.

Carol: That's why you're such a good speller. Now tell me about your last try [pointing to *latghter*].

Christopher: I was seeing if there was *t* there or not and I didn't think so.

The extent of Christopher's cognitive engagement with this word dispels any notion that spelling is simply a matter of memorization. Rather, it entails active hy-

pothesizing about orthographic features, testing these hypotheses, and then confirming or rejecting them. It also entails knowing what to do to confirm or to reject attempts. Christopher's decision to try out the alternative spellings on the back of the worksheets represents one such strategy—one that successful adult spellers use often. In addition, his explanation of his response to Item 3 on the Spelling Survey revealed his awareness about textual resources: "Well, after I stretch it out, I read it to check if I spelled it right 'cuz I may have accidentally read it wrong and then I would go into the dictionary if I had one and check it that way."

Christopher's attention to the visual aspects of words also was found in his writing samples. In his "Magic Train" story (Figure 7-1), he experimented with the word *conductor*. His original attempt was *conducter*; but he rejected the phonemic information. Instead he relied on his visual sense of the word, erasing the *e* and replacing it with an *o*. A number of other examples of his ability to self-edit using the visual strategy are evident in this story and in his journal entries such as *poepal* edited to *people* and *messijes* to *messages*. According to Christopher, he edits as he goes. When I asked if he proofread after a piece was finished, he said, "if the teacher makes me I do."

Curious about his ability to proofread text after the fact, I handed him a copy of a page from his journal and asked him to show me how he proofreads and fixes mistakes. He read the text from top to bottom and recognized all but one of his spelling errors (see Figure 7-6 on page 77). I asked him to try another spelling for each word. Once again, his adoption of the alternate spellings strategy is evident. Without any prompting, he tried four versions of *special*, thinking aloud at times: "*shh*, but there's no *h* . . . no that doesn't look right . . . I think *al* is at the end." When I gave him four options, he circled the correct spelling of *special* without hesitation. When I asked how he chose the correct version, he replied, "I know it. I read it." His response prompted me, in a later ses-

FIGURE 7-5 Christopher's Three Versions of the Word *Laughter*

sion, to present him with a list of all his misspelled words (from his journal and story) in correct form. He read all seventy words quickly and correctly. While he may not be able to retrieve the exact letter strings of some multisyllabic words when he edits, his advanced word recognition skills scaffold his proofreading efforts and ensure successful edits once he takes that next step to use textual or human resources.

Morphemic (Meaning-Bearing Units) Strategy

After Christopher completed the Strategy Inventory (Figure 7-3), I asked him which group of words was the easiest and why. To my surprise, he pointed to the Group C words. The following conversation reveals his evolving understanding about the semantic dimension of our orthography:

Carol: Christopher, why do you think the words in Group C are the easiest?

Christopher: Well, because, these were easy words (pointing to *skiped* and *burned*).

Carol: When I say the word *skipped*, what sound do you hear at the end—*skipped.*

Christopher: t.

Carol: So why did you write *ed* at the end of *skipped* instead of *t?*

Christopher: Because our teacher taught us about that.

Carol: What did she say?

Christopher: Don't write *t* even if you hear it.

While Christopher can't verbalize his knowledge about the past-tense marker *ed*, he understands it intuitively and uses it with much success in the inventory and in his writing samples. As the following examples from his "Magic Train" story and from his journal show, he understands that *ed* is a morphemic unit that remains constant regardless of the final sound (*t* as in *skipped*; *d* as in *planned*; *ed* as in *painted*):

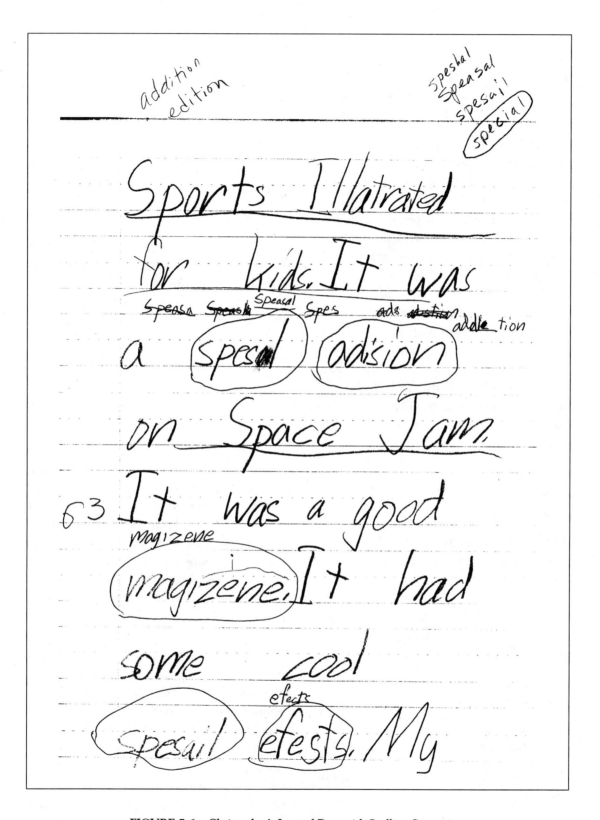

FIGURE 7-6   Christopher's Journal Page with Spelling Corrections

droped	named	heated
taped	studyed	started
skiped	sailed	Invented
	called	planted
	tryed	reminded

While Christopher hadn't discovered the principle of doubling the consonant before adding the *ed* ending (*droped*, *skiped*) or how to affix words ending in *y* (*studyed*, *tryed*), he concluded that past-tense marker is a highly stable unit—regardless of the sound heard, the *ed* ending remains intact—*when it is added to one-syllable words or to two- and three-syllable words in which the* ed *is a distinct syllable.* (Note his success with two- and three-syllable verbs—*planted*, *invented*—where the *ed* suffix is a distinct syllable.) However, he had yet to transfer this knowledge to two-syllable verbs in which the *ed* is part of the second syllable. Out of all of the past-tense markers found in this story and journal, only three were misspelled:

> *prepard*
> *happend*
> *sapost* (*supposed*)

With continued reading and writing, his understanding of past-tense markers will expand.

Returning to our discussion of the last word in Group C on the Strategy Worksheet, we note Christopher's thinking about the suffix *tion*:

Carol: Now, what about the last word, *action*? Was that a hard word to spell?

Christopher: No. I know that "un" is *t-i-o-n*. My mother taught me that *i-o-n* is *t-i-o-n*.

Carol: What do you mean when you say *i-o-n* is *t-i-o-n*?

Christopher: They both say "un."

Carol: So, tell me how you figured out the word *action*.

Christopher: I sounded it out *act, a-c-t* and *shun, i-o-n*.

Carol: How would you spell *motion*?

Christopher: [Sounding out *mosh*] *m-o-sh*, [sounding out *shun*] *t-i-o-n*.

Carol: Do you know what *tion* means?

Christopher: Motion, like moving around.

Carol: Do you know what we call endings like *tion*?

Christopher: A little word?

If we merge this data with the data found in his writing samples, we can appreciate the level of sophisticated hypothesizing that Christopher brings to spelling. Examine his spelling successes in the first column and spelling attempts in the second column:

action	moshtion
subtration	vacastion
demonstration	adision
	stasion

I suspect that Christopher has constructed the tacit rule: "If it starts with a word that I know, such as *act* in *action* or *subtract* in *subtration*, then I write the word and add *ion*. If the word starts with a word I don't know, such as *mo* in *motion* or *vaca* in *vacation*, then I represent the *sh* sound with an *s* and add *tion* or *ion*." Christopher's efforts show that children's spellings are grounded in logic and are not haphazard inventions (Read 1975).

Additional evidence of Christopher's morphemic knowledge can be found in his experimentation with homophones. Homophones require spellers to attend to meaning. On the first page of Christopher's story in Figure 7-1, we note correct usage of the homophone *there*; on the last line of the second page, we note that Christopher also uses *there* to mark possession. (*There* and *their* are among the twenty-five most frequently misspelled words by children in grades one through six (Buchanan 1989). We also note the alternate spelling of *herd* on page one, and the correct spelling on the tenth page of the story in the sentence,

"Then they heard a noise." My initial conclusion was that while his story and his journal show correct usage of the homophone pairs *night-knight, of-off, tale-tail,* and *knew-new,* he has yet to sort out *herd-heard, there-their,* and *which-witch.* My conclusion was wrong. In a later session, I presented these three pairs. Christopher not only read each pair but independently explained what each word meant: "*Herd* is a herd of buffalo; *heard* is you heard someone talking . . . *There* is here and there; *their* is it belongs to someone." He understood the semantic nature of the written language and relied on this knowledge much of the time. He will achieve even greater accuracy when he learns to proofread consistently.

Taken together, this evidence shows that Christopher fits the profile of a good speller. He understands that while English is an alphabetic writing system, he cannot rely solely on the sound system to spell words. He attends to the visual sequence of letters in numerous words and retrieves those sequences consistently. He also attends to the semantic demands of written language, and he uses his knowledge of the meaning-bearing units such as affixes, homophones, and compound words when spelling. Most importantly, he knows when to rely on what strategy and to check his spelling attempts to see if they "look right." Furthermore, he cares about spelling. He explains that he likes to think of himself as a "not-so-good speller" because "I think in my mind it helps me to work better . . . I pretend that I'm not [a good speller] because it makes me work harder to be a better speller." Such wisdom for one so young.

Spelling Acquisition and Development

Considerable agreement exists among the experts not only about the cognitive complexity of the spelling process but about its developmental evolution. The seminal work of Charles Read (1971, 1975) in the area of invented spelling alerted us to the remarkable reasoning abilities of preschool children who puzzle out the intricacies of written language in accordance with a system of "rules" they invent. He concluded that young children possess a tacit knowledge about the phonological system and use this knowledge to construct rules that govern their attempts at spelling. As exposure to print increases, their hypotheses are tested against new information and confirmed or rejected accordingly. While Read (1971, 1975) delighted in the developmental evolution of young children's hypotheses, he did not suggest any fixed course of spelling development.

Subsequent research corroborated and extended Read's findings (Bissex 1980; Schickedanz 1990). Over time, a number of researchers sought to compress their findings into distinct stages and to argue that children's acquisition of spelling moves along this fixed path of development (Buchanan 1989; Gentry 1985; Gentry and Gillet 1993). Others, however, argued against any notion of fixed, hierarchical stages (Clay 1975, 1991a; Wilde 1992) and urged us to acknowledge global shifts in development while simultaneously appreciating children's diverse responses.

The continuum of spelling development (Jenkins 1996), presented in Figure 7-7, attempts to capture the ebbs and flows of young children's spelling. It delineates the developmental research findings of experts while recognizing that children, at any point in time, may zigzag across the points on the continuum and experiment with alternative ways of thinking about written language. Our work as assessors is not to pigeonhole children's orthographic thinking into a discrete point on the continuum. Rather, it is to appreciate the richness and versatility of their thinking, and to be able to describe their developmental shifts over time.

To examine Christopher's developmental shifts across time, we begin with "The Picnic," a piece he wrote in kindergarten (Figure 7-8). Using the criteria in Figure 7-7, it is evident that Christopher is a developing

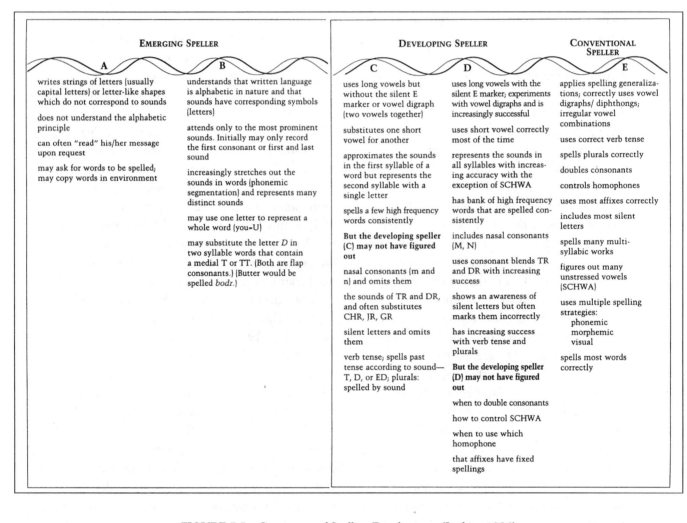

FIGURE 7-7   Continuum of Spelling Development (Jenkins 1996)

speller (point C). What separates developing spellers from emergent spellers is the acute attention that developing spellers bring to the encoding process. Developing spellers are adept at segmenting sounds in one-syllable words and at representing each sound with a letter. How they represent these sounds, in particular the short vowels, is indicative of their developmental understandings. For example, characteristic of spellers at point C on the spelling continuum is the substitution of one short vowel for another (Read 1971). Such substitutions are not random. Rather, they are governed by tacit rules that the young speller has constructed. For example, when Christopher spelled the word *went* as *wnat*, he reasoned "When I hear the short sound of *e*, I decide which letter of the alphabet sounds closest to this short *e* sound—*eh . . . A* or *eh . . . E*." Concluding that his mouth is in the same position when he says short *e* and the letter *a*, he writes *wnat* for *went*. He repeats this process with the word *ever*. Impressive also in this piece is the large number of words spelled correctly (*red, had, was, he, apple, house, and, the, end*). In these instances, Christopher relies on his strong visual memory to retrieve spellings. Characteristic also of developing spellers (C) is Christopher's handling of two-syllable words such as *pinc* (picnic). While he attends carefully to the sounds in the first syllable, he represents the second syllable with one letter. Not surprisingly, developing spellers at point C have little, if any, awareness of silent letters. Nor do

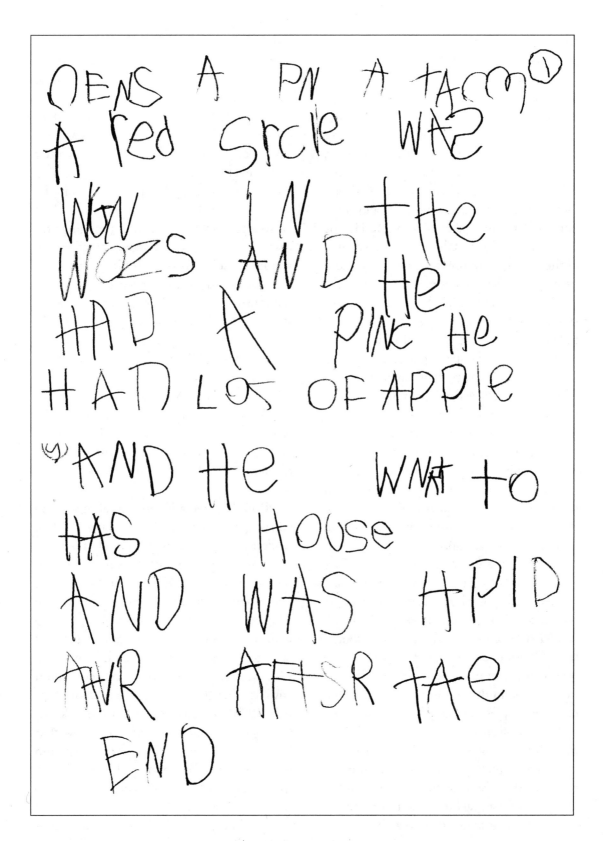

FIGURE 7-8   Christopher's Story "The Picnic"

they understand the fixed nature of affixes such as past-tense endings.

Analysis of Christopher's spelling two years later (Figures 7-1, 7-2, and 7-4) shows greater competence with short vowels (*dressed*, *sister*, *scrub*, *window*) and with two-syllable words (*express*, *castle*, *conductor*, *aboard*, *people*, *Titanic*). With respect to the spelling continuum in Figure 7-7, these examples suggest that Christopher is at point D or point E, or somewhere in between. Having been impressed with Christopher's command of the orthography, I suspect that he is a conventional speller at point E on the continuum.

Most significantly, he uses multiple strategies (phonemic, visual, and morphemic) to figure out unfamiliar words. In addition, he applies many of the spelling rules with regard to vowels and correctly spells many multisyllabic words. However, completion of the continuum worksheet, shown in Figure 7-9, suggests that Christopher is an accomplished second-grade speller who is straddling the continuum between points D and E.

While he has not fully problem-solved orthographic features such as double consonants, schwa, and affixes, his successes in each of these categories show a nascent awareness of these features and a readiness for instruction. For example, one of the primary challenges facing Christopher as a speller is schwa, the short *u* sound found in the unaccented syllable of a word. Like most youngsters, Christopher consistently represents the schwa sound with a vowel *a*, taking his cue from the noun determiner *a*: *a* book, *a* boy, *a*. . . . Examples include *illatrated*, *dasaster*, *anamal*, *spesal*, *mastakes*, and so forth. However, his writing samples reveal three instances in which he overrides the urge to represent the schwa sound with the vowel *a*: *prisoner*, *skeleton*, *and demonstration*, indicating his readiness for instruction with this skill.

The Reading-Spelling Connection

While good readers can be poor spellers, good spellers are good readers. As Frank Smith (1982) notes, "Spelling is primarily learned through reading . . . if you want to write with reasonably conventional spelling then there can be no substitute for reading" (187, 204). Manolakes (1975) found that, on average, children from grades two to six can spell 75 percent of the words in their grade-level spelling books *before* receiving any instruction and 64 percent of the spelling words one grade level *above* their current placement. In addition, spelling programs introduce, at the most, six thousand words to elementary children. Even if spelling programs are carried through high school, there is no way this cumulative instruction can account for the thousands and thousands of words we can spell as adults (Wilde 1992). We learn this vast corpus of words by reading.

Given what we know about Christopher's spelling ability, we can predict that he is a strong reader—a prediction that is borne out by conversations with Christopher and his mother and by an analysis of his oral reading.

Running records and retellings from Christopher show that he is a self-extending reader: one who reads third-grade texts fluently with appropriate phrasing; one who has an impressive corpus of sight words; one who keeps meaning at the forefront; one who takes corrective action when meaning is disrupted; one who relies on a variety of cues to problem solve unfamiliar text and who cross-checks one source of information with another (Clay 1991a; Fountas and Pinnell 1996). In addition, Christopher's engagement with and love of story show that he reads not only with his mind but also with his heart. He connects life and literature without being asked to do so. He understands story as "an exploration and illumination of life" (Peterson and Eeds 1990). Christopher is not only a strategic reader, he is a passionate reader.

Self-extended reading does not imply that Christopher faces no challenges as a reader. At present, Christopher approaches

Continuum Worksheet

Developing Speller
_____D_____

Conventional Speller
_____E_____

	Evidence of Success	Evidence of Approximation		Evidence of Success	Evidence of Approximation
* uses long vowels with the silent e marker; experiments with vowel digraphs and is increasingly successful	pine cone home bike freeze train beach		* applies spelling rules: vowel digraphs/diph-thongs; irregular vowel units; nasal consonants (m/n);		
* uses short vowel correctly	scrub fantastic pencil	mind read	* uses correct verb tense		
* represents the sounds in all syllables with increasing accuracy with the exception of schwa	Titanic computer microscupe	thermeter librairy dasaster	* spells plurals correctly		
*uses consonant blends tr and dr with increasing success	train dressed droped	childen	* doubles consonants		
* includes nasal consonants (m,n);	pumpkin sank spring		* controls homophones		
* has increasing success with verb tense and plurals	skiped studyed burned	happend sapost Finshist	* uses affixes effectively		
* shows an awareness of silent letters but often marks them incorrectly	knight muscle wrote	briye niney	* includes silent letters		
* has bank of high frequency words that are spelled consistently	because would friend		* spells most multi-syllabic words		

But the developing speller may not have figured out

	Evidence of Success	Evidence of Approximation		Evidence of Success	Evidence of Approximation
* when to double consonants	summer soccer tennis better	colect tomorow writen	* figures out unstressed vowels (schwa)		
* how to control schwa	skeleton demonstration	illutrated anamals mastakes favorat	* uses multiple spelling strategies: phonemic, morphemic and visual		
* when to use which homophone	eignt off night	herd witch break	* spells most words correctly		
* that affixes have fixed spellings	officer	especuley lueklly stasion			

FIGURE 7-9   Christopher's Completed Continuum Worksheet

all texts with the same operating principle: the faster I read, the better a reader I am. In easy texts, such as *Runaway Ralph* (Cleary 1970), he is able to read quickly while successfully manipulating the cue systems. However, as the gradient of text increases, his fast reading rate at times interferes with fluency and compromises his control of the cue systems. During his reading of *Amos and Boris* (Steig 1971), Christopher often got lost in complex sentences, inserting punctuation where there wasn't any and omitting punctuation that was present. His limited exposure to complex sentences and his fast rate caused him to lose meaning periodically. In addition, while Christopher has an impressive bank of advanced sight words (*universe, overwhelmed, miserable, iodine, desperately*), his impulse to partially decode long, unfamiliar words and to take or leave the results appears to be tied to his "reading race" mindset. With guidance on what good readers do with regard to rate, and with formal instruction in syllabication and affixes, Christopher will strengthen his self-extending system.

Taking Stock: Reading and Writing the Word

There are striking parallels, highlighted in Figure 7-10, between Christopher's word knowledge and usage across the processes of reading and spelling. Take a moment to assess Christopher's competence by answering the questions in Figure 7-10.

Christopher is a competent reader and speller. He brings a strong command of the English language to texts he is reading and writing. His sense of the world and his sense of the word drive his engagement with text. When meaning or accuracy is disrupted, he monitors his work and takes corrective action with a high degree of success. When presented with challenging words, he taps multiple sources of information. This is not to suggest that he problem solves every challenge. It does suggest that he has achieved what Clay (1991a) calls "inner control"—"a network of strategies for operating on or with text" (326). Undergirding this inner control is his affinity for the word—his love of language and his commitment to excellence.

Reading	Spelling
Does the child:	Does the child:
use multiple cue systems:	use multiple spelling strategies
meaning?	morphemic?
syntax?	phonemic?
print (visual)?	visual (letter sequence)?
self-monitor when meaning disrupted?	proofread for accuracy?
self-correct for meaning and accuracy?	self-correct for accuracy?
care about reading words accurately?	care about spelling words accurately?
have an extensive sight vocabulary?	have an extensive bank of spelling words?
read fluently?	write fluently?

FIGURE 7-10   The Strategic Aspects of Reading and Spelling

Spelling Assessment Worksheet

	Evidence	Conclusions
Use of strategies: phonemic		
visual		
morphemic		

Strategic Control:	Evidence	Conclusions
proofreads and edits during writing		
proofreads and edits after writing		
cares about accuracy		

Spelling Knowledge:	Evidence of success	Evidence of approximation	Conclusions
short vowels			
multisyllabic words			
past-tense endings			
homophones			
other			

Developmental Profile:
Developing Speller (C) _____
Developing Speller (D) _____
Conventional Speller (E) _____

FIGURE 7-11   Spelling Assessment Worksheet

Both reading and spelling have at their core meaningful communication. Both demand activation of language knowledge beyond sound-symbol relationships. Both necessitate constructive, strategic processes.

Reading and spelling are related processes, but they are not identical. While readers use their linguistic knowledge to sample and, subsequently, to confirm or to reject the graphic information in the text, spellers must attend to word detail. While readers depend on sentence/paragraph context, spellers can only depend on word context. While readers, at times, can skim and even skip text without losing essential meaning, spellers are locked into a process that demands precision. While a strong correlation exists between reading and spelling achievement in the early grades, successful reading does not ensure successful spelling.

One study examined the spelling ability of kindergartners whose word recognition and decoding skills matched those of second graders and found that the early readers spelled words with much less proficiency than the older readers (Bachman 1983). Frith's (1980) investigation of children who were strong readers but poor spellers also reinforced the notion that spelling was not just the inverse of reading. As Smith (1982) pointed out, "Writing places a much heavier burden on memory than reading. It takes much more experience and skill to write words than to read them. This is partly because it is far easier to recognize something than to reproduce it. . . . Reproduction requires skill of a quite different order from recognition" (147). Christopher's writing samples are consistent. When presented with a list of seventy words that he had misspelled in his journal and story, he read each word without hesitation.

Getting Started with Spelling Assessment

Good assessment is seldom a linear proposition. Rather, good assessment is the continual interplay of "sensitive observation" (Clay 1991a) and keen reflection. It assumes that we know what it is that we are seeing when we observe children's literacy behavior. It assumes that we understand that one bundle of data usually leads to new questions and to revised hypotheses. It assumes that trustworthy conclusions hinge on the corroboration of data.

There are some broad guidelines for the assessment of spelling. Central to a child's profile as a speller is the range of evidence that informs our analysis. They include observations and anecdotal notes, conversations with children, conversations with parents (and other teachers), writing samples (first draft and final), surveys, interviews, informal tests, running records, and retellings. It is through the skillful merging and analysis of these data that we can make good conclusions.

Guidelines for Assessing Knowledge of How Words Work

Pull together what you know about the speller as a reader and writer.
Spelling assessment can't be divorced from reading and writing assessment. Reading is the spelling lifeline. Good readers often are good spellers; good spellers are often good readers.

But, reading alone will not ensure good spelling. Readers need to write. Writing allows spellers to put into practice what they have learned from extensive exposure to print (Smith 1982). Through running records, we can observe evidence of the strategies children use to process print. Writing samples provide evidence of the strategies children use to produce written language. Responsive spelling assessment captures children's developing control of useful strategies.

Examine the tangible evidence and analyze spelling strategies used.
On one level, spelling is delightfully easy to assess—the word is either right or wrong. If we fail to examine children's spelling approximations, however, we close the window on the cognitive strategies that spellers adopt to puzzle out unfamiliar words. One essential dimension of spelling assessment, then, is the determination of the writer's knowledge and use of three prominent strategies (phonemic, visual, and morphemic) and the writer's understanding of when to use what strategy.

Buttress tentative conclusions about spelling strategies with insights from spellers.
In addition to informal conversation, it is helpful to ask spellers to complete a version of the Spelling Strategy Inventory (see Figure 7-3) that you design, keeping in mind grade-level appropriateness. The resulting data help to affirm or to reject the preliminary conclusions that are made from writing samples. The inventory also provides an important teaching vehicle. Once spellers' awareness has been heightened, they can include self-reflections about these spelling strategies in their writing portfolios. Asking students to complete a Spelling Survey (Figure 7-4) provides additional insights about their strategy usage at particular points in time and across time.

Check spellers' efforts to self-monitor and to self-correct.
"Independent reading requires strategic control" (Clay 1991a, 288); so too does spelling.

Essential to such independence is the ability to detect when a word doesn't look right and to take corrective action. Spellers' erasures and/or crossouts provide behavioral evidence of this self-regulating behavior.

Proofreading efforts both during and after the act of writing are important to observe. Because many young spellers edit as they go and are not inclined to reread pieces unless specifically asked to do so, it is important to build proofreading opportunities into our assessment procedures.

◼ Make a copy of a child's writing that contains a few spelling errors.

◼ Ask the writer to reread the piece, starting at the bottom of the page and reading backwards, and to circle words that don't look right.

◼ Beside each circled word, have the child write two or three attempts and check off a final choice.

Prompted proofreading events give important information about spellers' detection/correction strategies as well as skill knowledge. Unprompted proofreading attempts mark true strides toward spelling independence. As good spellers know, final proofreading efforts sometimes take us to resources such as dictionaries or more-knowledgeable others. Assessing spellers' awareness of resources can be attained through Spelling Surveys (Figure 7-4) and through direct observation.

Determine what spellers know about the orthography and what they need to know.

The English orthography is governed in part by bundles of spelling rules and spelling patterns (regular and irregular). Assessment of all spelling patterns and rules would be a painstaking task indeed. Fortunately, thanks to the work of Charles Read (1971) and others, we can focus our analysis on specific markers of growth. These markers are highlighted in the developmental continuum in Figure 7-7. In general, the two most discriminating markers of growth are the short vow-

els and two- or three-syllable words. Using the Spelling Assessment Worksheet (see Figure 7-11 on page 85), record the speller's successes and approximations with short vowels, and assess whether the vowel sounds are included, are substituted one for another, or are represented accurately. Do the same for multisyllabic words, assessing whether both (or all) syllables are represented in part or in full. In addition, track past-tense endings (and the three prominent spelling rules: double the consonant before adding *ed*; change the *y* to *i* and add *ed*; and drop the *e* before adding the ending) and homophones. In the Other category, log any pronounced pattern that marks success or that may need attention (e.g., *r*-controlled vowels). This evaluation signals areas of instruction that may be warranted as well as evidence to guide decisions about the speller's developmental profile.

Encourage spellers to self-assess their knowledge and strategy usage.

There is much agreement among literacy experts about the importance of student self-assessment (Graves 1994; Tierney, Carter, and Desai 1991). If children are to remain invested in their learning, they need to assess their own progress as readers, writers, and spellers, and to set goals for future learning. This reflective process begins with asking children to examine their writing samples, and to explain how their spelling has improved from one marking period. Of course, such invitations are contingent on minilessons in which we help children think about what to look for as they self-assess and how to set attainable goals (Jenkins 1996). Additional self-assessment data are available from the Spelling Inventory and Survey. These instruments, administered at the beginning, middle, and end of the year, reveal shifts in thinking.

Merge data across spellers and teach, teach, teach.

The goal of student self-assessment is matched in importance with the goal of instructional decision making. We assess so that we know what to teach. When we detect the prevalence of the phonemic strategy in our second- or third-grade spellers, we design a series of whole-class minilessons to illustrate the values and limitations of this strategy and to introduce students to the other strategies. When we determine that certain fourth graders use the homophone trio *there*, *their*, *they're* interchangeably, we pull them together for small-group instruction. When we notice that a fifth grader has not learned that past-tense markers are fixed units, we provide one-on-one instruction in a conference. At every grade level, we teach children how to proofread, edit, and care about their spelling. At every grade, we instill in children our love of language.

Suggestions for Professional Development

1. Using the guidelines for assessing knowledge of how words work, identify one younger student at the end of first grade or in second grade and one older student in fourth or fifth grade. For each student, read through two or three writing samples that were written around the same time. Using the worksheet in Figure 7-11, record examples of words that show evidence of each spelling strategy. Draw some preliminary conclusions about each strategy and discuss your results with colleagues.

2. Ask both students to complete a Spelling Survey (Figure 7-4). This information will give you some additional insights about their use of strategies at this particular point in time.

3. Try some prompted proofreading with each student by making a copy of the child's writing that contains a few errors and then asking the child to:
   - Reread the piece, starting at the bottom of the page and reading backwards.
   - Circle words that don't look right.
   - Make two or three attempts beside each circled word.
   - Check off a final choice.

What can you discover about the student's ability to recognize words that are not quite accurate? What can you discover about the student's word knowledge in successive attempts to spell each word?

4. Compare the two students and think about the implications for designing word study activities.

5. As a follow-up, read and discuss Chapter 10, "Assessing What Children Know," Chapter 11, "Word-Solving Strategies: Organize to Teach," and Chapter 13, "Word Explorers: Teaching Strategies That Promote Active Inquiry" from the companion volume to this book, *Word Matters: Teaching Phonics and Spelling in the Reading/Writing Classroom.*

Language Play and Word Study

From their earliest experiences, children learn language as they use it in their interactions with others. They find that language is a way to communicate and to achieve some control over the world in which they live. They use language as a tool for finding out about the world and for representing their experiences. Interest in language naturally grows as young children use it in different contexts, for different purposes. Language is not only a useful tool; it is something to be enjoyed. Children delight in such experiences as chants, rhymes, songs, and poetry. Stories that they hear read aloud capture their attention because of the content or characters, but the words and the way they are put together also bring a response from children. Why else would they ask to hear favorite stories like *Goodnight Moon* over and over? We would say that all of these ways of finding pleasure in language are "childlike." But, in fact, they are not. People of all ages enjoy language. They read poetry many times, listen to favorite music, watch television shows or movies, and go to see a favorite comedian use language in humorous ways.

People even enjoy studying words themselves, as they do when they complete crossword puzzles or play Scrabble.

Participating in oral language activities such as poems and nursery rhymes introduces children to word study because it invites them to attend to language and aspects of words. In this section our authors describe the connections between oral and written language from language play to sophisticated word study. Designing effective word study is challenging for us as teachers because it must be interesting and enjoyable, involve children in active rather than passive learning, promote interest in words, and motivate children to engage in their own inquiry about how words work. When you provide word study, you are not only thinking of interesting activities, you are plumbing the learning potential of these activities. You want your students to learn strategies, not simply isolated words. You are also faced with an additional challenge: you are making instructional decisions for a particular group of children who vary in their knowledge and experiences. The word study experiences must be within children's capability yet offer enough challenge to be interesting and productive for learning. When appropriately applied, word study has a high payoff: students learn powerful principles about how words work and develop skills that they can use in reading and writing.

In the first chapter in this section, Booth describes oral language play and its role in helping children learn about written language. As they play with words through games, poems, and songs, children develop sensitivity to the sounds of language and connect spoken and written words. Booth describes a variety of experiences that will help children enjoy playing with language. He also provides examples of written resources.

Two chapters describe active word study approaches that have practical use in the classroom. Zutell focuses on word sorting, a way of helping students actively investigate and connect words. By manipulating and categorizing words, students develop the ability to notice how words are connected by sound, visual pattern, meaning, or other characteristics, and in the process they develop knowledge of principles for word solving in reading and writing. Hall and Cunningham provide a wide range of classroom activities that will help students learn about words, and they also create resources such as word walls and word charts that children can learn to use as they read, write, and proofread.

DeFord draws us back to the continuum of learning from the development of critical cognitive processes involved in learning oral language to the sophisticated ways that advanced learners use and analyze words. All of the chapters in this section are directed toward extending our understanding of a curriculum that involves reading, writing, and word study. While this section focuses on word study, it's evident that word study is based on oral language learning and is connected to reading and writing continuous text.

Language Delights and Word Play

The Foundation for Literacy Learning

David Booth

Introduction

Think about something that you learned quickly, easily, and well. Chances are you also remember having some fun while learning the skill or concept. Throughout this book, we and our colleagues offer language as both the foundation for learning and a legitimate topic of focus. As human beings, our enjoyment of language is evident. We play with it, tell jokes, use and appreciate language in ironic and satiric ways, sing songs, enjoy reading poetry again and again, and listen to the rhythm of the rhymes and chants of our culture. Playing with language brings it to our conscious attention so that we can enjoy multiple aspects of language: alliteration, rhyme, and playful and intriguing uses of words.

When children are invited to enjoy language by playing with it, they learn many critical early concepts effortlessly. We agree with Booth, the author of this chapter, that word play is a legitimate and valuable classroom activity even after children have become readers and writers. It helps children consciously examine oral and written language while they learn to manipulate and control it. Word play provides numerous opportunities to learn how words work and how they are connected by pattern and sound. Indeed, our understanding of gram-matical concepts such as synonyms and homonyms arises from our enjoyment of playing around with words. Children find word play delightful; they focus not on a "lesson" but on their own pleasure. As a teacher, you can intentionally use this natural urge to participate in language as a foundation for helping your students develop key understandings about language.

In this chapter Booth provides numerous examples of books and extension activities that will propel young children into word play and invite them to notice essential features of words, letters, and sounds. He discusses how repeated readings of stories help young children attend to the sounds of words in different ways, and he also provides a rich source of jokes, riddles, puns, alphabet books, and poetry. Games, too, are included as a way to help young children learn about the sounds of language.

A language-rich classroom enables children to hear and say many varieties of language, experiencing word play, rhyme, and repetition for themselves. Children need a rich oral foundation for learning about letters and words. Before they can make connections between sounds and letters, children must be able to hear the sounds in words. Indeed, phonics learning begins with oral language.

▮ Children need to hear and say the words that, one day, they will read and write.

▮ Children need to enjoy the sounds of language before they are asked to engage in word analysis.

▮ Children build their interest in words and in the way language sounds through oral language experiences.

▮ Children experience language as a tool they can use for such functions as joining in, sharing information, or asking questions.

▮ Children absorb the meanings, the vocabulary, and the syntax of language through their engagement with oral language, thus expanding their capabilities as language users.

The Joy of Language

In *Babushka's Mother Goose*, Patricia Polacco (1995) presents us with rhymes and stories as told by her Russian grandmother, and we run our tongues around the unusual names *Natasha, Ivana, Katushka, Anushka, Diadushka, and Babushka*. The words delight the listening children, who are involved in the sounds of language from the very first page. Teachers can use young children's inherent love of the sounds of language to create a climate in which children enjoy and find satisfaction in acquiring word power. As well, playful and adventurous experiences with words can contribute to a better understanding of the technical aspects of the complexities of language—the spellings, sounds, rhythms, and incongruities of this complex and vital communication system.

Educator Bill Moore (1985) says that we need to share with children words "that taste good," that tickle the tongue, tease the ear, create images in the mind's eye, delight us with their trickery, and amuse us with their puzzles and complexities. As children come to realize that words have a power of their own,

they begin to take control of the medium and the message, becoming apprentice wordsmiths. Their confidence in using language and their knowledge about how language works explode; their flexibility and versatility with word patterns and meanings multiply; and their love of language and their need for specific and apt words expand and deepen.

As children play with language, they begin to notice the interplay among words, the patterns of similarity, the incongruities of sound-symbol relationships, and the amazing potential of letter clusters to represent diverse meanings. To be truly useful for developing young readers and writers, word play must incorporate a wide spectrum of activity, including:

▮ Simple oral "call and response" chants.

▮ Pencil-and-paper games.

▮ Chances to experiment with rhythm and rhyme in poetic structures.

▮ The satisfaction of reading aloud with a buddy the crafted dialogue of a humorous novel.

▮ The joy of participating in a choir that sings songs of such delight that the lyrics remain in the memory forever.

Children begin to grow aware of the "bits and pieces" of language, focusing on the smallest elements that are the building blocks of literacy.

Jack Prelutsky, in his funny and irresistible collection of poems *A Pizza the Size of the Sun*, offers children chants and cheers, made-up words and backwards words, and rhymes and rhythms that are perfect examples of word play that lead to word power. It is almost impossible to read the following poem without trying to say some of it aloud!

The Fummarummalummazumms
I'm succumbing to those numbing
Fummarummalummazumms
They are humming strumming
   thrumming on and on

Now they're drumming as they're
   humming.
I can't wait till morning comes,
And those Fummarummalummazumms
   are gone. (Prelutsky 1996, 155)

Dav Pilkey's *The Dumb Bunnies* series depends on word play for impact. For example, the sign for the African lion in *The Dumb Bunnies Go to The Zoo* (1997) reads, "Bitus Yourarmus Offus." When children explore print that is memorable, written with graphic power, full of rhyme and rhythm, and containing predictable patterns or puzzles, they develop a sense of ownership of the print they are learning to incorporate into their literacy lives. They begin to recognize and retain words and elements of words that are meaningful to them. Developing a fascination with language through activities that cause children to think about and use words in meaningful contexts helps children build, acquire, and retain vocabulary through the years.

Word Power from Story Power

David McPhail has given parents and teachers a treasure with his three volumes of porcine antics—*Pigs Aplenty, Pigs Galore!* (McPhail 1993), *Pigs Ahoy!* (McPhail 1995), and *Those Can-Do Pigs* (McPhail 1996). These stories told with rhyming couplets draw the children inside the words immediately as they join in and call out the rhyme combinations:

   In the cupboards
   On the floor
   Pigs aplenty
   Pigs galore! (1993)

When we read books to children and they join in on the second or third reading, they begin to feel that they are readers, and they take pride in demonstrating real reading behavior. The story, the images, the sounds, the rhythms, the words all come together to make "literary sense." Bill Martin, Jr., (1972) invites us to consider "the ingen-

uous, cumulative coupling of sequences" in his *Brown Bear, Brown Bear*:

The coupling has nothing and yet everything to do with reading. Momentarily banished are the restrictions of print, the preoccupation with eye movements from left to right, and "today's new words" drill. The literature creates its own life. The linguistic dance of the question and answer in *Brown Bear* is so pervasive and appealing that the reader is caught up in it and responds without labored awareness of technicalities and rules.

The important meaning of these and other books is not the story facts. It is irrelevant which animal Brown Bear saw or what trick was performed on which floor of the apartment house. The humanly worthwhile meanings are found in the playfulness of the language, in the interrelations of color and design and story development, and in the inculcated awareness that life is worth living.

Nonsense Books

Many children's books offer us opportunities for sharing innovative and memorable word play experiences with young people. As children laugh at the slapstick and nonsense, the funny and exaggerated characters, or the silly and ridiculous situations, the words and expressions pop up and jiggle the funnybone, and the letters, patterns, and refrains remain in their long-term memories. Check out the following:

- *A Dark Tale* (Brown 1981).
- *Funnybones* (Ahlberg and Ahlberg 1980).
- *Jake Baked the Cake* (Hennessy 1990).
- *The Napping House* (Wood 1984).
- *The Teeny Tiny Woman* (O'Connor 1986).

Books that focus on word play can give children opportunities to pick out specific words or letters, match and find words with similar beginnings, recognize frequently repeated words or phrases, ask questions and make observations about what has been read, and anticipate and predict what will work.

Alphabet books, counting books, books of verse, books full of word puzzles, books based on culturally significant sequences such as days of the week or months of the year, books that use recurring patterns from one page to the next—all allow children to enter the print world with confidence.

Puns and Expressions

Children love puns and expressions that conjure up amusing images. Riddle and joke books are excellent resources for integrating listening and speaking with reading and writing. Starting the year with such word play, perhaps by pairing children to read a joke book together and then create their own riddle and joke books to share with others, indicates that words and how they go together will be an interesting focus for learning.

The following excerpt from *Zoodles* by Bernard Most (1992) is typical of the sort of language play that twists words inside out and upside down and helps children to think about, listen for, and see the shapes and meanings of words and sentences:

> What do you call a kangaroo that wakes you up every day?
> Answer: A kangarooster.

Many picture books, joke and riddle books, poetry anthologies, and reference books contribute to children's understanding of technical aspects of language such as phonics, spelling, homonyms, derivations, and idioms. These books, of course, are popular with the children not because they teach but because the "bare bones" of language hold surprise and delight. *King Kong's Underwear* by Mike Thaler (1986), and the pop-up book *Knock! Knock!* by Colin and Jaqui Hawkins (1990) have been recent favorites.

Jokes and Riddles

Many jokes and riddles hinge on the irregularities between letters and sounds in English that draw the child into careful readings to discriminate between discrepancies. A number of jokes and riddles involve homo-graphs (words that are spelled the same but differ in meaning, origin, and often pronunciation), or homophones (words that sound alike but differ in meaning, origin, and sometimes spelling). *Go Hog Wild!* by Peter Roop (1984) is a collection of riddles about farming and farm animals. Other riddle books include:

- *Tyrannosaurus Wrecks: A Book of Dinosaur Riddles* (Sterne 1979).
- *What Do You Call a Dumb Bunny? And Other Rabbit Riddles, Games, Jokes, and Cartoons* (Brown 1983).
- *What's a Frank Frank? Tasty Homograph Riddles* (Maestro 1984).

Books About Words

Marvin Terban has written a series of books that celebrate word play. *Superdupers!* (1989) explores more than one hundred terms such as *wishy-washy*, *okey-dokey*, and *razzmatazz* that have become part of our everyday vocabulary. *Eight Ate: A Feast of Homonym Riddles* (1982) laughs at the vagaries of English spelling. *In a Pickle and Other Funny Idioms* (1983) examines the origins of idioms such as "a chip off the old block" and "a frog in his throat." *Funny You Should Ask* (1992) helps children use word play to compose their own jokes and riddles. The titles of other books in the series are self-explanatory: *I Think I Thought and Other Tricky Verbs* (1984); *Your Foot's on My Feet! and Other Tricky Nouns* (1986); *The Dove Dove: Funny Homograph Riddles* (1988); *Too Hot to Hoot: A collection of Funny Palindrome Riddles* (1985). Charles Keller gives children more than one hundred examples of word-craft in *Daffynitions* (1991). Fred Gwynne's books on puns and idioms, *A Little Pigeon Toad* (1984), *The King Who Rained* (1970), *Chocolate Moose for Dinner* (1976), and *The Sixteen Hand Horse* (1980), have hilarious illustrations.

Children can collect idioms, word pictures that make language more colorful, from the books they are reading and listening to. Some books of idioms to begin exploring with children include *A Hog on Ice and Other Curious Expressions* (Funk 1948) and *In a Pickle and Other Funny Idioms* (Terban 1983).

Tongue Twisters

Encouraging the use of tongue twisters in the classroom actively involves children in playing with words and enjoying the sounds of the language. Like joke, riddle, and pun books, collections of tongue twisters provide reasons for reading, encouraging auditory and visual discrimination and physical articulation.

Many tongue twisters involve the children in alliteration, an important poetic device. Alvin Schwartz gives us *Busy Buzzing Bumblebees and Other Tongue Twisters* (1992). In *Jamberry* by Bruce Degen (1983), a rhyme for every kind of berry can be found in these poems, which are full of word play and pictures. The seven children in *Rosie Sips Spiders* by Alison Lester (1989) work and play in their own unusual way. In *Sheep on a Ship* by Nancy Shaw (1989), sheep on a deep-sea voyage run into trouble when it storms. *Silly Sally* by Audrey Wood (1992) is a rhyming story.

Palindromes

Two interesting books of palindromes (words that read the same way forward and backward) are *Go Hang a Salami! I'm a Lasagna Hog! and Other Palindromes* by Jon Agee (1991) and *Too Hot to Hoot: Funny Palindrome Riddles* by Marvin Terban (1985). Children can find other palindromes in names (Anna), common words (pop), and even phrases (Madam I'm Adam). As well, children can incorporate their newfound palindromes in guessing games (What time is lunch? Noon.).

Anagrams

Children can make anagrams by transposing letters in existing words or phrases to make new ones. Beginners could turn *ant* into *tan* and *meat* into *tame*, while more advanced players could turn *kitchen* into *thicken*. Simi-

larly, children could look for small words in larger words, such as *read* in *bread*. They can unscramble nonsense words to form words, such as *tendust* to *student*. Bernard Most has children look for words inside words in *There's an Ant in Anthony and Pets in Trumpets* (1990). Alvin Schwartz has written several books of word play that are useful with all ages of children: *The Cat's Elbow and Other Secret Languages* (1982); *Chin Music: Tall Talk and Other Talk* (1979); *Tomfoolery: Trickery and Foolery with Words* (1973); and *Flapdoodle* (1990).

Words and Language Concepts

Many books teach skills by focusing on a particular theme or language concept. For example, William Steig's *CDB* (1968) and *CDC* (1984) challenge the reader to think about the sounds of words by solving rebus puzzles. Author/illustrator Ruth Heller uses rhyming text and richly detailed paintings to provide young readers with some basic concepts about parts of speech. In *A Cache of Jewels and Other Collective Nouns* (1987), Heller introduces children to such words as a *batch* of bread and a *fleet* of ships; in *Kites Sail High* (1988), the children explore the variety of uses and meanings a single verb can have; *Many Luscious Lollipops* (1989) discusses adjectives; and *Merry-Go-Round* (1990) explores nouns. So does *Your Foot's on My Feet! And Other Tricky Nouns* by Marvin Terban. Children can also push and pull the levers of grammar in *The Amazing Pop-up Grammar Book* by Jenny Maizels (1996).

Weird! The Complete Book of Halloween by Peter R. Limburg (1989) discusses definitions and the historical background of words associated with Halloween. Alphabet books such as *Animalia* by Graeme Base (1987) and *Q Is for Duck* by Mary Elting and Jack Folsom (1980) also help children identify letters as they inspect words. Counting books such as *One Watermelon Seed* by Celia Lottridge (1986) not only help children with numbers but also encourage an understanding of the use of the singular and plural.

Dr. Seuss's word play, a significant component of all his books, uses strong phonic cues: *Green Eggs and Ham* (1960); *Mr. Brown Can Moo, Can You?* (1970); *The Cat in the Hat* (1957); *One Fish Two Fish Red Fish Blue Fish* (1960). Books such as these draw children into the fun and delight of words. Riddles, rhymes, and surprises sharpen reading, spelling, and thinking skills. As the children laugh, they cannot fail to take time to notice the puzzles, tangles, and peculiarities of English, learning to make sense of this complicated word jungle.

The Magic of the Alphabet

Children enjoy playing alphabet games on automobile trips all over North America. For example, one person says "Alaska," and the next says "British Columbia," and so on through the twenty-six letters. Alphabet books, like Mother Goose rhymes, were among the earliest books published for children. Today these artistic creations are available with a variety of subjects and styles, providing children of all ages with much to look at, to think about, and to talk about (Booth 1997). Hundreds of authors and artists have created alphabet books for children; and although we know which letter is next, the text constantly surprises us.

Alphabet Books

New alphabet books are published every year to add to our growing classroom collections. The bright colors and interesting items for each letter in an alphabet book attract and hold the children's interest. Once children have grasped basic letter forms or shapes, we can help them focus on the style of letters as they make connections between each letter and its sounds within words. In *Jeremy Kooloo*, Tim Mahurin (1995) revisits an old rhyme pattern with his story of a mischief-making cat who spots four glasses of milk on the table:

A Big Cat
Drank
Every Full Glass . . .

Tomorrow's Alphabet by George Shannon (1996) includes twenty-six riddles that incorporate the letters inside a puzzle framework that challenges the children to predict the answers:

A is for seed
Tomorrow's . . .
Apple.

One class of children reworked their illustrated version, calling it *Yesterday's Alphabet*:

B is for eggs,
Yesterday's birds.
H is for bald,
Yesterday's hair.

Creating ABC Books

Using word play, children can create their own versions of alphabet books, brainstorming words beginning with the same letter and making up sentences using these words; designing alliterative poems; graphing letter frequency; drawing up alphabetical lists; and building collections of words, phrases, and sentences, which they can organize alphabetically on word charts, word files, alphabet posters, friezes, pictures, or in big books. Perhaps the class can create an illustrated alphabet book, a mixture of images as children draw one or two pictures for each letter of the alphabet. The variety of computer fonts can add to the repertoire of these budding graphic artists.

The Sounds and Sights of Poetry

Golden trees
Stand around me
Green hills
Sleep beside me
Swan-like clouds
Fly above me
And my soul rings
Like a church bell
Kevin (8 years)

The Russian poet Chukovsky (1927–1963) said that, in their early years, youngsters exhibit a kind of linguistic genius as they master intricate aspects of language form and function. Word play is a large part of that process. As they play linguistically, children are learning valuable information about how language works.

Poets continually remind us that how something is said is as important as what is said. Through poetry, children can isolate, scrutinize, magnify, and elaborate their store of words. Poetry is a perfect test for what language can do; it is full of word play. Poets have always used language in special ways, and in poetry, we have a vehicle for looking at the use of words, the choosing of the one special word that fits perfectly.

Sound Poems

It is fun to create sound poems using letters, groups of letters, or made-up words to stand for sounds. We can twist and play with sounds and words.

Peter Spier has compiled two books of sound words: *Gobble Growl Grunt* (1988), in which each letter of the alphabet is linked to a particular animal sound; and *Crash! Bang! Boom!* (1972) about the sounds people and machines make. In *Hoot Howl Hiss* by Michelle Koch (1991), children are introduced to a variety of animals and the sounds they make. In Jakki Wood's *Moo Moo Brown Cow* (1992), a kitten wanders through a barnyard asking mother animals about their babies. In *The Cow That Went Oink* by Bernard Most (1990), a cow that oinks and a pig that moos are ridiculed by the other barnyard animals until each teaches the other a new sound.

School-Yard Rhymes

In *Dr. Knickerbocker and Other Rhymes* (Booth 1993), children meet a hundred of the most memorable (and naughtiest) school-yard rhymes from recess, from the bus ride, and from all the anthologies the children read. Included in the wit and wisdom of the young are skipping rhymes, jingles, riddles, sayings, superstitions, taunts and teases, catcalls and retorts, autograph verses, street songs, counting-out rhymes, ball-bounce chants, tongue twisters, join-in rhythms, ac-

tion songs, nonsense verses, lullabies, jokes, silly rhymes, parodies, nicknames, slogans, and ads, all shouted and sung in the freedom of the playground. These verses form the folk poetry of childhood.

Nursery Rhymes

Nursery rhymes often provide children's first introduction to poetry. The word play, the imagination, the sounds, the rollicking rhythms, the merriment, and the excitement all introduce the child to poetry. Contemporary poets have taken the well-known rhymes, the slapstick humor, the wit, the comic spirit, and used similar techniques for their own writings. Because nursery rhymes feature sounds and rhythms that appeal strongly to children, and because they also are so close to the children's own oral folk poetry, they form the basis of our work. We can speak the words and invite them to join in. Many of the traditional nursery rhymes will be unfamiliar to the children, and the opportunity for them to feel the rhythms and try out the vocabulary should be as pleasurable as we can make it. Even though archaic words and expressions and unfamiliar vocabulary are used, this seldom poses any barriers to the children's imaginings. The images created by the nursery rhymes are powerful and evocative, the characters we meet in them stay with us throughout our lives, and the stories they tell or hint at are rich with possibilities for the children's own story making. Check out the following books:

- *Alligator Pie* (Lee 1987).
- *Butterscotch Dreams* (Dunn 1987).
- *Garbage Delight* (Lee 1970).
- *Jelly Belly* (Lee 1983).
- *Nicholas Knock & Other Rhymes* (Lee 1977).
- *There Was an Old Man...A Collection of Limericks* (Lear 1994).
- *There Were Monkeys in My Kitchen* (Fitch 1992).
- *The Wheels on the Bus* (Kovalski 1987).

Extending Word Play into Writing

Rhymes and verses, chants, cheers, and songs offer a variety of occasions for contextualized word play. Once the words of a song are learned by the children, they can be incorporated into language activities. We can write the words on the overhead transparencies and ask the children to read along while they sing; we can leave out certain words of a song, and ask the children to fill in the missing ones.

Out-Loud Poetry

We need to encourage young children to browse alone or with classmates through the many illustrated picture books of poems available today, but most of all, we must encourage the public sharing of poetry out loud. Taking time to read selections by contemporary poets and introducing children to the different sounds and different worlds of long-ago poets, such as Walter de la Mare, Christina Rosetti, or Robert Louis Stevenson, will broaden the children's language and literature base.

Out-loud poetry represents the joy of literature and the power of making meaning with the words of others. We listen and celebrate, we read and wonder, we sing and laugh. When the children come to meeting print on their own, it will be with the knowledge of the full satisfaction reading can bring, and with the excitement that lies ahead. They will mine and forage and dig for meaning in the dust of the print, and in the sounds of their lives.

Games for Learning

Games belong at the heart of childhood, and they help us remember the child in each of us. When we, as grown-ups, engage in play, we can often free ourselves of many of the restrictive overlays that we have gathered over the years, and we find ourselves released into new learning through play (Booth 1994).

Because games belong to the world of the child, we must be careful in using them for purposes of directed learning. Perhaps we can harness the energy of play for the business of learning, but it must not be at the expense of the spirit of the game. Games can't be used all of the time to teach all things, but they can be a medium for altering attitudes and abilities in safe, enjoyable contexts. Often games require the players to plan strategies, use memory, make decisions, solve problems, suggest alternatives, recognize patterns, analyze and synthesize, sequence, and evaluate. Depending on how it is used, a particular game can promote different areas of growth. Games can teach children to apply rules, give and follow directions, understand cause and effect, detect irregularities, generate possibilities, and use probabilities. Games work from inside the children's world, propelling them toward discovery and creativity, building skills along the way.

New games arise from old ones. Once the control concept of a game is understood, inventing new ones is comparatively easy for the children. Rules can be changed, minimized, or clarified; numbers of players can be increased or made into teams; and tensions can be added to increase the learning. A whole new game may emerge from the children's ideas. They will be building games out of games, developing imagination and thought as they play. Games can generate new thought and spawn new structures for learning.

In "What Works in Play," Moffett and Wagner (1993) make a case for the importance of games in learning how letters and sounds relate:

Most games depend on social interplay. Players pool their knowledge. Game materials such as cards, letter cubes, and pull-through or spinning devices usually provide the sight, or spellings; but players have to provide the sound, or oral language. Collectively, they have enough knowledge of word recognition and sound-spellings to play the game; but while one player may only be practicing a sound-spelling or word she already knows, another player in that game may be learning from her that sound-spelling or word for the first time. Similarly, given a certain game, players will alternate between presenting spellings to each other and sounding out spellings presented to them by their partners.

Such games are vestiges of folkways of learning that existed before public schools, which have, in their insecure professionalism, usually been scornful of them. As a result, parents tend to distrust games, and the society has drawn a sharp line between playing and learning. But it is precisely this sort of mistaken professionalism trying to make an exclusive place for itself that has resulted in the concept of reading as an activity requiring special practices and programs. Actually, being read to, dictating, and inventing spelling teach initial literacy because they are games, too, as attested by the fact that children will choose to do these things out of school for their own satisfaction. Play works.

Computers, in one form or another, are a part of the daily lives of many children. There are dozens of games that can be played on screen using the Internet or prepared programs. With the computer, children can search and discover several games, then make a "gameplan" for others to follow, keeping track of the results or printing the outcomes.

Children enjoy doing crossword puzzles that are challenging but manageable. The words could be listed at the bottom to make the activity easier for children in lower grades. A crossword could also be designed by a teacher or a group of children in response to a story, novel, or nonfiction book experienced in class. Computer programs allow teachers to employ their own word lists and clues to make crossword puzzles that children can work on during free time, simplifying the activity a great deal (Booth 1997).

Board games such as Pictionary and Junior Scrabble, which involve reading, spelling, and cooperative skills, motivate children and encourage learning and can also be used in cooperative learning lessons to encourage working in groups. Volunteers can bring in a variety of board games that are popular with children and discuss how each works before making them available to the class (Booth 1997).

Ten Classroom Games for Word Play
Larry Swartz, in "Spelling Games" (1994), has put together a series of activities that promote word play.

1. *Sentence in a Word*. Partners decide on a word of five to eight letters. Then each player uses each letter of the word to start another word and create a sentence. Partners compare answers to determine which words are similar and which sentence makes the most sense. For example: G-A-R-B-A-G-E = Go and read books and get enlightened.

2. *Wordchain*. Partners or small groups create a chain of words. Player #1 writes down any word: *begin*, for example. The next person must begin the next word with the letter that ends the first word (in this case, *n*). If Player #2 writes the word *never*, the next word must begin with an *r*, and so on. The words are written in a continuous chain (e.g., *begineverealizenteroad*). The game could be played with a special topic, such as names, cities, colors, birds.

3. *Letter Switch*. In pairs or small groups, one player begins by saying any word that comes to mind. The next player makes a new word by changing one letter. The third player then changes one letter of the new word. The game should proceed quickly without repeating the same word twice. It is recommended that four or five letters be used for the most success. An example would be *land, lane, sane, sang*.

4. *No Space*. Children write a number of words together with no spacing between

them. Then someone finds as many words as possible (a time limit can be set): *bookreadarkindoordeal*. Words can be arranged in a circle without any spaces between letters. Partners can list all the words they can find in the circle going clockwise. Small words that are found within bigger words can be counted separately.

5. *I Love My Friend with an "A."* In this alphabet game, the first player says, "I love my friend with an A because. . . ." Then, depending on the version that is decided on, Player #1 adds an adjective, or an occupation, or something that he or she likes. The next player repeats the sentence with the letter B, and so on. An example would be *I love my friend with an "A" because she's adorable, I love my friend with a "B" because she's bold.*

6. *Alliterative Headlines.* Players decide on a letter of the alphabet. In a set time limit of five minutes, they write three-word phrases that might appear as a newspaper headline using that letter to begin each word. For instance, for the letter *s*, the headline might read *Superman Saves Saskatchewan.* As an extension, players can write longer headlines. The one with the longest headline is the "winner."

7. *What's My Word?* Working in pairs, each player thinks of a word that consists of an agreed-upon number of letters. Each then writes on a piece of paper as many dashes as there are letters in the word. Player #1 chooses a letter of the alphabet and inquires whether the letter is in the opponent's word. If it is, the second player must write the letter over the dash that represents it and show this to the first player. If the letter is used more than once in the word, it must be written wherever it occurs. The first player, seeing the letter written in one or more spaces on the opponent's paper, continues asking about other letters until the letter called out is not in the word.

Player #2 then takes a turn to ask about the letters in the first player's word. The game continues in this way until one of the players successfully guesses the other's word from seeing its letters gradually filled in.

8. *Antonyms and Synonyms.* In a group, the first player calls out a word. Almost any word will do, although adjectives are probably the easiest to handle. The second player gives an antonym of that word, the third player gives a synonym for the second player's word, the fourth player gives an antonym of the third player's word, and so on. If stuck, a player may use a rhyming word. An example would be *hot, cold, cool, warm, fresh, stale, pale* (rhyme), *vivid.*

9. *Vanishing Vowels.* One player begins with a simple sentence, removing all the vowels. A partner tries to reconstruct the original sentence: *Spelling games can be lots of fun. sp-ll-ng g-m-s-c-n b- l-ts -f f-n.*

To make the game more challenging, you can eliminate the dashes so that the puzzle looks like this: *spllng gms cn b lts f fn.*

10. *Word Pyramids.* Verbal pyramids are built from the top down. They start with the apex, which consists of a single letter—the same letter for all players. Each player then works independently, adding one letter at a time to make new words, rearranging previously used letters if necessary. These new words are listed below the original letter to form a pyramid. The player who writes down the most words in a given amount of time wins the game—counting only those words that are spelled correctly. Here is an example of how two players might form pyramids starting with the letter *I:*

I	I
it	it
mit	kit
timer	knit
merits	think
	knight
	knights

Word pyramids can be made more difficult if the players are not allowed to change the order of the letters from word to word.

In classrooms where children delight in letters, words, and the sounds of language, literacy learning is propelled forward. Oral language provides the impetus and the foundation. Children see themselves as language users and language creators who can read and write language for themselves.

Suggestions for Professional Development

1. Collect many of the book titles listed in the collections of books in this chapter. Use the Recommended Children's Book List (see Figure 8-1, page 102).

2. Investigate the collection and discuss its specific potential for letter, word, and language learning. Think about:

   ▮ What can children learn about letters and sounds from these books?

   ▮ What can children learn about words and their meaning?

   ▮ What can children learn about ways to use language?

   ▮ What can children learn about how words are connected?

3. Try several of the books with children. Observe and note how children respond and to what they attend. What did they learn from the experience? What learning do they use in other settings?

4. Meet with colleagues to discuss what you learned about your students and your teaching.

5. As a follow-up, read and discuss Chapter 1, "Eight Principles of Literacy Learning," and Chapter 6, "What Teachers Need to Know About Language," from the companion volume to this book, *Word Matters: Teaching Phonics and Spelling in the Reading/Writing Classroom.*

Agee, J. 1991. *Go Hang a Salami! I'm a Lasagna Hog! and Other Palindromes.* New York: HarperCollins.

Ahlberg, A., & J. Ahlberg. 1980. *Funnybones.* London: William Heinemann.

Base, G. 1987. *Animalia.* Toronto: Irwin.

Booth, D. 1993. *Dr. Knickerbocker and Other Rhymes.* Illus. M. Kovalski. Toronto: Kids Can Press.

Brown, M. 1983. *What Do You Call a Dumb Bunny? And Other Rabbit Riddles, Games, Jokes, and Cartoons.* New York: Little, Brown.

Brown, R. 1981. *A Dark Tale.* New York: Scholastic.

Degen, B. 1983. *Jamberry.* New York: Harper & Row.

Elting, M., & J. Folsom. 1980. *Q Is for Duck: An Alphabet Guessing Game.* New York: Clarion.

Fitch, S. 1992. *There Were Monkeys in My Kitchen.* Toronto: Doubleday Canada.

Funk, C. E. 1948. *A Hog on Ice and Other Curious Expressions.* New York: Harper & Row.

Gwynne, F. 1970. *The King Who Rained.* New York: Dutton.

———. 1976. *Chocolate Moose for Dinner.* New York: Dutton.

———. 1980. *The Sixteen Hand Horse.* New York: Prentice Hall.

———. 1984. *A Little Pigeon Toad.* New York: Simon & Schuster.

Hawkins, C., & J. Hawkins. 1990. *Knock! Knock!* London: Walker.

Heller, R. 1987. *A Cache of Jewels and Other Collective Nouns.* New York: Putnam.

———. 1988. *Kites Sail High: A Book About Verbs.* New York: Putnam.

———. 1989. *Many Luscious Lollipops: A Book About Adjectives.* New York: Putnam.

———. 1990. *Merry-Go-Round: A Book About Nouns.* New York: Putnam.

Hennessy, G. G. 1990. *Jake Baked the Cake.* New York: Viking Penguin.

Keller, C. 1991. *Daffynitions.* New York: Simon & Schuster.

Koch, M. 1991. *Hoot Howl Hiss.* New York: Greenwillow.

Kovalski, M. 1987. *The Wheels on the Bus.* Toronto: Kids Can Press.

Lear, E. 1994. *There Was an Old Man . . . A Collection of Limericks.* Toronto: Kids Can Press.

Lee, D. 1970. *Garbage Delight.* New York: Macmillan.

———. 1977. *Nicholas Knock & Other Rhymes.* New York: Macmillan.

———. 1983. *Jelly Belly.* New York: Macmillan.

———. 1987. *Alligator Pie.* New York: Macmillan.

Lester, A. 1989. *Rosie Sips Spiders.* New York: Houghton Mifflin.

Limburg, P. R. 1989. *Weird! The Complete Book of Halloween.* New York: Macmillan.

Lottridge, C. 1986. *One Watermelon Seed.* Toronto: Oxford University Press.

McPhail, D. 1993. *Pigs Aplenty, Pigs Galore!* New York: Dutton.

———. 1995. *Pigs Ahoy!* New York: Dutton.

———. 1996. *Those Can-Do Pigs.* New York: Dutton.

Maestro, G. 1984. *What's a Frank Frank? Tasty Homograph Riddles.* New York: Clarion.

Mahurin, T. 1995. *Jeremy Kooloo.* New York: Dutton.

Maizels, J. 1996. *The Amazing Pop-up Grammar Book.* New York: Dutton.

Most, B. 1990a. *The Cow that Went Oink.* New York: Harcourt Brace.

———. 1990b. *There's an Ant in Anthony and Pets in Trumpets.* New York: William Morrow.

———. 1991. *Pets in Trumpets and Other Word Play Riddles.* Orlando: Harcourt Brace Jovanovich.

———. 1992. *Zoodles.* Orlando: Harcourt Brace Jovanovich.

O'Connor, J. 1986. *The Teeny Tiny Woman.* Illus. R. W. Alley. New York: Random House.

Pilkey, D. 1997. *The Dumb Bunnies Go to the Zoo.* New York: Scholastic.

Polacco, P. 1995. *Babushka's Mother Goose.* New York: Philomel.

Prelutsky, J. 1996. *A Pizza the Size of the Sun.* New York: Greenwillow.

Roop, P. 1984. *Go Hog Wild!* New York: Lerner.

Schwartz, A. 1973. *Tomfoolery: Trickery and Foolery with Words.* New York: J. B. Lippincott.

———. 1979. *Chin Music: Tall Talk and Other Talk.* New York: J. B. Lippincott.

———. 1982. *The Cat's Elbow and Other Secret Languages.* New York: Farrar, Straus & Giroux.

———. 1990. *Flapdoodle.* New York: HarperCollins.

———. 1992. *Busy Buzzing Bumblebees and Other Tongue Twisters.* New York: HarperCollins.

Seuss, Dr. 1957. *The Cat in the Hat.* New York: Beginner Books.

———. 1960a. *Green Eggs and Ham.* New York: Beginner Books.

———. 1960b. *One Fish Two Fish Red Fish Blue Fish.* New York: Beginner Books.

———. 1970. *Mr. Brown Can Moo, Can You?* New York: Beginner Books.

Shannon, G. 1996. *Tomorrow's Alphabet.* Illus. D. Crews. New York: Greenwillow.

Shaw, N. 1989. *Sheep on a Ship.* New York: Houghton Mifflin.

Spier, P. 1972. *Crash! Bang! Boom!* New York: Dutton.

———. 1988. *Gobble Growl Grunt.* New York: Doubleday.

Steig, W. 1968. *CDB.* New York: Windmill.

———. 1984. *CDC.* New York: Farrar, Straus & Giroux.

Sterne, N. 1979. *Tyrannosaurs Wrecks: A Book of Dinosaur Riddles.* New York: Crowell.

Terban, M. 1982. *Eight Ate: A Feast of Homonym Riddles.* New York: Clarion.

———. 1983. *In a Pickle and Other Funny Idioms.* New York: Clarion.

———. 1984. *I Think I Thought and Other Tricky Verbs.* New York: Clarion.

———. 1985. *Too Hot to Hoot: A Collection of Funny Palindrome Riddles.* New York: Clarion.

———. 1986. *Your Foot's on My Feet and Other Tricky Nouns.* New York: Clarion.

———. 1988. *The Dove Dove: Funny Homograph Riddles.* New York: Clarion.

———. 1989. *Superdupers!* New York: Clarion.

———. 1992. *Funny You Should Ask.* New York: Clarion.

Thaler, M. 1986. *King Kong's Underwear.* New York: Avon.

Wood, A. 1984. *The Napping House.* New York: Harcourt Brace.

———. 1992. *Silly Sally.* San Diego: Harcourt Brace.

Wood, J. 1992. *Moo Moo Brown Cow.* San Diego: Harcourt Brace.

FIGURE 8-1   Recommended Children's Book List

Sorting It Out Through Word Sorts

Jerry Zutell

Introduction

In this book we recommend focused and engaging word study. Effective word study involves children as investigators of words. Word sorting is a specific, active word study experience that helps students discover important principles about the written language system. Word sorting involves active exploration of various aspects of words that students have encountered in other literacy activities. Combined with learning about words through reading and writing, as part of a comprehensive word study program, word sorting brings important aspects of words to the fore. When they manipulate the words for themselves, thinking about word parts, letter patterns, sound-letter relationships, and meaning, children notice the aspects of words that will help them make useful connections. They learn what to look for as they come to understand words.

As children sort words according to various criteria or criteria they generate themselves, they discover connections between words. Exploring these connections helps them make generalizations about words and discover important spelling principles. Word sorting can be used with children who are just beginning to learn to spell a few words,

but it is also useful for helping older students explore complex, sophisticated underlying principles. In this chapter, Zutell describes word sorting and discusses the historical and conceptual base of this powerful instructional approach. He also provides examples of word sorts and talks about how you can vary the activity to help students learn more about words.

The Historical and Conceptual Base for Word Sorting

The study of words has historically been a key element of the language experience approach (Hall 1981; Lee and Van Allen 1963; Stauffer 1980). In language experience, teachers act as the scribe to produce students' own experience-based texts. Reading both group- and individually dictated stories has at least three important advantages for children:

1. It heightens awareness of the relationship between oral and written language.

2. It strengthens the connection between literacy and personal experience.

3. It provides highly memorable texts for reading.

With these advantages, not only are children supported in accurately matching spoken and written words, an activity essential for acquiring a beginning sight vocabulary, but they develop greater enthusiasm for and a more positive attitude toward reading and writing.

In the highly supportive context of language experience, words are read and reread. As the contextual support is gradually reduced, words are written on sentence strips and individual cards. The "known word" cards are then added to children's individual word banks. As children learn these words through their experience with texts, they can also practice the words and develop fluency with them through a variety of activities. For example, they might assemble words into old and new sentences, match them back to the stories from which they were originally acquired, or review words with a partner.

Research on the language experience approach has revealed that the number of words in the word bank of first graders typically consists of a fairly equal blend of high-frequency "irregular" words and the slightly lower-frequency "patterned" words (Henderson, Estes, and Stonecash 1972). Thus word banks provide a rich source of data students can use to unravel the patterns and relationships that help show how English spellings are put together.

Our understanding of student spellings across a wide range of ages and ability levels has been informed by two research directions:

❚ First, analytic studies of the relationships between English pronunciation and spelling have revealed that, while these relationships are complex, systematic interactions among letter-sound correspondences, visual patterns, meaning elements, and historical sources are ultimately taken into account (Chomsky and Halle 1968; Cummings 1988; Venezky 1970). What might seem arbitrary in spelling are actually connections between words in how they sound, look, and mean.

❚ Second, Read's (1971) study of young children's attempts at spelling revealed that the attempts were based on reasonable analyses of the relationships between letter names (or "sounds"), phonetic features, and points of articulation in the mouth (for example *JR* for the *dr* in *dragon*). This research helped teachers make sense of young children's attempts and demonstrated the children's ingenuity in exploring and working with words.

Henderson (1981, 1990), his colleagues (Templeton and Bear 1992), and others have extended the work initiated by Read. Four important principles of learning have emerged from the continuing research that they have conducted:

1. Learning to spell is more than a matter of rote memorization; it includes a strong conceptual component. Students not only learn individual words but acquire progressively more complex ideas about "how words work."

2. Word familiarity and concept formation are mutually supportive. Relationships or patterns are first recognized in familiar words. Then concepts are extended to less familiar words, and these words become easier to remember as they are fitted into an overall scheme. As students expand their sight and spelling vocabularies, they have more examples for making sense out of more complex patterns, and so a powerful cycle for word learning is established.

3. Word knowledge in reading and spelling are closely connected. Both processes require a level of control over the same system, English spelling. Spelling and reading inform each other. Through reading, one develops visual knowledge of words, and that supports learning to spell. Through writing, children acquire knowledge of word forms and patterns that may speed word identification and word solving in reading.

4. Development follows a broadly defined set of stages marked by advances in correct spellings and more sophisticated misspellings. Children move from having a limited understanding of the match between sounds and letters to grasping the basic phonetic principle that letters and sounds go together in systematic ways. Once they get this idea and begin to acquire a substantial beginning sight vocabulary (50–100 words), they move beyond simple sound-letter matches to recognize the importance of combinations of letters—chunks and patterns—first in single-syllable and then multisyllable words. At later stages meaning-spelling connections and combinations of prefixes, roots, and suffixes become salient and useful.

Thus, the findings from research on developmental spelling support an approach to learning about words that focuses on the discovery of categories and relationships by building on previously acquired word knowledge (Zutell 1996).

From Word Banks to Systematic Study

Students' personal word banks are excellent sources of words for comparing and contrasting regular patterns and relationships. The words are familiar, so they are within students' control. As word banks expand, students have to rely on more complete sets of visual cues to distinguish among the words.

These word banks provide the teacher with a good indication of the number of words students know and the characteristics of them. Looking at these word banks, along with information about stages of development, provides teachers with a rough guideline for deciding which word patterns and contrasts should be studied. Of course, as students' sight vocabularies grow beyond beginning levels, keeping physical collections of all known words becomes impractical; still, the concept of beginning with a collection of well-known words—a subset of the

student's "mental word bank"—is an essential feature of a developmentally based word study program.

Word sorting blends the use of word bank words with the study of the patterns and relationships within and among those words. Word sorting is a focused experience in word study, so it may be seen as "decontextualized" in nature; that is, students work on words that are not embedded within a text. There is, however, a strong link between words learned in and through context and word study "out of context." The clear advantage of this kind of "out-of-context" study is that patterns and relationships can be examined and studied in more focused and systematic ways.

The Concept of Word Sorting

Organizing objects, events, and experiences into categories and classes is a fundamental way we make sense of the world around us. Animals are wild or domestic; foods are sweet, sour, or salty. We recognize the power of this way of thinking when we purposefully ask young children to compare objects that are rough or smooth, round or pointed—that is, to notice features that help us distinguish among objects in some clear and/or useful ways, extending what we often do automatically to a more conscious level of organization. Of course, for most real-world categories, boundaries are rarely rigid or absolute, but it is often in the examination of the features of examples that don't quite fit that we sharpen our understanding of how things do and don't go together.

Word sorting is a more formal, direct extension of this basic strategy to the study of words and how they work. It is a technique in which key words are written on individual cards and then organized into columns according to patterns of similarities and differences among the words, with words that are alike placed together in the same column. As with other complex relationships, there are typically words on the boundaries that don't seem to fit or that are exceptions to the

e: tent, egg, thread, wrench; *i:* drill, fish, clip, ship; *u:* drum, bug, brush, plug

FIGURE 9-1   Picture Sort: Short Vowel Sounds *e, i, u*

general pattern, so we almost always include a "question mark" category as well.

What Are the Basic Types of Word Sorting?

There are several types of word sorts, each of which may be used at different times depend-ing on your purpose, the needs of your stu-dents, and the nature of the words being sorted (see also Bear et al. 1996; Zutell 1998).

Picture Sorting

A considerable body of research supports the value of phonemic awareness in learning to read and write. Children at the beginning stages of word knowledge can clearly benefit from some focus on the sounds in words, their order, and their similarities and differences. Along one of these dimensions, students can listen for beginning sounds, long or short vowel elements, rhyming patterns, and so on, and judge spoken words as the same or different. The ability to attend to and classify the sounds in words will serve students well in later sorting tasks such as matching pronunciations and letter patterns. Picture sorting (Figure 9-1) is a way to help younger children:

■ Say words and think about the order of sounds in the word.

■ Make connections between the sounds in words before they can actually recognize the visual features of words.

■ Gain experience in thinking about aspects of words and categorizing them.

Concept or Meaning Sort

Words represent a variety of properties that are independent of their pronunciation and/or spelling. For example, the word *mountain* can be classified as a natural object, *Teflon* as a man-made substance, *beauty* as an abstract concept in the eye of the beholder. These distinctions have nothing to do with the number of syllables in the words, their beginning letters, vowel patterns, or other features. Teachers often use simple and familiar concept sorts (Figure 9-2) as a means of introducing the idea and procedures for sorting to students who are unfamiliar with sorting activities. At a more sophisticated level, concept sorts are also closely related to, and can be used as a variation on, the use of semantic feature analysis and categorization to develop comprehension and critical thinking in content area instruction.

Spelling Sort

Spelling sorts (Figure 9-3) focus specifically on relationships between pronunciation, visual pattern, meaning units, and/or word origin and spelling. They range in difficulty across the full spectrum of orthographic complexity, from matching initial consonant sounds to a beginning letter to recognizing the connection between the silent *g* in *ensign* and the hard *g* in *insignia*. The great majority of sorts done in a word study program are usually spelling sorts.

Closed Sort

Word sorting is more of a "closed" activity when you decide categories that will address words you feel your students are ready to learn and need to learn. In a *closed sort*, you:

Concept Sort: Animal Names (Adults and Children)

Adult	Child
bear	calf
cat	chick
chicken	cub
duck	duckling
dog	kid
goat	kitten
sheep	lamb
swan	puppy
whale	cygnet

FIGURE 9-2   Concept Sort: Animal Names (Adults and Children)

Spelling Sort: The k Sound with Different Vowel Patterns

kick	cake	soak	?
back	smoke	cheek	talk
luck	bike	cook	folk
clock	take	speak	hawk
neck	strike	book	

FIGURE 9-3   Spelling Sort: The k Sound with Different Vowel Patterns

■ Choose key or master words to head each category.

■ Limit the sort initially to a specific subset of student-known words.

■ Create a "question mark category" for those words not corresponding to the categories.

Later, students can add to the words to be sorted through word hunting and/or brainstorming. In these situations, you will want to lead the activity in a way that most effectively extends student thinking and promotes word learning. (The sorts in Figures 9-2 and 9-3 are illustrations of closed sorts.)

Open Sort

Word sorting is an open-ended activity when students choose the categories for sorting and then organize their words (or subsets of them) into columns based on those categories. After a student completes an *open sort*, you and the other students (either in a small-group meeting or with the whole class) try to "solve" this open sort by hypothesizing about the features of each category and why words are placed as they are. "Solving" the sort sparks a learning conversation in which students share the learning and discover what's involved in the sorting activity—you and/or your students might challenge a particular word placement, and

the sorter then shares the reasoning behind her decision. Open sorts serve two important functions:

1. They put the students in charge of organization and decision making, giving them a greater sense of control over their own learning.
2. They provide the teacher with a window into how students "look at words," which can be helpful in organizing future sorting tasks.

An extension of open sorting is to have students sort the same set of words in two or three different ways. This task of *multiple sorting* (Figure 9-4) requires students to focus on different aspects of the words in quick succession. Multiple sorting encourages flexibility in thinking about words and helps students recognize the different parts and features a word can have (Figures 9-5 and 9-6).

How Does Word Sorting Help Students Learn?

As a student-centered and active learning approach to word study, word sorting is compatible with instructional models that build on the concept of teachers' "scaffolding" or assisting students to advance their learning. Through providing structured, well-designed word-sorting tasks and interacting with students about their work with words, teachers assist students in using what they know to construct new understandings. Learning

---

Words for an Open Sort with Multiple Sorting

bat	goat	mouse	star
bike	hawk	pig	stone
chick	house	robin	swan
duck	jay	shark	whale
eagle	lion	sheep	

FIGURE 9-4   Words for an Open Sort with Multiple Sorting

First Open Sort: Student Categories: Only on Land, In the Sky, In Water, On Water

chick	bat	shark	duck
goat	eagle	whale	swan
lion	hawk		
mouse	jay		
pig	robin		
sheep	star		
bike			
house			
stone			

FIGURE 9-5   First Open Sort

Second Open Sort: Student Categories: Short Vowels, Long Vowels, Other Vowels, Two Vowels

chick	bike	hawk	robin
duck	whale	house	lion
pig	stone	mouse	eagle
swan	goat	shark	
	jay	star	
	sheep		

FIGURE 9-6   Second Open Sort

---

does not happen at a particular point in time but keeps moving from socially supported action to independent control. Thus, with careful support, the teacher is helping children do more than they could do without assistance. In Vygotskyian terms, the children are working in the "zone of proximal development"; they are within the range between successful independent and successful assisted performance (Bodrova and Leong 1996; Vygotsky 1986; Wood, Bruner, and Ross 1976).

The teacher chooses tasks and activities connected with the students' own experiences to help them construct their own knowledge. The activities must also be challenging enough to extend their learning and understanding.

A Word-Sorting Cycle

Word sorting will not be effective unless the activities are designed to meet students' needs. Teachers should think about a cycle of decision making directed toward designing appropriate word-sorting activities for a particular group of students. The cycle is described in the following section.

Information from Observation

First, the design of word sorting is based on the teacher's observations of student performance across a variety of spelling and word study activities. Teachers use that information to decide what students need to know next. For example, teachers might use developmental spelling inventories, previous word sorts and spelling lessons, and independent and assigned writing as a basis for finding the word patterns that students already know or almost know (see Pinnell and Fountas 1998).

There is generally a broad order in which certain features are learned. Instruction is most effective when it is focused on patterns and relationships that students are "using but confusing." (Students have some known examples of a pattern and an awareness of the concept, but no clear and consistent understanding of how and when it is to be applied [Invernizzi, Abouzeid, and Gill 1994].) Teachers consider the developmental process to determine the order in which to address concepts that are used but confused. For example, issues such as marking long vowels (like "silent *e*" in *name*) would be addressed before more complex problems like consonant doubling (*sit, sitting; run, running*).

Ongoing Decisions About Direction, Support, and Independence

During the cycle, the teacher makes ongoing decisions about:

❚ Balancing opportunities for student discovery with the need for modeling and openly discussing the basis for deciding how words are classified.

❚ Using peer support to build toward independent performance.

Steps in the cycle, all of which require decision making, are illustrated by the closed word sort lesson described in Figure 9-7.

The "buddy sorting" described in this cycle not only provides students with the intermediate support of their peers as they work out concepts and relationships, but it also provides the opportunity for them to take on and use in a natural way the language needed to clarify, justify, and extend their own thinking about words. By the end of the cycle, students will have worked with a combination of whole-class/group words and ones of their own finding. From these sets they can negotiate with the teacher about which ones they are responsible for sorting independently.

Varying the Demands of the Task

The teacher also supports student learning by varying the demands of the task in terms of:

❚ The information available.
❚ The complexity of relationships.
❚ The output required.

Word sorts vary in difficulty depending on the amount of information available to students when they make their decisions, and on how they are asked to respond. All things being equal, visual sorts are easier than auditory sorts; writing to the sort is more demanding than either.

❚ In a *visual sort*, students have the opportunity to look at the word, examine its features, and compare it to the other words in the various columns as they decide where to place it.

❚ In an *auditory sort*, a teacher, an aide, or a classmate reads the word to the student and the student decides on placement without the advantage of seeing the word first. Once a decision is made, the word card is put down, and the student then can check to

---

A Word-Sorting Cycle

- ■ The teacher chooses the basic concept the children will explore, drawing from her observations of students as well as from her knowledge of the linguistic system and the general order in which patterns are acquired.
- ■ The teacher introduces the material in a small-group setting. A pocket chart provides a clearly visible place for the teacher to lay out the key words at the heads of columns.
- ■ The teacher may then initiate discussion about why these words and categories have been chosen.
- ■ The teacher underlines the specific letters or letter combinations to help students focus their attention on the orthographic features they are examining.
- ■ Depending on the feedback she receives from the students, the teacher considers if and how quickly she will turn over decision making to the group or individuals.
- ■ Often the teacher specifically verbalizes how she chooses where the words will go—"I am going to put this word under here because . . ."—to give students a clear sense of how the process of decision making and the product, the final sort, are connected.
- ■ On succeeding days students often sort in pairs, either working together on each word or taking turns, but coming to agreement about where and why each word is placed. (They then check their results with either the teacher, other students, or a key.)
- ■ Students may also work together brainstorming and/or searching familiar books and their own work to find other examples of words that fit the patterns under examination. They can add more examples to individual banks and/or a class or group set that can be displayed as a class chart or notebook or on a word wall.

FIGURE 9-7   A Word-Sorting Cycle

see if visual or sound or meaning features correspond.

■ In a *speed sort,* the student is asked to work quickly as well as accurately, in order to build more automatic, fluent processing.

■ When students *write to the sort* (Figure 9-8), they have the key words available for reference and have the words read to them, as in an auditory sort. The task is for the students to write the words correctly in the appropriate column. This task is more demanding because it requires students to actually produce the full, correct form of the word. The process encourages close attention to visual detail, especially in cases in which two spellings are equally allowable (for example, *herd* vs. *heard*). Writing to the sort can thus form a scaffold that supports student control and preparation for a final,

independent check of learning (traditionally the end-of-the-week test). In fact, teachers have reported instances in which students have, on their own, chosen to write the words on their tests in sorted columns, rather than in the traditional single, numerically ordered list.

Over time and across cycles, teachers can increase the demands and complexity of the sorts by moving from simple contrasts to more complex relationships. For example, in building a sense of short- and long-vowel spelling patterns, teachers may choose to begin with a single vowel and two patterns (*back* vs. *bake*). A later activity might add the contrasting patterns for long-vowel spellings (*fast* vs. *same* vs. *rain* vs. *play*). An even more complex sort could compare vowel-consonant patterns for long- and short-vowel spellings across more than one vowel (*hat* vs.

Writing to the Sort: The *k* Sound with Different Vowel Patterns (Teacher Dictates Words in Random Order)			
kick	cake	soak	?
back	smoke	cheek	talk
luck	bike	cook	folk
clock	take	speak	hawk
neck	strike	book	

FIGURE 9-8   Writing to the Sort

best vs. *time* vs. *float*). Certainly this last sort would require significant previous experience with and examination of individual vowel patterns. Student success with it would indicate a high level of understanding of the complex relationships between English vowel-consonant combinations and the pronunciation of single-syllable words. It would also provide a powerful base for the further development of extensive sight and spelling vocabulary.

Versatility and Flexibility

Word sorting is a versatile and flexible tool for helping students attend to words and their features. A word sort can be designed to highlight almost any aspect of words that students might study. Word sorts may be used effectively with younger children, helping them look at simple ways to place words into categories (for example, by number of letters or first letter). Word sorts are also effective in helping older children to look at very complex aspects of words. A teacher may engage an entire class in word sorting at the same time, may work with a small group, can set children up as partners to sort words, or can rotate children in and out of a word study center (Pinnell and Fountas 1998) in which a word-sorting task, previously introduced in a minilesson, is set up. Word sorting is multilevel; there is always room for children to discover more about words as

they work with them. Word sorting is a "thinking" activity that will help children acquire deeper understandings about the ways words work—understandings that they can take away from the word-sorting activity and apply in reading and writing.

Suggestions for Professional Development

1. After reading this chapter, meet with grade-level colleagues to construct some word sorts that will be at the appropriate level for your students. What aspects of words would be most appropriate for your students to explore through word sorting?

2. Make the following types of word sorts and share them with each other.
    - ❚ Concept sort
    - ❚ Open-ended spelling sort
    - ❚ Closed spelling sort
    - ❚ Multiple sort

3. Discuss how you can vary the use of these sorts by making them visual or auditory, or by having students "write to the sort."

4. Try out at least one word sort with a small group of children.

5. Meet again to discuss the results.

■ Was the activity at an appropriate level (not too easy or too hard)?

■ Were students able to perform the task quickly and independently?

■ What did students discover about words while sorting?

■ Did students become more knowledgeable about the aspects of

words that the sort brought to their attention?

6. As a follow-up to this session, read Chapter 13, "Word Explorers: Teaching Strategies that Promote Active Inquiry," from the companion volume to this book: *Word Matters: Teaching Phonics and Spelling in the Reading/Writing Classroom.*

Multilevel Word Study
Word Charts, Word Walls, and Word Sorts

Dorothy P. Hall and Patricia M. Cunningham

Introduction

In a rich language and literacy classroom, there is evidence everywhere that children are discovering interesting facts about how words work. When you engage children in learning about words, you are not just teaching them a few words. You are teaching them how to look at words and how to make connections. Hall and Cunningham help us visualize active word learning in the primary classroom by using proven techniques for focusing children's attention on aspects of words.

They explain word walls, which provide a constant visual reference for children as they progress in learning about words. Hall and Cunningham also describe predictable charts and other activities, used in an ongoing way to help children derive word-solving principles as they connect words in categories. The authors discuss the process of creating and using word walls and multilevel activities to support learning. They also describe "making words," an activity designed to help children learn how words work.

Because of the wide variation in knowledge and experience among any group of primary-age children, you will want to provide some small-group work to help children in writing and in spelling. But there may be very practical reasons for providing some word study lessons for the entire class of children, such as limited time. Hall and Cunningham invite us to think about word study as "multilevel" in nature. They have organized their chapter to extend our understanding of multilevel approaches that have the greatest potential for helping all children in the class move forward in their development of word knowledge.

Word study, with the goal of being able to decode and spell words, begins in the primary grades. Yet, whether or not spelling should be directly taught—and if so, how and for which words—continues to be a subject for debate and decision making. Since within every primary or elementary classroom we see both a wide range of abilities and several stages of spelling development, we cannot find the answers in any one textbook or approach. Cramer (1993) suggests that the typical elementary classroom contains spellers at five different grade levels and that teachers should have at least three different spelling groups. Morris (1992) looked at the spelling growth of third graders who were all being taught with a third-grade spelling book. Children whose actual beginning spelling level was below third-grade learned the words for the weekly spelling test but did not retain these words and showed little growth in their spelling ability.

The words children are learning to spell and what teachers need to do within their classrooms varies depending on the grade level and characteristics of children. Kindergarten spelling instruction will look different from instruction in the first and second grade; spelling instruction in third, fourth, and fifth grades varies also. Within grade levels any activities that take place with the entire class need to be *multilevel* so that all the children in the class can move forward in learning to spell.

Why Use Multilevel Spelling Activities

We have found that through multilevel spelling activities, spelling instruction that meets the needs of a wide range of students can be provided without grouping for spelling (see Hall, Cunningham, and Cunningham 1995). For children who are already spelling above the grade level, the type of spelling instruction received does not seem to matter. Some children are good spellers, and given some kind of spelling instruction and opportunities to write, they will continue to grow in their spelling abilities. But this is not true for children who are struggling to memorize words and learn to spell at the same time. Compared to a traditional spelling approach, a combination of multilevel spelling activities enables below-grade-level and at-grade-level spellers to improve markedly in their spelling development.

How are multilevel spelling activities different from traditional spelling activities?

1. They involve both the teacher and the students.

2. They are active, hands-on activities in which students are asked to think about words and patterns and then respond in a variety of ways.

3. There is something for everyone in the classroom to be able to respond to and think

about regardless of their spelling development and ability. Teachers who know their students also know who to call on and when. However, the most important difference is that children actually enjoy these activities!

We will first describe how kindergarten teachers can help young children focus on print, and then we will extend the description to first and second grade. Finally, we will describe instructional experiences that extend the word knowledge of third-, fourth-, and fifth-grade children.

Kindergarten

Learning to read and write appears effortless for some children. For others, it is a struggle. Recent findings from emergent literacy research have demonstrated that when children have had a variety of experiences with reading and writing before coming to school, they can more easily profit from school literacy instruction and are more likely to learn to read easily (Cunningham & Allington 1999). From these experiences they develop the critical understandings that are the building blocks of their success. Most important, children learn that reading and writing provide both enjoyment and information, and they develop the desire to learn to read and write. They also learn many new concepts and add words to their speaking and listening vocabularies. They learn print concepts, including left-to-right directionality. They develop phonological awareness, including concepts of rhyme. They learn to read and write some words that are interesting to them, such as their names, *Pizza Hut, cat, and bear*. Finally, they learn some letter names and sounds, usually those that are connected to the interesting words they have learned (Hall & Cunningham 1997).

Children who depend on school for their early learning about literacy need a variety of experiences that simulate those at-home reading and writing experiences. For example, at home, children watch parents write shopping lists, notes, checks, and other messages. As children watch people write, they increase in their desire to learn to write, notice important print concepts, and begin to learn some familiar words. These experiences also need to be provided for children at school.

Shared Writing with Predictable Charts

One important activity that helps children learn about writing words is watching the teacher write a morning message or a journal entry at the end of the day. This kind of adult writing model can be made even more powerful by creating predictable charts. To create a predictable chart, a teacher records class experiences (one sentence for each child), as follows:

❚ Teachers use the same sentence pattern for each sentence so that it is predictable ("I saw a bus"; "I saw a bird").

❚ After writing and reading the charts with the children, the teacher writes corresponding sentence strips and cuts apart the words in the sentences.

❚ Each child puts the words together to build his or her sentence.

❚ Finally, each child glues the words of his or her sentence in order on a page and illustrates the page; together, the children then make a class book.

In addition to increasing the children's desire to learn to write, shared writing with predictable charts helps children focus on print concepts. Because the texts follow predictable patterns, most children can read the charts and the books made from them. They learn some words and begin to notice some letters and sounds.

The activity is multileveled:

❚ Some children are reading the entire chart and are learning to spell many high-frequency words.

❚ Other students can read only their own sentence and are learning about letters and sounds and how they can represent words.

❚ Still others, those to whom writing is new, are learning what letters are and how letters are used to make up words, as well as other important early print concepts.

Getting to Know You!

In addition to reading and writing, parents often help children notice the print in their worlds. Children want to read and write their names along with the names of their brothers, sisters, pets, and stuffed animals. They notice and want to read calendars, signs, cereal boxes, soft drink cans, and the names of stores and restaurants. In kindergarten, it is appropriate to help children read and write some of these words that interest them. An activity called "Getting to Know You!" is designed to help children build letter-sound associations based on these interesting words (Hall and Cunningham 1997).

Most kindergarten teachers begin their year with some get-acquainted activities. As part of these get-acquainted activities, they often focus on a special child each day. In addition to learning about each child, teachers can focus attention on the special child's name and use the name to develop some important understandings about words and letters.

A Sample Lesson

To prepare for this activity, write all the children's first names (with initials for last names if two or more names are the same) with a permanent marker on sentence strips. Cut the strips so that long names have long strips and short names have short strips. Place the strips in a box.

Put all the names into a box. Each day, reach into the box and draw out a name; reserve a bulletin board and add the child's name to the board. Then, call that child forward and name her "Star of the Day." Lead the other children to interview this child and find out what she likes to eat or play, or where she goes after school. Does the "Star of the Day" have brothers? Sisters? Cats? Dogs? Mice? Record this information on an experience chart with shared or interactive writing.

Now focus the children's attention on the child's name—for example, Jasmine. Point to the word, *Jasmine*, on the sentence strip, and point out to the children that this *word* is Jasmine's name. Tell them that it takes many *letters* to write the word *Jasmine*, and let them help count the letters. Say the letters in *Jasmine—J-a-s-m-i-n-e*, and have the children chant along. Point out that the *word Jasmine begins* with the letter *J*. Explain that the *J* looks different or big because it is a *capital J* and the other letters are *small letters* (or use the terms *uppercase* and *lowercase*).

Take another sentence strip and, with the children watching, write *Jasmine*. Have them chant along. Cut the letters apart and mix them up. Let Jasmine arrange the letters in just the right order so that they spell her name. Have the other children chant to check that the order is correct. Jasmine can then choose another child to do the same thing.

Give each child a large sheet of drawing paper. Have them write *Jasmine* in crayon in large letters on one side of the paper. Model at the board how to write each letter as they write it. Do not worry if what they write is not perfect (or even doesn't bear much resemblance to the actual letter), and resist the temptation to correct what they wrote. Remember that children who write at home before coming to school often reverse letters and make them in funny ways. The important understanding is that names are words, that words can be written, and that it takes a lot of letters to write them.

Finally, have everyone look at Jasmine and talk about what she is wearing. Then let the children draw a picture of Jasmine on the other side of the drawing paper. Let Jasmine take all the pictures home. Teachers who want to make a class book can save Jasmine's own picture with her name printed on the back to put in the class book.

On the next day, pull another child's name—David. Make David the "Star of the Day" and do the same interviewing and chart making. Focus the children's attention

on David's name. Say the letters in *David* and have the children chant along. Help the children count the letters and decide which letter is *first*, *last*, and so on.

Write *David* on another sentence strip and cut it into letters. Have children arrange the letters to spell *David*, using the first sentence strip name as their model. Put *David* on the bulletin board under *Jasmine* and compare the two. Which has the most letters? How many more letters are in the word *David* than in the word *Jasmine*? Does *David* have any of the same letters as *Jasmine*?

Continue with picking a name, interviewing, making a chart, chanting, writing the name, and drawing the pictures. As each name is added, compare it to the others. Who has the longest name now? Which names have the same letters? Are the same letters in the same places in the names? If you have a *Joseph* and a *Julio* or a *Sheila* and a *Sam* or a *Carol* and a *Charlie*, help the children notice that some letters have two sounds and that some letter combinations have a special sound. Point out that it is the *sh* in *Sheila* that gives *s* its different sound. Most of the children who are just beginning to learn about how letters and sounds are related would not need to know this. But those who were already reading when they came to kindergarten probably know the single-letter sounds and are ready to realize that some letter combinations have different sounds.

Finally, at about the halfway point in adding the names, let the children take charge of noticing the similarities and differences between the names. Instead of pointing out that Rasheed's name starts with the same letter and sound as *Robert*, say: "What do you notice about the letters and sounds in Rasheed's name and the other names on our wall?"

There is a system and a pattern to the way letters in English represent sounds. Our instruction should point out these patterns. Children who see a new word and ask themselves how that new word is like the other words they know can discover many patterns on their own. "Getting to Know You!" is a truly multilevel activity. Some children are actually learning to spell the names. Others are using the names as interesting bridges to an understanding about how our English spelling system works.

First and Second Grade

As children engage in lots of reading and writing, they grow in their understanding of how our alphabetic language works. Children learn that English is not a language in which one sound is always represented by one letter and that "spelling it the way it sounds" will often result in a word that's readable but not conventionally spelled.

The letter-sound relationships in English are complex and often irregular, but they do exist. It is strange that r-i-g-h-t is the correct way to spell right and t-i-o-n spells the "shun" part of vacation. But there is a method to the madness. If you can read the word right, you can also read tight, fight, and bright. The tion at the end of vacation works the same way as it does at the end of nation, action, election, and hundreds of other words that end in t-i-o-n. (See Jenkins, Chapter 7.)

As children work with words in first and second grade, we have two priority goals. We want children to learn to spell high-frequency words, many of which do not follow spelling patterns. We also want them to learn the patterns that allow them to decode and spell lots of words.

Word Wall for High-Frequency Words
Our major activity for helping children learn to spell high-frequency words is the word wall. The word wall for high-frequency words is usually located above or below the alphabet. The words are written with thick black marker on colored paper and are placed with the letter they begin with. Five words a week are added until there are between 110 and 120 words on the wall. For about ten minutes each day, students practice new and old words by looking at them;

saying them; clapping; chanting, or snapping the letters; writing the words on paper; and self-correcting the words with the teacher.

First-grade teachers usually choose words to add to the wall from the selections children are reading. They consult a high-frequency list (Cunningham and Hall 1997c) and then add the most frequent words from what has been read. There is no particular order in which to add the words, but we try not to add two in the same week that begin with the same letter. We also try to include some easier words (me, go, in) along with some of the trickier ones (what, friend, there). Many teachers add what, do, you, see, and at after reading Brown Bear, Brown Bear (Martin 1970).

In addition to high-frequency words, many teachers like to have a word on the wall to represent each of the beginning sounds, along with sh, ch, th, and wh. Figure 10-1 contains a list including high-frequency words, a few words that are frequently written by first graders (favorite, sister, brother), and an example for all beginning sounds (Cunningham and Hall 1997c). Underlined words have a helpful spelling pattern and will help children spell lots of rhyming words.

In second grade, we base our word selection more on what we observe in children's writing than on what words they have read during guided reading. The emphasis is still on high-frequency words, but we select those that are irregularly spelled and particularly those that we see misspelled in their first-draft writing. Many second-grade teachers begin their word walls with the words they, said, was, have, and because, words most second graders can read but many cannot spell. These hard-to-spell high-frequency words are often on the first-grade word wall and then put back again on the second-grade word wall.

Once we have included the hard-to-spell high-frequency words, we include an example word for letter combinations including ch, sh, th, wh, qu, ph, wr, kn; the less

High-Frequency Words for Grade One

after	<u>down</u>	I	out	they
<u>all</u>	<u>eat</u>	<u>in</u>	over	<u>thing</u>
<u>am</u>	favorite	is	people	this
<u>and</u>	for	it	<u>play</u>	to
animal	friend	<u>jump</u>	pretty	up
are	from	<u>kick</u>	<u>quit</u>	us
<u>at</u>	<u>fun</u>	<u>like</u>	<u>rain</u>	very
be	get	little	<u>ride</u>	want
<u>best</u>	girl	<u>look</u>	said	was
because	give	<u>made</u>	<u>saw</u>	we
<u>big</u>	go	<u>make</u>	school	<u>went</u>
<u>boy</u>	good	me	<u>see</u>	what
brother	<u>had</u>	<u>my</u>	she	<u>when</u>
<u>but</u>	has	<u>new</u>	sister	where
<u>can</u>	have	<u>nice</u>	some	who
can't	he	<u>night</u>	<u>talk</u>	<u>why</u>
<u>car</u>	her	no	teacher	<u>will</u>
children	here	<u>not</u>	<u>tell</u>	with
come	<u>him</u>	of	<u>that</u>	won't
<u>day</u>	his	off	the	you
<u>did</u>	house	<u>old</u>	them	your
do	<u>how</u>	on	there	zoo

FIGURE 10-1   High-Frequency Words for Grade One

common *c* and *g* sounds; the most common blends (*bl, br, cl, cr, dr, fl, fr, gr, pl, pr, sk, sl, sm, sn, sp, st, tr*); and the most common vowel patterns:

cr<u>a</u>sh, m<u>ake</u>, r<u>ain</u>, pl<u>ay</u>ed, c<u>ar</u>, s<u>aw</u>, c<u>aug</u>ht

w<u>e</u>nt, <u>eat</u>, gr<u>ee</u>n, sist<u>er</u>, n<u>ew</u>

<u>in</u>to, r<u>ide</u>, r<u>igh</u>t, g<u>ir</u>l, th<u>ing</u>

n<u>o</u>t, th<u>ose</u>, fl<u>oat</u>, <u>or</u>, <u>out</u>side, b<u>oy</u>, sh<u>oo</u>k, sch<u>ool</u>, h<u>ow</u>, sl<u>ow</u>

b<u>u</u>g, <u>use</u>, h<u>ur</u>t

wh<u>y</u>, ver<u>y</u>

Finally, we include the most commonly written contractions: *can't, didn't, don't, it's, that's, they're, won't*; homophones: *to, too, two; there, their, they're; right, write; one, won; new, knew*; and example words with *s, ed,* and *ing*.

Figure 10-2 contains a list of words (Hall and Cunningham 1998) that includes all of these. This list provides a beginning point for thinking about second-grade word walls. Words with an asterisk are often also included on first-grade word walls. Underlined words have spelling patterns that help children spell lots of rhyming words.

Because patterns exist in words, they are there for children to find. Some children, through lots of reading and writing, learn to read and spell many words and then figure out how to use the patterns found in these words to read and spell other words. Other children read and write and learn some words but never quite figure out "how it works." Two of the most popular activities to nudge children along in learning how words work are "rounding up the rhymes" and "making words."

Rounding Up the Rhymes

Rounding Up the Rhymes is an activity to follow up the reading of a book, story, or poem that contains lots of rhyming words.

High-Frequency Words for Grade Two

about	every	mail	*saw	trip
*after	*favorite	*make	*school	truck
again	first	many	shook	two
*are	float	more	*sister	use
beautiful	found	name	skate	*very
*because	friends	*new	slow	wanted
before	*girl	*nice	small	*was
*best	green	*not	snap	*went
black	gym	*off	sometimes	were
*boy	*have	one	sports	*what
brothers	*here	or	stop	*when
bug	*house	other	tell	*where
*can't	*how	our	than	*who
*car	hurt	outside	thank	*why
*caught	*I	*people	that's	*will
*children	into	phone	their	*with
city	it's	played	*them	won
clock	joke	*pretty	then	*won't
could	*jump	*quit	*there	write
crash	junk	*rain	*they	writing
crashes	kicked	really	they're	
didn't	knew	*ride	*thing	
don't	line	right	those	
drink	*little	*said	*to	
eating	*made	sale	too	

FIGURE 10-2   High-Frequency Words for Grade Two

A Sample Lesson

In this section we provide an example using that timeless book *In a People House* (LeSieg 1972).

The first (and often second) reading of any text should focus on meaning and enjoyment. *In a People House* is an engaging story with wonderful "Seussian" language. As the mouse shows the bird what is in a people house, mundane things such as bottles, brooms, and pillows come to life.

Returning to the book for the second or third time, we draw the children's attention to the rhyming words. As we read each page or two, we encourage the children to chime in and try to "hear the rhymes they are saying." (We used to ask them to listen for the rhymes we were saying but have discovered that children with limited phonemic awareness are much more successful hearing rhymes when they say the words and hear—and feel— themselves making the rhyme.) As children tell us the rhyming words, we write them on index cards and put them in a pocket chart.

We continue having children chime in with us as we read the pages until we have six or seven sets of rhyming words in the pocket chart. (If there are many more rhyming words, as is the case with *In a People House*, teachers can revisit the text later to discover more rhymes. Too many rhymes in one activity can confuse and frustrate some children.) Here are the rhyming words that would be in the pocket chart after reading the first half of the book:

mouse chairs brooms thread door pails
house stairs rooms bed more nails
floor

Next, we remind the children that the spelling pattern in a short word includes all the letters beginning with the first vowel and going to the end of the word. After naming the vowels—*a, e, i, o, u*—we pick up the first set of rhyming words, *mouse* and *house*, have the children tell us the spelling pattern in each (*-o-u-s-e*), and underline the spelling pattern. We decide that *house* and *mouse* rhyme and have the same spelling pattern. We emphasize that we can *hear* the rhyme and see the spelling pattern. We put *house* and *mouse* with their underlined spelling pattern back in the pocket chart and pick up the next set of rhymes—*chairs* and *stairs*. Repeating the procedure, we underline *airs* in both, decide they have the same spelling pattern, and put them back. We do the same for *brooms* and *rooms*.

Next we pick up *thread* and *bed*. We say them together and hear once more that they do rhyme. We then underline the spelling patterns: *ead, ed*. They do rhyme but they have a different spelling pattern. We remind the children that words that rhyme usually have the same spelling pattern but that sometimes they have different spelling patterns. Because we want to have in our pocket chart only words that rhyme and have the same spelling pattern, we toss *thread* and *bed* in the trash can! (Throwing these cards away is hard for some teachers to do, but doing so has a dramatic effect on the children.)

Next we take *door, more,* and *floor,* underline the spelling patterns, return *door* and *floor* to the pocket chart, and throw away *more.*

Finally, we underline the spelling patterns in *pails* and *nails*, decide they are the same, and return them to the pocket chart. We now have five sets of words that rhyme and have the same spelling pattern in our pocket chart:

h<u>ouse</u> ch<u>airs</u> br<u>ooms</u> d<u>oor</u> p<u>ails</u>
m<u>ouse</u> st<u>airs</u> r<u>ooms</u> fl<u>oor</u> n<u>ails</u>

The last part of this activity is to use these words to read and write some other words. This is the transfer step and is critical to the success of this activity for children who "only learn what we teach." So far, we have taught what rhyming words are and that many words that rhyme have the same spelling pattern. If we don't show them how to use this knowledge to decode and spell new words, they have not learned anything they can actually use. We begin the transfer part of this activity by telling children something like this:

You know that when you are reading books and writing stories, there are many words you have to figure out. One way many people figure out how to read and spell new words is to see if they already know any rhyming words or words that have the same spelling pattern. I am going to write some words and you can see which words with the same spelling pattern will help you read them. Then, we are going to try to spell some words by deciding if they rhyme with any of the words in our pocket chart.

Next we write two or three words that rhyme and have the same spelling pattern as the sets of words in our pocket chart. As we write each word, the children help us decide which letters to underline for the spelling pattern, and then a child puts that word in the pocket chart under the other words with the same spelling pattern. We then use the rhyme to decode the words.

Finally, we remind the children that thinking of rhyming words can help them spell words when they are writing. We say something like this:

What if you were writing and wanted to tell how your new bike zooms down the road? Let's see if we can find some words that rhyme with *zooms* and probably have the same spelling pattern.

We then lead the children to say the rhyming words and *zooms*: "mouse, house, zooms; chairs, stairs, zooms; brooms, rooms, zooms." After deciding that *zooms* rhymes with *brooms* and *rooms*, they help us spell *zooms*. We write *zooms* and put it in the pocket chart under *brooms* and *rooms*.

Here are the words rounded up from *In a People House*, along with the new words read and spelled based on their rhymes and spelling patterns at the conclusion of this activity.

h<u>ouse</u>	ch<u>airs</u>	br<u>ooms</u>	d<u>oor</u>	p<u>ails</u>
m<u>ouse</u>	st<u>airs</u>	r<u>ooms</u>	fl<u>oor</u>	n<u>ails</u>
bl<u>ouse</u>	p<u>airs</u>	z<u>ooms</u>	p<u>oor</u>	sn<u>ails</u>

Rounding Up the Rhymes is a multilevel activity, an activity that has something for everyone. Struggling readers and writers whose phonemic awareness is limited learn what rhymes are and how to distinguish rhymes from beginning sounds. Other children whose phonemic awareness is better developed may learn lots of spelling patterns and also that words that rhyme often share the same spelling pattern. Our most advanced readers and writers become proficient at the strategy of using words they know to decode and spell unknown words. This proficiency shows in their increased fluency and in the more sophisticated nature of the invented spellings in their writing.

Making Words

Making Words is an activity in which children are given some letters and use those letters to make words (Cunningham and Cunningham 1992; Cunningham and Hall 1994a and 1994b; Cunningham and Hall 1997a and 1997b). With the teacher, they make little words and then bigger words until the final word is made—a word that always includes all the letters. Children are eager to figure out what this "secret" word is. After making words, they put the letter cards away and the teacher leads them to sort the words into patterns and then use those patterns to decode and spell some new words. (The final step in Making Words is just like the final step in Rounding Up the Rhymes.)

A Sample Lesson

Give children cards with the vowels *a* and *i* and the consonants *c*, *h*, *n*, *p*, and *s*. Cards should have the uppercase letter on one side and the lowercase letter on the other side. The consonant letters are written in black and the two vowels are in red.

In the pocket chart at the front of the room, place some large cards with the same letters, which have been treated the same way.

Begin by making sure that each child has all the letters needed. Ask, "What two vowels will we use to make words today?" The children hold up their red *i* and *a* and respond appropriately.

Then write a 3 on the board and say, "Let's begin with some three-letter words. Take three letters and make *nap*. Everyone say *nap*."

The children quickly spell *nap*, and one child who has it made correctly is chosen to go and spell *nap* with the pocket chart letters.

Put the index card with the word *nap* in the pocket chart.

Next, say, "Just change your vowel and you can change *nap* to *nip*. Everyone say *nip*. A little dog will nip at your shoes."

The children make *nip* and then make four more three-letter words—*sip*, *sap*, *pin*, and *pan*.

Write a 4 on the board; tell the children to add just one letter to *pan* and they can make the word *span*. Because this word is unfamiliar to some children, explain that the part of a bridge that goes over the river is called the *span*. "We say that the bridge spans the river. We also talk about how long an animal lives by calling it the life span. The average life span of a dog is about twelve years."

Next, change one letter to change *span* to *spin*. At this point, you might say, "Don't take any letters out and don't add any. Just change where the letters are and you can change *spin* into *snip*."

The children then make two more four-letter words—*snap* and *pain*.

Then, write a 5. The children use five of their letters to make the word *Spain*.

End the word-making part of the lesson, as usual, by asking, "Has anyone figured out the secret word—the word that can be made with all the letters? If you know, make that word in your holder and I will come and see what you have."

Walk around and find a child who has figured out the secret word. Send the child to the pocket chart to manipulate all the letters to make the big word. As the child gets almost to the end, the other children realize what the word is. For the example described here, the children would say, "It's spinach!" and then make *spinach* in their holders.

After all the children have made the secret word in their holders, have them close their holders. Then together they read all the words they have made, which are lined up in the pocket chart: *nap, nip, sip, sap, pin, pan, span, spin, snip, snap, pain, Spain, spinach.*

After making words, the children sort these words into patterns and then use these words to read and spell other words. The patterns they sort for include beginning letters, endings (*s, ed, ing, er, est*), and rhyming words. The sample lesson described here included only words that begin with *s, p, n, sp,* or *sn.* Have children sort the words according to the beginning letters, which they know are all the letters up to the vowel. The words sorted for beginning letters would look like this:

n̲ap	s̲ip	p̲an	s̲pan	s̲nap
n̲ip	s̲ap	p̲in	s̲pin	s̲nip
		p̲ain	S̲pain	
			s̲pinach	

Help the children notice the beginning sounds, and particularly the sound of *sp* and *sn* blended together at the beginning of words.

The next sort is for the rhyming words. Ask, "Who can come and find some rhyming words that will help us spell and read other words?" Have several children come up and sort the words into rhymes like this:

n̲a̲p	n̲i̲p	p̲i̲n	p̲a̲n	p̲a̲in
s̲a̲p	s̲i̲p	sp̲i̲n	sp̲a̲n	Sp̲a̲in
sn̲a̲p	sn̲i̲p			

When the rhymes are sorted out, write on index cards a few new words that can be decoded based on these rhymes (*flip, twin*). Have children put the new words under the words with the same spelling pattern, and help them use the pattern and the rhyme to figure out the words.

Finally, remind the children that thinking of rhymes can help them when they are writing, too. Say, for example, "What if you were writing and you wanted to write *We set a trap to catch the mouse in our house.* How would you spell *trap?*"

The children may decide that *trap* rhymes with *nap, sap,* and *snap* and will probably be spelled *t-r-a-p. Trap* is written on an index card and put with its rhyming counterparts. A similar procedure is used to decide that *brain* rhymes with *pain* and *Spain* and is probably spelled *b-r-a-i-n.*

Like Rounding Up the Rhymes, Making Words activities help children look at words, sort those words into patterns, and use those patterns to read and spell some other words. Making Words is also a multilevel activity. Advanced readers are challenged to figure out the secret word and learn how thinking of rhymes and spelling patterns helps us read and spell lots of other words. Struggling readers are usually able to make some of the shorter words and change the beginning letter, ending letter, or vowels to make new words. They also develop phonemic awareness as they say words slowly while making them, and as they sort the words made into beginning letter patterns and rhyming patterns.

Third, Fourth, and Fifth Grade

Teachers in the intermediate grades often wonder if they need a word wall. This question can be easily answered by looking at the first-draft writing of the students. If many students are misspelling common words or using the wrong *to, too, two* or *their, there, they're*, then a word wall is probably needed. Figure 10-3 contains a list of words for consideration for a third-grade word wall and Figure 10-4 contains high-frequency words for an upper-grade word wall (Cunningham and Hall 1998a and 1998b). In addition to high-frequency words, the third-grade list contains:

▌ The most frequently misspelled words at the third-grade level.

▌ The most commonly confused homophones (*to, too, two; write, right*, etc.).

▌ The most common contractions.

▌ The most common compound words.

▌ A word beginning with each letter, including examples for the *s* sound of *c* (*city*) and the *j* sound of *g* (*general*).

▌ Examples for the common endings and suffixes (*s, es, ed, ing, ly, er, or, ful, less, ness, en, able, ible, tion, sion*) with common spelling changes (drop *e, y* changes to *i*, consonant doubling).

▌ Examples for the most common prefixes (*un, re, dis, im, in*).

Selection of words for the word wall depends on the students' spelling knowledge and on grade-level expectations. In addition to high-frequency words, older children need to learn the patterns that will help

---

High-Frequency Words for Grade Three

about	exciting	our	unhappiness
again	favorite	people	until
almost	first	pretty	usually
also	friendly	prettier	vacation
always	getting	prettiest	very
another	general	probably	want
anyone	governor	question	was
are	have	really	wear
beautiful	hidden	recycle	weather
because	hole	right	we're
before	hopeless	said	went
buy	I'm	schools	were
by	impossible	something	what
can't	independent	sometimes	when
city	into	terrible	where
could	its	that's	whether
community	it's	their	who
confusion	journal	then	whole
countries	knew	there	winner
didn't	know	they	with
discover	laughed	they're	won
doesn't	let's	thought	won't
don't	lovable	threw	wouldn't
enough	myself	through	write
especially	new	to	your
everybody	no	too	you're
everything	off	trouble	
except	one	two	

FIGURE 10-3   High-Frequency Words for Grade Three

High-Frequency Words for the Upper Grades

a lot	biologist	discourage	happiness(y)
accident	buy	doesn't	heard
adventure	caught	don't	hopeless
again	communities(y)	employee	I'm
all right	competition	endurance	impossible
almost	confidence	especially	indescribable
always	confusion	everybody	international
amazing(e)	crazier(y)	everyone	into
another	delicious	everything	irresponsible
apologize	depression	except	it's
beautiful	didn't	favorite	know
because	different	finally	let's
biggest	disagreement	friend	misunderstanding
nonsense	relative	there	usually
off	reporter	they	want
our	restaurant	they're	we're
outrageous	said	thought	went
outside	something	through	were
overwhelmed	sometimes	to	when
people	substitute	too	where
predictable	supervisor	transportation	which
prettier(y)	swimming	treasure	whole
probably	that's	two	would
professional	their	unfriendly	write
really	then	until	you're

FIGURE 10-4 High-Frequency Words for the Upper Grades

them spell lots of other words. These patterns include more complex rhymes and chunks used exclusively in polysyllabic words. The following section describes some of the multilevel spelling activities we use to help students learn the patterns.

What Looks Right?

What Looks Right? is an activity designed to help children learn (1) that good spelling requires visual memory, and (2) how to use their visual memory for words along with a dictionary to determine the correct spelling of a word. In English, words that have the same spelling pattern usually rhyme. If readers come to the unknown words *plight* and *trite*, they can easily figure out their pronunciation by accessing the pronunciation associated with other *ight* or *ite* words they can

already read and spell. The fact that there are two common spelling patterns with the same pronunciation is not a problem when trying to read an unfamiliar word, but it is a problem when trying to spell it. If a writer were trying to spell *trite* or *plight*, these words could as easily be spelled *t-r-i-g-h-t* and *p-l-i-t-e*. The only way to know which is the correct spelling is to write it one way and see if it "looks right" or check the probable spelling in a dictionary. What Looks Right? is an activity to help children learn how to use these two important self-monitoring spelling strategies (Cunningham and Hall 1998a and 1998b).

A Sample Lesson

Using an overhead or the board, create two columns and head each column with a word, such as *bite* and *fight*, which most of the children can both read and spell.

Have the children set up two columns on their paper to match the model.

Have the children pronounce and spell the words and lead them to realize that the words rhyme but have a different spelling pattern.

Tell them that there are many words that rhyme with *bite* and *fight* and that you can't tell by just saying the words which spelling patterns they will have.

Next, say a word that rhymes with *bite* and *fight* and write it both ways, saying, "If *kite* is spelled like *bite*, it will be *k-i-t-e*; if it is spelled like *fight*, it will be *k-i-g-h-t*."

Write these two possible spellings under the appropriate word.

Tell the children to decide which one "looks right" to them and to only write the one they think is correct.

As soon as each child decides which one looks right and writes it in the correct column, have children work collaboratively to find that word in the dictionary. If they cannot find the one that looked right, then have them look up the other possible spelling.

Compare what they have found, and then erase or cross out the spelling on the board that is not correct and continue with some more examples. For each word, say something like, "If *flight* is spelled like *bite*, it will be *f-l-i-t-e*, but if it is spelled like *fight*, it will be *f-l-i-g-h-t*."

Write the word both ways and have each child write it, check to see if it looks right, and then look in the dictionary to see if the word is spelled the way the child thought.

With words such as *site/sight* and *mite/might*, write them both ways and have children discover when they go to the dictionary that both spellings create words and that the dictionary—a most helpful book—will let them know which spelling has which meaning!

Figure 10-5 shows what the columns of words might look like after several examples.

To make the lesson more multilevel, include some longer words such as *invite*, *delight*, *unite*, and *polite*, in which the last syllable rhymes with *bite* and *fight*. Proceed just as before to write the word both ways and have children choose the one that looks right, write that word, and look for it in the dictionary.

What Looks Right? is an active response activity through which children can learn a variety of important concepts. As a versatile strategy, What Looks Right? can be used to help children become better spellers of longer words. In addition to the common two-letter vowel patterns, teachers could focus lessons on words like *motion* and *pension*

---

ite/ight Chart	
<u>bite</u>	<u>fight</u>
kite	kight
quite	quight
spite	spight
tite	tight
mite	might
frite	fright
site	sight
flite	flight

FIGURE 10-5   **ite/ight Chart**

as the heads of columns. The words the teacher writes end in either *sion* or *tion*, and the children use the same procedure.

Word Sorts

Traditional Word Sorts

Word sorts have long been advocated as an activity to help children develop the habit of analyzing words to look for patterns (Cunningham and Hall 1998b; Henderson 1990; Zutell, Chapter 9 in this volume). There are a variety of ways to do word sorts, but the basic principles are the same. Children look at words and sort them into categories based on spelling patterns and sound. Children say the words and look at how they are spelled. They learn that to go in a certain category, the words must "sound the same and look the same." There is variation in the amount of teacher input given to the sort. In a closed sort, the teacher gives the children the category headings. In an open sort, the children determine what the categories should be.

It is important that children develop speed and automaticity as they sort. Here are some general guidelines:

1. Many teachers begin by showing the children the words. They have the children say the words and then put them in appropriate categories.

2. When the children are good at looking, saying, and deciding, the teacher leads them in some blind sorting by calling out the same words already sorted but not showing them to the children, who then decide in which column the teacher should place the word. Then the teacher shows them the

word to confirm and places the word in the correct column.

3. The final stage in developing automaticity in spelling certain patterns is the *blind writing sort*. The teacher calls out the previously sorted words and children write them in the appropriate column before seeing them. Once the children have written the word, the teacher shows the word so that they may confirm their spelling and categorization.

Word Hunts

Word sorts are followed by word hunts. Many teachers post charts with the categories the class has worked on and encourage children to add words that fit the pattern any time they find them in anything they are reading. Some children keep word notebooks and add words they find that fit particular categories. Hunting for words is a critical transfer step because it draws children's attention to spelling patterns in the real materials they are reading.

A Sample Multilevel Word Sort

As traditionally done, word sorts are not very multilevel. Children begin by sorting for initial letters and then for words with one vowel, two vowels, etc. We have had good success giving our word sorts a multilevel twist by including the vowel patterns used in short and longer words. Here is an example using patterns for the vowel *u*.

Reading sorts. On the first day, each child had a sort sheet and the teacher had a transparency that looked like Figure 10-6.

The children folded their sheets so that they couldn't see the last two columns—*sure*

Transparency of Word Sort: Day 1

Other	u	ue	u-e	ur	sure	ture
	us	sue	use	burn	insure	nature

FIGURE 10-6   Transparency of Word Sort: Day 1

and *ture*. (Those columns were also covered on the transparency.)

The teacher then showed the children fifteen to twenty words that had the vowel *u*. As she showed them each word, the children pronounced the word and then wrote it in the column where they thought it belonged.

They then told the teacher which column to put it in on her transparency. At the end of that first lesson, the sort sheets looked like Figure 10-7.

On the second day, they used the same sheet again and kept the last two columns covered. Another fifteen to twenty words were sorted into the first five columns. Some of these words had more than one syllable, and the teacher reminded the children that they were focusing on the syllable with *u*.

On the third day, they opened their sheets so that all columns were visible. They sorted words that cut across all columns. At the end of the third day the sheets looked like Figure 10-8.

Blind sorts. The first three days of sorting activities had been devoted to reading sorts—that is, the children looked at and pronounced each word before deciding on the appropriate column. On the fourth day, they did a blind sort. The children got a new sorting sheet just like the one they used the first three days, and the teacher used a new transparency.

Some of the same words used on the first three days were used on the fourth day, but this time the teacher said the word without showing it. The children indicated where they thought it belonged by putting a finger on the column. The teacher then showed the word and both the teacher and the children wrote it where it went.

Blind writing sort. The final activity with these words was a blind writing sort. The teacher said the word and the children tried to write it in the correct column before the teacher showed the word.

Word hunt. Next, the children moved from word sorting to word hunting. The children were given another clean sheet with the columns. They had one week to find other words that fit the patterns and write them on their sheets. They were encouraged to hunt for words everywhere—around the room, on signs, in books they were reading, and even in science, social studies, and math. They did this hunting on their own and were all eager to have lots of words—especially big words—to contribute to the final sort.

For the final sort, the teacher put a huge piece of butcher paper all the way across the chalkboard. Columns were set up to make the original sort sheets, using different colors for each. The children took turns coming up and writing one word in its correct column, pronouncing that word, and, for an obscure word, using it in a sentence. Words

Transparency of Word Sort: Day 2				
<u>Other</u>	<u>u</u>	<u>ue</u>	<u>u-e</u>	<u>ur</u>
	us	sue	use	burn
menu	run	true	mule	turn
	must	blue	mute	urban
	snub	due	cute	turtle
	runt		amuse	

FIGURE 10-7   Transparency of Word Sort: Day 2

Transparency of Word Sort: Day 3

Other	u	ue	u-e	ur	sure	ture
	us	sue	use	burn	insure	nature
menu	run	true	mule	turn	measure	creature
tuna	must	blue	mute	urban	assure	picture
	snub	due	cute	turtle	treasure	mixture
	runt	statue	amuse	return	pleasure	mature
	strum	value	reuse	hurt	pressure	adventure
	bus	rescue	compute			
	minus	continue				
	numbers					
	sunset					
	summer					
	submarines					

FIGURE 10-8   Transparency of Word Sort: Day 3

were added until the children ran out of words or until there was no more room in a particular column. The easy columns (*u* as in *us*, *ur* as in *turn*) were quickly filled, but children ran out of words before the *ture* and *sure* columns were full. The teacher hung the mural along the back wall and children continued to write words for these patterns.

We have used many similar multilevel word sorts with success. By limiting the first day's sorting to the most common patterns and one-syllable words and then increasing to longer words and the patterns found in longer words, we provide opportunities for children at all different levels of word knowledge. We can summarize the procedure in three steps:

1. Begin with *reading sorts*, in which the children look at and pronounce the word first.

2. Move to *blind sorts*, in which they must decide where the word goes before seeing it.

3. Finally, use *blind writing sorts*, in which they must write the word before seeing it.

The hunting is multilevel. Children tend to find words at their own level of developing word knowledge because they must be able to pronounce any word they are going to add to the word sort mural and, if it is not a commonly known word, use it in a sentence. The most advanced children hunt for big words because they soon learn that there is almost always space left in the columns for big word parts.

In all of these multilevel activities, there is something to be learned by everyone in a class, regardless of their ability. That is why we call them "multilevel activities." When children are actively involved in their decoding and spelling instruction, they learn how words work. Once children find out how words work, they can move forward in their ability to decode and spell lots of words and use these strategies when reading and writing.

Suggestions for Professional Development

1. Meet with grade-level teachers. Each teacher should bring a particular word study activity that provides various opportunities

for children who bring different understandings of how letters and words work.

2. Select a spelling principle or pattern. With a partner, construct a word sort that is multilevel. Take turns having the group engage in the word sort developed by each teacher pair. Then discuss the insights you gained by engaging in the activity. Discuss the implications for working with your students.

3. As a follow-up, refer to Chapters 3, 12, and 13 in *Word Matters: Teaching Phonics and Spelling in the Reading/Writing Classroom.*

CHAPTER ELEVEN

Learning Links in Language and Literacy

Diane E. DeFord

Introduction

When children learn to become word solvers, they are learning important linguistic systems that are related to their broader knowledge of the world and of language. Analysis and categorization are important aspects of learning for young children, and they perform these complex cognitive operations—with meaning as a base—as they learn an oral language to talk about their world. In this chapter DeFord reminds us that learning about words is part of the whole process of learning language and learning about language. She describes links between oral language and written language. She also explains how relating the spoken and written word helps young learners to develop word-solving strategies.

Learning words, learning about words, and learning how words work is not something that is accomplished at a particular time through particular activities. These important understandings are part of the whole language-learning process, a process that begins at (or even a little before) birth. DeFord suggests, in broad strokes, a way of looking at early, intermediate, and advanced learning in reading, writing, and word study, and she also suggests that we

learn about the power and structure of words all of our lives.

Helen Keller was blind and deaf by the time she was about eighteen months old. She lived for the first seven years of her life in a world of silence, darkness, and frustration. A victim of a terrible fever, Helen later wrote about those first years as her "long night" (Kudlinski 1991, 4). Many thought she was deranged, others pitied her, and although her parents loved her dearly, no one knew how to reach out to her, to break the frustration of silence in a darkened world. Without words, she couldn't get her needs met, communicate with others, or solve her own problems. Through tantrums, Helen cried out from her confining world in the only way she could; she cried out for understanding of her own need to learn.

Her teacher, Annie Sullivan, worked daily during their first month together to help Helen learn sign language to speak with her hands. Helen learned the "finger games" but did not understand their purpose. Helen's breakthrough occurred when Annie took her to the water pump and signed *w-a-t-e-r* in the cool stream that flowed from the pump; *w-a-t-e-r* was a finger pattern they had practiced before. Helen began to tremble with her new insight. "I knew then," she wrote later, "that *w-a-t-e-r* meant the wonderful cool something that was flowing over my hand. That living word awakened my soul, gave it light, hope, joy, set it free" (16). She had finally discovered a way to communicate her own thoughts and to share in the thoughts of others: "It was as if I had come back to life after being dead. Sweet strange things that were locked up in my heart began to sing" (16). Within a day, Helen learned thirty words: the swinging wood that was a *d-o-o-r* could *o-p-e-n* or *s-h-u-t*; the woman who had fought with her and made her do all these new things was *t-e-a-c-h-e-r*. She now had language—a tool of the mind, a tool for learning.

The insight that Helen had is recreated anew for every child as a learner. Every child learns about patterns of sounds and letters and about their order within the child's name and other frequently used words. Children learn that their name and other words stand for particular things, events, and ideas. Language, whether it is oral or written, stands for meaning and makes meaning.

Developing a System of Language Competence

Helen Keller's learning about one word gave her access to a language system through which she was able to communicate and think about her world. There is evidence that this process normally begins before birth. Within minutes after birth newborns show they recognize their own mothers' voices, and they react differently to unfamiliar stories than to familiar stories that they heard repeatedly in their last weeks before birth. They are even able to discriminate between an unfamiliar language and their "mother tongue" (Cooper and Aslin 1989; DeCasper and Fifer 1980; DeCasper and Spence 1986; Mehler et al. 1988). The newborn is very sensitive to language.

This sensitivity to language allows chil-

dren to listen to the flow of language and link it to other forms of communication— such as posture, emotions, patterns of gesture and movement, and timing of movement—to begin to form a system of relationships. They associate meaning with the language used around them, the actions of others, the tools they use, and the objects in their world. Across settings children learn the sounds of the language, the words of the language, the rules for putting words together to communicate their intentions, and the social rules of interaction with others. Parents and caregivers guide the child's participation in cultural activities in ways that help children learn (Rogoff 1990). The parent who holds a telephone to a child's ear and says "Talk to Grampa!" is engaged in this process.

As the child's world broadens to include other settings besides the home, children shift from the support of their caregivers to others, learning from activities and experiences more distant from those of the home. In this way, the child's ability to use oral language and make sense of the world becomes the first self-extending system (Clay 1991a, 317). In other words, the child's strategies for using language and meaning get better within activities in which language is used.

These powerful self-extending systems are forged and expanded as children interact with people and objects in their world. For example, as children participate with others in activities, "extra" learning is taking place. The children are also learning *about* language—the generative rules that allow them to produce new sentences that they have never heard before. And, they are learning how to use language as a tool for learning, storing information, and analyzing ideas. As they use language as a tool, they are always improving that tool.

Two particular capabilities transform the child's sensitivity to language into this dynamic system of language competence: (1) the ability to organize information into categories; and (2) the ability to link new information to known information through analogy. These abilities are critical to expanding oral language and beginning to read and write, and the process begins in the home.

Children categorize actions and objects in their world every day, and language helps them do this. Words represent categories of things (nouns), actions (verbs), and so on. Words such as articles (*the*) help us put words together in meaningful units so we can see the relationships among categories (*The cat ran*). For children, simple categories form around such things as activities that are fun to do (*I like to jump*), favorite toys (*my bear*), things the child doesn't like (*I hate spinach*), family members versus strangers (*my dad; that man*), and so forth. These categories all become associated through language. As a child interacts with others, categories are extended throughout a lifetime, and the associations with language and experiences become more complex and refined.

If language use is encouraged in the classroom setting, children will show teachers they are continuing this process. Cazden (1992) reported an incident she overheard in her own classroom in San Diego. Everett, a tiny first grader, sat quietly whispering, "*Little* is a big word, and *big* is a little word." When he saw the word *on* written on the chalkboard, he said, "You take the *n* off *on* and put it in front and it'd be *no*." Yet another time, he came to the word *what* when he was reading and asked, "What's this word?" She told him *what* and he laughed, saying "When I asked you 'what's the word,' I said it myself!" As children engage in reading and writing events in home and school settings, they meet challenges that fuel continued learning. Wood (1988) indicates that learning language requires that the child find solutions to problems that are specific to language itself.

With a category system in place, analogies are used to relate one known quantity to something new and to relate one category to another. For example, Fodor, Bever, and Garrett (1974) suggest that knowing one's

name is linked in complex ways to a host of information. The knowledge of how to write a name connects to the knowledge of speaking it, writing it, and reading it. A network of relationships is established between a name and other information, just as Everett made a link between the word *on* and a known word, *no*.

Translations of the writing of Luria and Vygotsky (Luria 1973; Vygotsky 1978) have provided us with a great deal of insight into the power of language as a tool for learning. They talk about language as a tool for intellectual activity, a means of communication in the use and transmission of information. Language provides a multidimensional tool within intellectual activity.

The power of language is to provide the bridge from what is known to new ways of thinking and acting. The construction of this system of language competence, then, grows from the interaction of the following characteristics and abilities within the learner:

■ Sensitivity to language.
■ Ability to synthesize rules of interaction.
■ Ability to organize information into categories.

Ability to Learn Through Analogy

The ability to analyze language is of interest to us as literacy educators because in reading and writing that is precisely what we are asking children to do. To understand and use words in oral and written settings, for example, one would use the following language analyses:

1. Acoustic or phonemic analysis to hear and discriminate language and articulate responses (*set it here* vs. *step right here*). For Helen Keller, of course, this information was unavailable, so she had to find a route in through the finger motions taught by Annie.

2. Organized networks of word groups with similar features (*don't* and *won't*) and

semantic groups (hospitals, schools, and police stations as public institutions). Helen could use words (or combinations of finger motions) to name categories and represent her world to herself and others.

3. Transformation of thought into speech (and vice versa) using sentences and narrative structures. Helen learned to communicate meanings to family members by sign or gesture, and they responded by speaking.

Oral language, world experiences, and the growing ability to analyze and learn from language form the foundation for learning about written language. For young children, written language is a new symbol system, and as children learn about this new system, key understandings that they forged in the oral language system must be related to the new information. Key terms used by Vygotsky and Luria offer a guide to help us think about what children must learn anew as they move from the use of oral to written language:

■ A structure for the analysis of written language that involves acoustic and phonemic discriminations, organizing networks, and the transformation of thought.

■ A method of analyzing, organizing, and categorizing written language.

■ Operations or strategies that aid in abstracting, generalizing, drawing conclusions, making decisions, and regulating the use of written language.

A Structure for the Analysis of Written Language

Learning written language prompts further learning in oral language. In fact, this new learning makes a unique contribution to oral language. When children learn written language, they rethink and also refine their understandings and use of oral language. Let's remember some important aspects of language learning in general:

■ Language is structured; there are rules by which words are put together. These rules are "generative" in that an infinite number of sentences and meanings can be generated once we understand the "rules." They are not the rules of correct grammar but simply the way we put words together. Every speaker of the language knows them unconsciously.

■ The brain is well suited to the analysis language itself allows. The brain has built into its very cells ways of receiving, analyzing, processing, and regulating information.

Children entering kindergarten or first grade encounter written language and, usually, try to match it up with oral language, often encountering some things they find puzzling. These peculiarities may occur in the way they try to match oral language with print. For example, children are familiar with phrases of oral language such as "Happy birthday to you." When they first encounter the printed representation of these familiar phrases, a set of anomalies arises. The teacher might say, "Find the first word"; "What is the first letter of the word *Happy*"; or "Point to each word and read." This kind of direction guides the children to think about aspects of language that are very different from those they have had to think about before. In this case, the teacher uses language to talk about language, a concept that is quite abstract for the young child. Children have the challenging task of coordinating knowledge of the oral expression with the visual display—that is, matching oral speech to written form.

The fact that *happy birthday* includes two words, four syllables, nine different phonemes, and fourteen characters (including the space) is an earth-buckling concept for children! In many ways, this understanding is what Helen Keller meant when she said that she finally understood "that *w-a-t-e-r* meant the wonderful cool something that was flowing over my hand. That living word awakened my soul, gave it light, hope, joy, set it free." During kindergarten and first grade, children learn that a word is a "complex, multidimensional matrix of different cues and connections (acoustic, morphological, lexical, and semantic)" (Luria 1973, 306). The concept of a word in both speech and writing (which Luria refers to as the basic unit of language), and the sentence (the basic unit of narrative) are the center of the child's linguistic tutoring in the early grades. In Figure 11-1, a young girl whose name is Candy knows one word, and—like Helen—she finds that this word is the basic unit of language she uses in her first forays into learning about written language.

As Candy learns how this new written symbol system works, her name forms the basis of a set of analogies, or the nexus of a growing network in which new information is linked to known sets. For example, Candy is a member of a family (Mom, Dad, brother Randy), and her first written stories in the classroom are likely to come from this semantic group or to be about herself as a learner in the classroom. The first sentences she writes may be "I like my Mom and Dad. I like my brother." She will take on new words in writing (*I, my, like*) and explore the similarities and relationships these words have to meanings in her world. Categories will begin to form for the written symbols to the spoken words that help her define the similarities and differences she notes (*Candy* contains the words *and* and *can* and sounds like her brother's name, *Randy*). This is how a network of relationships that extend from a name is initially linked to other information. The knowledge of how to write a name, the sequence of letters that are required, and the sound correspondences that are formed establish a structure for this analysis—a link to the knowledge of speaking it, writing it, and reading it.

A Method of Analyzing, Organizing, and Categorizing Written Language

When a child constructs knowledge about written language, three linguistic systems are involved in linking new words and information:

1. Making acoustic discriminations and matching sounds with written representations of language.

2. Organizing networks of information for written language itself.

3. Transforming thought and meaning through written language.

Through the use of these linguistic systems, a child forges a method of analyzing, organizing, and categorizing written language. This method utilizes perceptual and conceptual processes, which aid in generalizing from one thing to another, drawing conclusions, making decisions, and regulating the use of written language.

The Role of Perception and Cognition

Perception is the process or act of perceiving, recognizing, and interpreting sensory information. *Cognition* is the thinking process that uses awareness, perception, reasoning, intuition, and judgment. Cognition, then, is the larger umbrella of mental activity that utilizes sensory information (e.g., visual, auditory, smell, taste, touch) as input. Visual perception is part of the inner processing system that readers and writers develop about how letters and words work as the building blocks of written language. As Clay (1991a) states:

The beginning reader has to give attention to visual information as well as the language and messages but gradually becomes able to use visual information without much conscious attention, freeing more attention for the messages and language of the text and for novel information which expands the system. (287)

Developmental psychologists report that for all children perception (auditory and visual) and cognition (thinking and problem solving) change remarkably between the ages of five and seven. Schooling contributes to

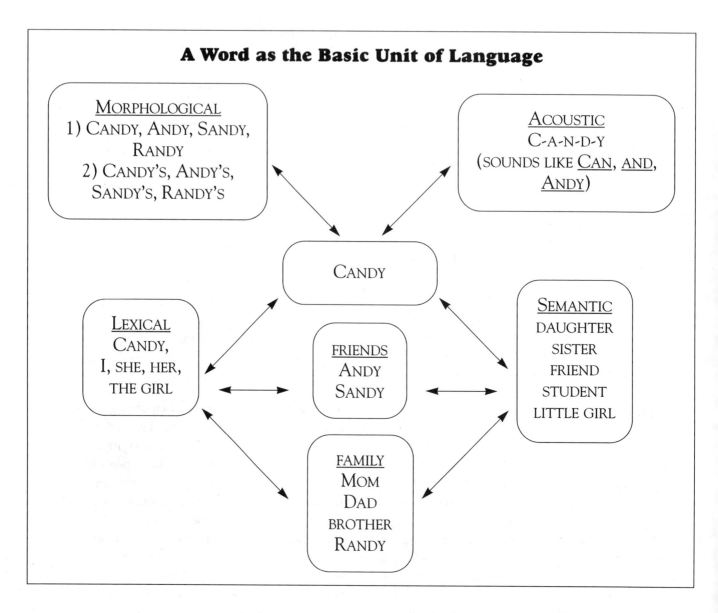

FIGURE 11-1   A Word as the Basic Unit of Language

these changes. Visual exploration and visual scanning of print are important learning tasks in the first year that must not be neglected by educators and researchers. Language skills are very important for reading but can only be applied to literacy tasks if children learn where to direct their attention as they explore the text with their eyes (Clay 1991a, 318). Young readers must learn what a word is, how to find it on the page, and how to relate it to the picture and to what they know about the world.

As they participate in early literacy experiences that involve meaningful print, children analyze, organize, and develop categories to identify and use letters, sequences of letters in words, and relationships between letters, sounds, and words. Each child learns how to use these varying sources of information within reading and writing settings. This categorical thinking eventually aids in the development of expertise in processing information as a reader and writer:

The good reader manipulates language, spatial and visual perception cues, and categorizes these efficiently, searching for dissonant relations and best-fit solutions. Familiar responses become habitual, require less and less processing and allow attention to reach out towards new information that was not previously noticed. (Clay 1991a, 321)

Through using knowledge of words in reading and writing, children learn more. The puzzles that they resolve help them make connections and form the generalized knowledge that underlies strategies. Their own problem solving supports the development of the internal processing system.

Strategy Development

As you observe your students during reading and writing, you can notice how they use directional concepts, recognize letters or letter clusters, work to get the word sequence right, read fluently, and locate and correct errors. Such behaviors signal that inside the children's heads other kinds of activity have possibly occurred, such as:

■ Anticipating what could follow.

■ Searching for more "information" in the print.

■ Self-monitoring, evaluating, and correcting.

■ Linking to prior knowledge.

■ Lining up a new item with an existing general rule and perhaps extending that rule (Clay 1991a, 321).

By focusing on how children are processing text and what they are attending to, teachers can assist learners in organizing experiences and help correct any idiosyncratic or unreliable concepts. To be effective in helping them understand learning, we must understand how children learn how words work and how best to support their efforts.

Learning How Words Work

What does all of this mean for helping children make the connections they need

to learn about words? If we understand something about how children learn and have a tentative concept of what the individual child knows, then we can make some decisions about what next steps the child must take.

Early Learning

In the first year of school children are learning foundational concepts as they engage in a wide range of literacy activities. These children are learning how to look at and think about print. At first, the stories they hear, write, and read help them learn what reading and writing are for, and their own roles and responsibilities in the school community. Certain words stand out in this new setting: signs for the principal's office, the boys' and girls' bathrooms, important words within the classroom, their names and those of their friends and family. In shared reading and writing settings, they learn about concepts of orientation and directionality. They also make their first generalizations about how stories, words, and print work in terms of words and voice matching, from which the first letter-sound correspondences emerge. They develop phonological awareness: how language sounds in written stories and sentences, and how language gets segmented from words, syllables, onsets, and rimes, down to phonemes.

Once children have developed these early concepts, this foundational literacy learning should be extended through more systematic instruction. At this point, children are learning conventions and how to talk about words and written language (beginnings and endings of words, sentences, capital letters, lowercase letters, periods, etc.). The goal is for them to learn how these principles work in a variety of settings so they become flexible and fluent with what they know. They begin to be more consistent in using the terms *word* versus *letter*, leaving spaces between words, and representing more of the consonant framework in words they write. They rapidly begin to add new words they know in both writing and reading.

At this critical point in learning about written and oral language, children indicate they have begun to attend to the details of print. If they know as many as ten letters that they consistently use to locate where they are in print, their knowledge of these correspondences seems to mushroom.

Intermediate Understandings

The next learning horizons are the flexible use of these concepts in increasingly demanding settings. Children must pay greater attention to within-word patterns and learn about inconsistencies in oral/written language conventions. Attention to visual discrepancies in how words are spelled versus how they are pronounced (*ate, eight; like, liked*) is crucial for children to learn to problem solve new words in reading and writing when the texts they use or create have increased linguistic complexity. The most difficult task for the child is to attend to and use this information "on the run" while reading and writing.

It is time for greater sophistication in word knowledge, linguistic relationships, and conceptual ties to be developed. More complex word study must be undertaken as well as more advanced experiences with reading and writing. Within these experiences, children begin to grapple with concepts such as:

- Blends and digraphs.
- Syllables in more complex words.
- Morphemic endings and markers, prefixes and suffixes.
- Meaning relationships across word categories.

In guided reading, you can help children learn to take words apart and use chunks of information within words, simultaneously coordinating that process with attention to meaning and language syntax. In writer's workshop, you can provide demonstrations of how to use known words to spell new ones and help children understand the discrepancies between sounds and orthography. You are asking them not only to think about letter-sound relationships but to retrieve visual patterns that they can notice in words and connect to meaning. By talking to students about word choices in their own writing (word play encouraging variation) and about authors' choices of words in the books they read, you can emphasize the importance of words in conveying their meanings.

Word sorting and word construction should emphasize these three different aspects of learning that feed into how the brain functions:

1. Extending learning through analogy—using what they know within sequences and clusters of letters (blends and digraphs, syllables, endings), in groups of words (conceptual, high-frequency, more complex analogies), in word families (onsets and rimes), and in vowels and spelling patterns.

2. Using knowledge of categories (rules) and probabilities to make words.

3. Developing regulation and verification systems in order to tell what looks right, to deal with discrepancies between oral and written language, and to check on oneself as a reader or writer.

Advanced Learning

As children move into advanced learning about how words work, there are several characteristics that you are likely to notice.

- In reading, students are developing fluency in problem solving that incorporates visual analysis of features of words; use of sequential, left-to-right analysis; and recognition of words' functions within a hierarchy of language—letters within words and words within phrases and sentences as part of a meaningful text.

- Students show evidence in their writing that they have incorporated the elements of consonant and vowel patterns that exhibit many of the rules (consonant[s], vowel, ending). Many vowels are accurately represented, signaling long vowels with two vowels together or with an *e* at the end.

❚ They use meaning and spelling rules together regardless of variations in sounds and orthography (*liked, wanted, dived*), as well as simple compound words and inflections and affixes.

Advanced word study promotes student exploration of word categories, idioms, similes, and tongue twisters. Students may derive rules for root words, homonyms, diphthongs, compounds, and the use of inflections and affixes by grouping and regrouping in open (undefined categories) and closed (defined categories) word sorts. Students are ready for and can enjoy sophisticated analysis of words (see Zutell, Chapter 9).

Lifelong Learning

I have talked about beginning, intermediate, and advanced learning, but in a sense, all of us are learning about words all of our lives. We have only to look at the many people doing crossword puzzles on paper and computer, using words to cruise the Internet, laughing at jokes that center around unusual or surprising uses of words, or simply talking over and using new words they have encountered in reading or in the media, to know that word learning, as part of language, is of interest to us all.

From birth, children are involved in a lifelong quest to expand their knowledge of words. The school time that they spend in word connecting and word exploration must be active and enjoyable—simply part of language learning. Improving literacy stems from a lifelong love of language itself. Instill this in the hearts of children and, like Helen Keller, they will feel an equal sense of personal freedom: "That living word awakened my soul, gave it light, hope, joy, set it free."

Suggestions for Professional Development

1. Gather two or three running records and two or three writing samples from students who evidence varying levels of literacy achievement in your classroom.

2. Using the descriptions of early, intermediate, and advanced learning on pages 137 and 138, put key descriptors on a piece of chart paper.

3. Take turns presenting the data on each child and placing the child in one of the three categories.

4. Discuss the specific teaching methods you are planning to use to further the learning of each group of children.

5. For a follow-up, read Chapters 6, 7, and 8 in *Word Matters: Teaching Phonics and Spelling in the Reading/Writing Classroom*.

4

Reading: Taking Apart
Letters and Words

It is often said that children learn to read by reading. And conventional wisdom tells us that when we practice something, we generally get better. Certainly, we know that becoming an accomplished reader demands lots of reading from a diverse range of reading material. Competent readers possess multiple strategies and are able to divide their attention among a complex array of reading tasks, maintaining meaning while they solve words rapidly and easily. Good readers sound fluent. That's because they process print as language, something they could not do if they were not constantly building their understanding of the whole text.

In a smooth, coordinated way, readers use many sources of information, including knowledge of the world, knowledge of language, and knowledge of the visual aspects of words (including letter-sound relationships). Good readers possess knowledge of words in multiple ways. Some words they recognize instantly; we should not forget that competent readers know thousands of words that require little or no attention while reading. Recognizing many words frees readers' attention for more important matters: thinking about the meaning of the text they are reading. Good readers also have ways of figuring out words that they do not know (or they nearly know). They can use parts of words, left-to-right analysis, letter-sound relationships, and words they do know in strategic ways. Competent readers actively search for ways to figure out a word; through problem solving their way through texts, readers get even better.

As adults we may not be fully aware of how our "self-extending" and "self-improving" systems operate in reading. We think about it momentarily when we meet a word we do not know, read an unusual use of language in a text, or lose the meaning because of the complexity of ideas we are encountering. Once we have puzzled out the problem (usually at such a rapid rate we hardly know we are doing it), we are more familiar with the word, idea, or language structure when we meet it again in other texts. In this way, not only are we extending our learning of the content of what we are reading, but we are expanding our knowledge of written language and how it works. That is the way the self-extending system operates—through this "reading work" that takes place within the head.

There are two important aspects to becoming a competent word solver. First, we want children to know about words. They need information that they can use as readers. They need to know about the letters, letter-sound relationships, and the patterns of letters in words. Even more important than the development of that knowledge (but impossible without it), we want children to use their knowledge while reading words that are embedded in phrases, sentences, paragraphs, and whole texts of different kinds.

As teachers we are fortunate that young children display so many reading behaviors overtly. We can observe them for evidence that they are searching for information or checking on themselves as readers. We can support the kinds of behaviors that are related to effective problem solving in reading and so help them to build self-extending systems. The "noticing teacher" is always looking for evidence that children are developing effective reading strategies. We can find ample evidence in children's reading to help us know how they are solving words while reading continuous text, and we can create instructional settings such as guided reading and shared reading that support the development of those strategies.

In this section we explore how teaching interactions support young readers as they engage in the problem-solving process. Askew provides a model for observing and thinking about the evidence of strategy use on the part of readers. She also provides examples of teaching interactions that support learners. Hundley and Powell explore the beginnings of reading through their descriptions of shared reading, an important instructional approach to support emergent readers. Shared reading provides a highly supportive context. It enables children to solidify their understanding of how print works and practice early behaviors such as moving left to right along a line of print and matching oral and written language. Both of the chapters in this section emphasize teacher decision making. Effective teachers direct children to clear examples that demonstrate successful reading and word solving.

Helping Young Readers Learn How to Problem Solve Words While Reading

Billie J. Askew

Introduction

As they work to construct meaning from a text, readers draw from multiple sources of information. They are able to divide their attention so that they can solve words while at the same time focus on the meaning. Readers are thinking about an interesting character (perhaps visualizing what that character looks like), becoming excited by the series of events that make up the plot, figuring out the mystery, or absorbing information that they will incorporate into their own understandings of a particular topic. And, all the time, they are engaged in rapid word solving. Readers are also recognizing many known words instantly and quickly analyzing words that they do not recognize.

Adult readers, of course, typically encounter only a few words they don't recognize in any given reading, but, for new readers, the process is often more difficult. The complex reading process—which demands divided attention—requires excellent, fast, automatic word-solving strategies. Otherwise, readers can become so bogged down in solving words that they lose the meaning. Selecting an appropriate text for young readers so that they can effectively use strategies is a key teacher decision. Once the text is selected, teaching interactions are critical to supporting the development of a self-extending system.

In this chapter Askew describes how young readers learn to use the print information while they read for meaning. She discusses how readers initiate action to read for meaning while solving words. She also explains how teaching interactions support a reader's development of a complex set of strategies for processing text.

Text: The fans were shouting in the stands.

Child: The fans were sh-out-ing shouting in the st-stands.

This child was reading a new text. There were some unfamiliar words. Yet he was able to problem solve quickly—on the run—to read this sentence. How did he do it?

We cannot presume to get inside the child's head to explain the processing; however, there is evidence that the child was using information from the text. His response was meaningful and linguistically/structurally acceptable, indicating his understanding of those requisites in reading. We also have evidence that within the search for a meaningful sentence, he was using the symbols and the sounds of his language to solve problems on the run. He was using his knowledge of letter clusters and their sounds and his knowledge of inflectional endings. Furthermore, he appeared to be using what he knew to solve new problems by analogy, possibly using known words such as *out* and *and* to help with *shouted* and *stands.*

We know that readers use a host of strategies when they read books or stories. This chapter focuses on the *visual* information that readers use from the text to solve problems, particularly when encountering new or unknown words.

Consider any child. What actions does the child take when facing difficulties while reading a story or a book? Does the child know enough about visual information within text to solve problems that can only be resolved through word analysis? Can this reader *use* current knowledge to analyze new words while reading? Or is the child's repertoire of strategies for problem solving words too limited? Is the reader willing to choose among alternatives? Can the reader act quickly and independently so that the meaning of the text is not lost?

Even beginning readers, when given appropriate, manageable texts, should be acquiring ways of working out new words in a text using their current responses. While these possible responses begin early, they are expanded and modified across years of problem solving while reading text.

There is always a danger in isolating one source of information for consideration. The complexity of the reading process cannot be simplified in that way. Rather, the complex interactions of the reader with many sources of information from texts lead to successful problem solving when reading. For example, the cohesion of the text, language codes, and the availability of redundant information in the text all contribute to efficient and effective reading of that text (Clay 1991a). A reader problem solves using three language-based sources of information: (1) the reader's understandings of what can happen in the world (meaning); (2) the reader's understandings of language (of words, struc-

tures, and sound sequences); and (3) the reader's understandings about several approaches to phonological information (Clay 1991a). The examples from the oral readings of first graders shown in Figure 12-1 demonstrate their use of multiple sources of information when reading texts.

In all of these examples, children were processing "on the run" while reading text, or they were commenting on the processing that enabled them to solve a problem related to the printed text. Because they processed visual information rapidly, they maintained the fluency needed to keep the meaning of the text. As Fountas and Pinnell (1996) note:

Being able to recognize words without slowing down helps maintain fluent processing. Fluent readers recognize features of words that they know and use these features to get to words that are unknown. Fluent reading means solving problems "on the run," something all readers must do if they are to gain understanding. (151)

This chapter is about problem solving during the act of reading "real" texts. The work of Marie Clay (1966, 1991a, 1993b), her comprehensive studies in which she observed reading and writing processes as children read or wrote *continuous* text, provides the underlying theory for this discussion. Within her theory of reading and writing continuous text is the understanding that *while* reading and writing text children develop a network of strategies that allow them to attend to information from different sources.

When they are embedded in continuous text, letters and words provide different kinds of information and support than they do when the child encounters them in isolation. The syntactic patterns of the language and the meanings of the text narrow the possibilities so that it is easier for readers to select and use the graphic symbols to take words apart as needed. Clay's (1991a) theory takes into account that reading is a complex

Analyzing Text Reading	
Example 1 Text: Can you put a hen in a pot? Child: Can you put a chicken/rooster/h/h/h/hen in a pot?	**Analysis** The child's first two attempts made sense and were structurally acceptable. However, he noted that the word in text looked different from his choices, and he worked to resolve this difference by using the initial letter and possibly more of the word and/or the meaning.
Example 2 Text: A purple elephant can reach in high cupboards. Child: A purple elephant can reach in high (long pause) cupboards. "That's a funny word. It starts like cup but it doesn't sound like cup. But cupboard is the only thing that would make sense there."	**Analysis** The child's verbalization of his problem solving suggests that he is aware of several approaches to phonological information. It also reveals that he knows that the word must make sense in the text even when he has resolved the pronunciation.
Example 3 Text: We must get rid of that mouse! Child: We must get rid of that mouse! "Look!" (using his fingers to frame the word mouse). "That looks like house!"	**Analysis** Having produced a meaningful and linguistically acceptable response, the child is sharing his awareness of words that share the same printed pattern.

FIGURE 12-1   Analyzing Text Reading

process in which we use multiple sources of information, including:

❚ The way space is used (space divides clusters of letters so we can read them as words).

❚ The way words are put together to form phrases and sentences (probabilities are lowered because we know the "rules" of grammar).

❚ The visual spelling patterns of words (we become familiar with many likely patterns and can see and understand them at a glance).

❚ The redundancy of words, where some meanings are given in several ways (as in two cents, where both words signal a plural).

We also attend to many different levels all at once:

❚ The discourse level, in which we are constantly processing the whole meaning of the extended piece of written language, relating one kind of information to another later in the text.

❚ The phrases and structures of the particular part of the text we are reading at the moment.

❚ The words and parts of words that we encounter and interpret.

■ The letter clusters and letter-sound combinations that we use to process individual words as needed.

Readers Use Visual Information

Reading involves recognizing and using the visual patterns in print and relating those significant patterns to the meaning and structures of our particular language. All of the systems of information must "match up" in a smooth, cohesive way while we are reading specific print on a page and putting together in our minds the meaning of a whole story or informational piece. Reading really involves thinking on several levels, all of the time, while our eyes move left to right along a line of print, seeing letters, letter combinations, and words in sequence.

In the task of learning to read, young children face three big challenges related to the serial order and the hierarchical structure of our printed language (Clay 1991a):

■ The English language is written in a serial order from left to right.

■ Print information is organized in a hierarchy of levels (letter, letter cluster, word, phrase, sentence, text) and the reader must know which level to attend to at a given time to be effective and efficient.

■ Attention must be given to serial order and the appropriate level of the language hierarchy *at the same time*.

Meeting these challenges is quite an awesome task for the beginning reader. In fact, the reader must divide attention.

When reading continuous text, children begin with the "message," taking in a sentence, its phrase structure, word elements, and parts of the word all at once. As they read, they are practicing the structure, meaning, words, sounds, intonation, and punctuation. They can pause and study any feature on any level of linguistic analysis, while keeping relationships between levels

intact. Focused word study while reading, however, should be relatively infrequent in practice (Adams 1990). Students' reading abilities are best advanced when they use texts in which most of the words are manageable (Rosenshine and Stevens 1984). Therefore, if students are stumbling on too many words, they probably need an easier text.

Visual Information and New Words

Readers gradually become able to use visual information without much conscious attention. The following selected categories will illustrate some ways in which young readers use visual information when reading and/or ways in which teachers support this process. Examples from early readers are provided for each category.

Initial and Final Letters

Teachers find that initial and final letters are good starting points for a child's analysis of words when reading. The examples in Figure 12-2 demonstrate a child's and/or a teacher's attention to initial and final letters.

In the first example, the child likely used the picture to predict *sucker*. However, when noticing the initial letter, he used some more information from the text, the initial letter and its sound, to immediately correct his choice. Note that he did not have to sound out the word; his sampling of visual information gave him an acceptable, meaningful substitution for his first attempt.

In Example 2, the child did not overtly monitor when he said *lion* for *tiger*. Perhaps there was little or no difference in the meaning for this child. Therefore, the teacher interacted in such a way that the child was learning an important principle—first letters are helpful when reading.

Example 3 illustrates the way a teacher can draw attention to the use of an initial letter without neglecting meaning. She acknowledged the use of one source of information, in this case meaning. She then challenged the child to use more than one

Using Initial and Final Letters While Reading Text

Example 1
Early evidence of child using beginning letter when reading.

Child: Can you put a *sucker/l/l/lollipop* in your mouth?

Example 2
Early teacher/child interaction about using beginning letters when reading.

Child: [Reads *lion* for *tiger*.]
Teacher: That sounds okay, but it doesn't look quite right.
Child: Tiger.
Teacher: How do you know that's *tiger*?
Child: Starts with a *t*.
Teacher: Okay, of course. *Tiger* starts with a *t*. Those first letters are important, aren't they?

Example 3
Teacher attending to use of initial letters without neglecting meaning.

Child: [Oral reading of text made sense but was not accurate.]
Teacher: I like how you're trying to make it make sense. Let's check the first letter and see if it looks right. It has to make sense and look right. Try it again.

Example 4
Early teacher/child interaction about ending letters.

Child: [Said *dog* for *dogs* and then corrected himself.]
Teacher: I like how you checked the end of the word. That's good when you can check the beginning *and* the ending.

FIGURE 12-2   Using Initial and Final Letters While Reading Text

source, in this case visual information, specifically the first letter.

In the fourth example, the teacher simply confirmed the child's attention to final letters. Her acknowledgment directed the child's attention to yet another source of visual information that may be helpful in solving problems.

Inflectional Endings

Teachers also find that most children learn very early about letters and letter clusters that are known as *inflectional endings*. The examples in Figure 12-3 illustrate the ease with which children seem to acquire this understanding about how words work. In example 3, the teacher and child were attending to more than the understanding of *ed* in the final position. The child was also developing a sense of possibilities about language that was not distorted by overemphasis on regularities.

Letter Groups or Chunks of Information

Good readers use phonological information from several levels of language, not just from the sounds of letters. Readers use letters, digraphs, clusters, syllables, prefixes and suffixes, root words, phrases, and so forth. Therefore, their uses of print-sound relationships are varied and are not limited to letter-sound associations. All readers tend to work in clusters or chunks when possible (Adams 1990; Clay 1991a; Treiman 1992). "Children may more readily learn links between groups of letters and groups of phonemes. Reading and spelling instruction that begins with larger units may be more successful than instruction that begins at the phoneme level" (Treiman 1992, 102).

Using Inflectional Endings While Reading Text

Example 1

Child noticing and using inflectional ending *ing* when reading.	Child:	(reading text) Jumping here, jumping there. Jigarees jump everywhere! (comment) Look! It's like in *going*! It ends the same way—/ing/.

Example 2

Teacher supporting child's use of the known inflectional ending to correct his reading.	Child:	(Text says: Ben helps Dad with the washing.) (Reads) Ben helps Dad with the wash—no, washing.
	Teacher:	Nice work. You used *ing* like in *going* to help you fix that up—and fast!

Example 3

Teacher/child interaction about endings.	Child:	(Text says: The lion walked up and down.) (Reads) The lion walk/walk-ed/walked . . . (comment) Hey, that sounds like a *t* instead of a *d* at the end.
	Teacher:	Sure does. Sometimes that *ed* ending says *t* like in *walked* and in *jumped*. But other times it sounds like a *d* like in *played*. That's good for you to notice. It may be different for different words.

FIGURE 12-3   Using Inflectional Endings While Reading Text

Good readers effectively search for different sources of visual information in print and shift rapidly to using chunks or patterns of information because it is more efficient. As shown earlier, the *ing* cluster is rarely segmented by beginners; it functions as a unit that organizes perception as soon as it is in the reading or writing vocabulary of the child. The child has to expend less energy and attention with larger pronounceable units.

The example in Figure 12-4 demonstrates the use of letter groups when children are taking words apart on the run while reading a new text. The child is using chunks of information rapidly to figure out new words within the meaningful context of a story.

Natural Breaks in Words

When we think of the components of words, we usually think of letters. However, in speech there are several kinds of natural breaks in words, such as a syllable break, an inflection break, prefix or suffix breaks, and onset and rime breaks (Goswami and Bryant 1990). As shown in the examples in Figure 12-5, children can use these breaks to assist them when reading texts. In all four of these examples, the child and/or the teacher were attending to natural breaks in words, in these cases syllables or onsets and rimes. Some of the syllable breaks were in fact prefix or suffix breaks.

Readers and writers also use correspondences based on units such as onsets and rimes (Goswami and Bryant 1990). In a one-syllable word, the onset comprises the letters up to the vowel, and the rime is represented by the vowel and all letters that follow the vowel. In example four, the child knew both the onset and the rime, yet did not initiate the problem solving. The teacher drew the child's attention to this way of generating new learning from existing knowledge.

Using Clusters of Letters While Reading Text

Example
Child analyzing new words using clusters of letters.

Child:

The boy tried to /r/ea/ch/—reach—the top /sh/elf/—shelf.

FIGURE 12-4 Using Clusters of Letters While Reading Text

Analogies to Known Words and Word Parts

It is important for children to understand that they can use their core of known words and known features of words to get to new words by analogy (Bruck and Treiman 1992; Ehri and Robbins 1992; Goswami and Bryant 1990). When children understand that words that have sounds in common also frequently share spelling sequences, they have a powerful way to figure out how to read and write new words. Younger children are considered by many to be capable of using analogies in reading if they are linking to their known words (Goswami and Bryant 1990; Baron 1977).

When a first-grade reader came to the word *landed* in a story, he appealed to his teacher that he did not know the word. She asked, "What do you already know about that word?" He immediately said, "*and*, oh, *land*, no *landed*." The following day he was reading a different book. He encountered the word *sandwiches* and cried out, "There it is again! *S-and-wiches!*" He had learned an important generative principle—that he can use what he knows about known words and known word parts to solve new words.

Children use analogy in unique and personal ways. They can use both their personal known vocabularies (the reading vocabulary and writing vocabulary) to solve new words. They also use clusters of letters from their personal corpus of known words to get to new words (see Figure 12-6).

In all three examples, the teacher was providing assistance for the child to learn that he must use what he knows to problem solve on new words. Again, this principle of generative learning will facilitate his future, independent learning.

Choices Among Alternatives

As children acquire understandings about how words work and how they can be taken apart on the run when reading stories, they also have to be willing to explore alternatives and choose among those alternatives. Independence comes from being able to operate flexibly using many sources of information effectively and efficiently. The example in Figure 12-7 illustrates the kind of flexibility, in this case about phonological information, needed by good readers. The child's first pronunciation of *most* was the predictable one. Yet he knew that choice was not an acceptable one, and he was free to explore other alternatives rapidly to solve the problem.

In order to choose among alternatives, a child must have opportunities to explore words and how they work. The child must flexibly accept exceptions and ambiguities within our language in order to be free to try other possibilities. This does not mean that rules and exceptions need to be systematically taught. It means that children should be flexible enough to try something else when their first trial is unsuccessful, and that they need a growing repertoire of what the most likely possibilities may be.

Running Records

Teachers can observe evidence of a child's use of visual information as the child reads

Using Natural Word Breaks While Reading Text

Example 1
Child analyzing a new word using sounds and syllables.

Child: (Text says: Purple elephants look different.)
(Reads) Purple elephants look /d/d/dif/er/ent, different.

Example 2
Teacher demonstrating use of syllables as natural breaks.

Child: (Text says: And it makes an excellent coat rack.)
(Reads) And it makes an (stops).
Teacher: (Uses finger to expose *ex*).
Child: (Reads) ex.
Teacher: (Uses finger to expose *cel*).
Child: (Reads) cel . . . excel . . . oh, excellent!
Teacher: Nice work. You used the first parts and then knew what made sense. Good work!

Example 3
Child dividing a word into syllables for analysis.

Child: (Text says: It can stop traffic if you want to cross the street.)
(Reads) It can stop trucks (then used finger to divide traffic into syllables) traf/fic/—oh, traffic . . . if you want to cross the street.

Example 4
Teacher/child analyzing a new word using known onset and known rime.

Child: (Stops at the word "stall" when reading.)
Teacher: Do you see a part you know in that word?
Child: (Frames the word *all* with his finger.) All. Oh, stall!
Teacher: Absolutely. So you know that this was *stall* by using a part that you already know. Keep reading.

FIGURE 12-5   Using Natural Word Breaks While Reading Text

text. Running records are a tool for ongoing assessment developed by Clay (1993a) to code, score, and analyze observable reading behaviors of young children. The teacher sits alongside a child and uses a simple coding system to record the child's exact responses as the child reads a book or story. Every attempt at problem solving, every error, and every self-correction can be analyzed to see how the child extracts information from print and uses letter analysis, syllabification, visual analysis by analogy, and syntactic and semantic information. Each word has several identities—orthographic, phonemic, grammatical, or semantic. The teacher can see how the child uses these identities and how the child checks one against the other (Clay 1991a).

The example in Figure 12-8 demonstrates how a teacher, while taking a running record of text reading, can observe for evidence of a child's use of visual information. This limited sample of a child's reading provides evidence of using letter clusters to quickly analyze words. There was also some evidence of flexibility with phonological information; however, his responses to some multisyllable words, even those with known parts, were less consistent. Additional analyses of running records for this child could provide the

Using Known Words to Get to New Words While Reading Text

Example 1
Teacher prompting to use known words to get to a new one by analogy.

Child:	(Having trouble with the word *shook* within a text.)
Teacher:	You know a word like that. You know *look*.
Child:	Shook!
Teacher:	Right! Now use what you know!

Example 2
Teacher/child interaction about using a cluster of letters from a known word to get to a new word when reading.

Child:	(Text says: He didn't get a bath. He got a shower.)
	(Reads) He didn't get a bath. He got a (stops).
Teacher:	You can get that word started. It starts like your brother's name, *Shawn.*
Child:	/sh/, oh, shower!

Example 3
Child/teacher analyzing a new word using known word and known chunk.

Child:	(Stops at word *bigger.*)
Teacher:	What do you know that might help you?
Child:	(Pointing to *big.*) big.
	(Pointing to *er.*) er.
	Oh, bigger!

FIGURE 12-6   Using Known Words to Get to New Words While Reading Text

teacher with important information about how he is using visual information to problem solve on the run while reading text. The teacher would then know how to assist the child in attending to print within continuous text. As Clay (1991a) notes, "The significant question at any stage of progress is not 'How much does he know?' but rather 'What operations does he carry out and what kinds of operations has he neglected to use?'" (313).

Other Activities

What children have opportunities to learn when they write has some relationship to opportunities for learning when reading (Clay 1982, 1991a; Teale and Sulzby 1986; Tierney and Shanahan 1991). While the relationship between reading and writing is not perfect, the store of knowledge that children use for spelling words is similar to the store of knowledge they use for reading (Treiman 1993).

Writing requires the child to deal with the distinctive features of letters, to learn about words and how they work, to acknowledge the importance of letter order and spatial concepts, and to learn about conventions such as punctuation and capitalization. Therefore, much learning and many operations needed in early reading are practiced in another form in writing.

Writing is a "building-up process," complementing the visual analysis of text reading, which is a "breaking-down process" (Clay 1991a). In essence, "It is about how the child takes words apart while reading a text. The constructive processes involved in writing provide numerous opportunities for children to learn about print and how language is written down" (Askew and Frasier, under review).

Children also need multiple opportunities

Choosing Between/Among Alternatives

Example

Child choosing between two alternatives.	Child:	And mŏst/mōst purple elephants are very good at games.
	Teacher:	I like the way you changed it when the first one didn't work. And you did that fast, too!

FIGURE 12-7   Choosing Between/Among Alternatives

to explore print and to learn how words work. In addition to learning about letters and words within the guided reading lesson while reading continuous text, children can benefit from other activities during the day to learn how letters and words work. Young children benefit from activities with magnetic letters and other manipulative activities with print. Word study or ABC centers, sorting activities, word walls, and word ladders may also contribute to their understandings about how words work (see Fountas and Pinnell 1996; Pinnell and Fountas 1998). There is also a joy in learning about printed language when the child is an active participant.

Visual Information and Reading

Examples in this chapter demonstrate that teachers can guide children in learning about the details of print and about the many kinds of visual units in print. Clay (1991a) suggests three considerations for teachers. First, teachers must find ways to gain the maximum benefit without spoiling the story. As stated earlier, focused word study while reading, however, should be relatively infrequent in practice (Adams 1990). Second, teachers must continue to check on whether children are increasing their control of the various kinds of visual information in print. Running records and other observations of reading behaviors will assist teachers in this check. Third, teachers should use what they have learned

about a child's control of visual information to replace unnecessary training exercises and drills with extensive reading of simple stories.

Assuming the child knows how to use particular kinds of visual information, the teacher will require the child to use this knowledge when reading, asking the child to do any of the following that are appropriate:

■ Find the error.
■ Try some alternatives.
■ Look at visual cues.
■ Sound parts of the word.
■ Make a choice.
■ Be flexible and change the response.
■ Be self-sufficient in solving the problem (Clay 1991a, 301).

Clay (1993b) cautions teachers to engage in only as much "taking words apart while reading" as is needed to foster visual analysis of the words within the book. It is only used when necessary and should relate to the problem the child is currently solving. We need to avoid the temptation to teach using examples that have no relation to *this* child's need to solve *this* word in *this* text.

The teacher must also create an expectation that the reader will actively work on a problem that is within the child's reach. The good reader is always actively *working* to solve problems quickly while reading. The work should not be hard. In fact, when it is not hard, the reader can proceed more efficiently and learn more about the process.

Observing for the Use of Visual Information While Reading

Interaction		Analysis
Text:	When he was a little boy, he lived in New York.	Child quickly chose between alternatives for *lived* to make it make sense, showing flexibility with phonological information; quickly used first letter of *York* to mediate appropriateness of possible response.
Child:	When he was a little boy, he lived [pronounced with long sound of *i*] lived [self-corrected] in New/Y/York.	
Text:	I went to stay with him each summer.	Child used known letter clusters *st* and *ay* to quickly blend the parts; same with *ea* and *ch*. Teacher showed child how to use his finger to look at word parts.
Child:	I went to st/ay with him ea/ch [stops].	
Teacher:	[Used finger to show two syllables of *summer*.]	
Child:	Summer.	
Text:	It was bigger than any place I'd ever seen.	Child used finger to divide word and used known parts to solve the word; used subword units of onset and rime to analyze *place* quickly.
Child:	It was big-ger [used finger to divide] than any pl/ace I'd ever seen.	
Text:	Maybe it was the biggest place in the world.	Child appealed before using what he knew. Teacher demonstrated importance of using what is known.
Child:	[Appealed on *Maybe*.]	
Teacher:	What do you know about that word?	
Child:	Be.	
Teacher:	What else do you know?	
Child:	May—oh, maybe.	
Teacher:	You have to use what you know—and do it all by yourself.	
Child:	[Reads] Maybe it was the *bigger*— [points to *est*] [Comments] It's not *er*. [Reads] Maybe it was the biggest place in the world.	Child self-corrected after expecting *er* on *biggest*, and then using visual information to search further.

FIGURE 12-8   Observing for the Use of Visual Information While Reading

When texts or tasks are too hard, the child will require more support from the teacher, thus taking the control away from the child (Askew and Fountas 1998).

We know that children attend to print in complex and uniquely personal ways. "It is, after all, one's personal experience with a word or spelling pattern that determines the strengths of the associations it evokes" (Adams 1990, 170). They differ in ways of extracting cues from print; they place varying dependence on letter analysis, syllabification, visual analysis by analogy, and syntactic and semantic information (Clay 1991a, 249). Therefore, "teaching" while a

child is reading text is connected to the child's current processing.

Note that in all examples shown in this chapter, the teacher does not have a teaching agenda about specific items of knowledge. Rather, the teacher is generally demonstrating or acknowledging ways in which the *child* can solve the problem at hand—using a strategy that will be useful in similar problem-solving situations in the future.

A Final Note

Reading is a complex process involving a network of strategies for solving text. As children read and write continuous text, they learn a host of things:

■ The aspects of print to which they must attend.

■ The aspects of oral language that can be related to print.

■ The kinds of strategies that maintain fluency.

■ The kinds of strategies that explore detail.

■ The kinds of strategies that increase understanding.

■ The kinds of strategies that detect and correct errors.

■ The feedback control mechanisms that keep their reading and writing productions on track.

■ The feed-forward mechanisms (like anticipation or prediction) that keep their information-processing behaviors efficient.

■ How to go beyond the limits of the system and how to learn from relating new information to what is already known (Clay 1991a, 326).

In order for children to engage in learning of this kind, they must be active processors of printed information. In addition, they must have massive opportunities to interact with rich texts. "The more meaningful read-ing that children do, the larger will be their repertoires of meanings; the greater their sensitivity to orthographic structures, and the stronger, better refined, and more pro-ductive will be their associations between words and meaning" (Adams 1990, 156). As children experience these rich opportuni-ties, they gradually become able to use visual information without much attention or con-scious effort.

Suggestions for Professional Development

1. For four weeks, take a weekly running record on one child who is reading at grade level. Ask your grade-level colleagues to do the same.

2. Examine the child's use of visual information (i.e., the use of letters and letter clusters) when trying to problem-solve a word. What is the child using, and what does he need to learn to use?

3. Look for changes across time in the child's use of visual information.

4. Share sets of records among colleagues at a grade-level meeting. Discuss observations from running records for each child.

5. As a follow-up, refer to Chapters 17 and 18 of *Word Matters: Teaching Phonics and Spelling in the Reading/Writing Classroom*.

Investigating Letters and Words Through Shared Reading

Susan Hundley and Diane Powell

Introduction

Shared reading enables children to behave like readers before they can actually read much for themselves. Shared reading is an excellent transition tool that helps children build those early, critical understandings and actions that must be acquired in beginning reading. In this chapter, Hundley and Powell define and describe shared reading. They discuss how shared reading can help children learn about directionality and print conventions, develop a reading vocabulary, and learn how to use visual information while reading.

Although when they first experience shared reading children are probably not doing much precise "decoding" of print, they are internalizing written texts and using conventions. As they participate more in shared reading, children start to notice features of words. In particular, they can connect what they are learning in writing and word study with the texts that they read together.

Teacher support for learning makes the difference. Hundley and Powell discuss teacher decision making in shared reading as well as the materials that support the process. They provide examples and descrip-

tions that help us understand how children move from their very first experiences with print to ways that shared reading can support more advanced readers.

Shared reading or shared book experience was first developed by Don Holdaway (1979) to replicate lap reading experiences of young children within the school setting and to provide support to those children with limited literacy experiences prior to school entry. He was particularly interested in helping children engage in purposeful reading activities while directing their attention to the role of print in the reading process. He made large-print books or "big books" as well as large-print charts that would allow the young children to join the adult in reading. Because the adult and children read together, the experience is called "shared reading." Holdaway worked closely with teachers to identify how they could provide support for children through a shared book experience. He and his colleagues determined that shared reading could be helpful when:

■ The choice of text is similar to the natural language of children and/or made easier to read by repetition and predictability.

❚ The first reading emphasizes enjoyment and understanding of the text.

❚ The teacher accepts and values different levels of participation as individuals read as much of the text as they can.

❚ The instruction reflects the children's interests, understandings, and needed reading skills.

In this approach, the children and teacher read and reread stories, rhymes, poems, and other texts. Often the children reread books, poems, and charts as well as reading new material. Each time they reread familiar text, children are able to notice new and different information. New material provides children with the opportunity to use what they know how to do and to broaden their repertoire of reading strategies.

Benefits of Shared Reading

Shared reading provides many benefits to children. Reading interesting texts in shared reading, enables children to:

❚ View reading as meaningful and pleasurable.

❚ Develop a sense of story.

❚ Use what they know about the world and language to make predictions.

❚ Learn about how the English language is represented in writing, especially the directionality concepts and word-by-word match.

❚ Build a knowledge of and skill in using the multiple sources of information found within a text.

❚ Learn more about reading in a socially supported context.

❚ Become a community of learners with common literacy experiences.

❚ Accumulate a set of materials they can reread.

In this chapter we address teaching children about letters and words through the shared reading experience.

Changes Over Time

When teachers understand both the reading process and the strengths of the children, they are able to build on what the children already know and match the instruction to what they need to learn next. Fountas and Pinnell (1996) describe children's development of a reading process through readers' increasing control in emergent, early, transitional, and self-extending stages. Of course, children are never really in discrete stages. Rather, they show many characteristics over time that reveal patterns of increasing control. Figure 13-1 provides an in-depth description of several essential skills necessary at each stage.

Learning About Directionality and Print Conventions

As a whole, print conventions are early learnings for children, and therefore teachers should focus their instruction with emergent readers not only on directionality concepts but other print conventions such as word-by-word matching and the use of space to define word boundaries. Emergent and early readers need to be taught how to differentiate letters from words and discriminate letter features so they can use this print information to help them check their own reading. Generally, teachers should begin teaching early readers about punctuation and specialized print (e.g., bold type); this instruction should continue across all stages as children encounter more types and uses of punctuation.

Developing a Reading Vocabulary

As children develop a reading vocabulary, they shift from a limited high-frequency reading vocabulary at the emergent level to a more extensive, complex, and specialized vocabulary at the advanced stage. This development is the result of initial instruction

	Emergent Readers	Early Readers	Transitional Readers	Self-Extending Readers	Advanced Readers
Directionality and Print Conventions	• Print carries the message and has a variety of uses. • Where to start reading. • Top-to-bottom and left-to-right movement. • Return sweep to left. • Read the groups of letters. • Word boundaries are defined by the spaces. • Discriminate letter features. • Difference between letters and words.	• Print appears in various layouts. • Print is smaller in size and closer in spacing. • Language expressed in print increases in length and complexity on the page. • Punctuation is a signpost for meaning. • Specialized print is a signpost for meaning.	• A minimum of conscious attention to print unless something unique occurs. • More forms and functions of punctuation. • More forms and functions of specialized print.	• Print is used differently in specialized genres. • Titles as a signal for connected meaning within extended text.	• Print conventions related to more complex specialized texts.
Building a Reading Vocabulary	• A few high-frequency words plus the child's name. • The principle of order; a word is constructed left to right in sequence. • The constancy principle; a word remains the same when the same letters appear in the same order.	• More high-frequency words that become characterized by more challenging visual features. • Giving of minimal attention to already known words. • Alternate letter forms don't negate the constancy principle. • A system for learning more words.	• A reading vocabulary that increases in complexity.	• A reading vocabulary that is more content specialized.	• A more content-specific reading vocabulary.
Using Visual Information While Reading	• There is a link between oral language and print that can be checked through word-by-word matching across a line of text. • Known words are used to visually check against meaning and language.	• The eyes can do the voice-print match without finger support. • Increased known reading vocabulary is a useful checking device. • Use of letter information (often beginnings and/or endings of words) to monitor reading. • The visual analysis of words using some letter-sound knowledge. • Larger chunks of visual information can be attended to rather than smaller units.	• When it is helpful to devote more attention to visual information. • Use only as much visual information as needed to solve problems. • Visual analysis of words using a variety of methods including analogy. • Problem solving of more complex words through visual analysis. • Integrate the use of visual information on the run in concert with meaning and language.	• How to quickly and flexibly use visual information on more complex words. • How some units of visual information such as affixes carry meaning within themselves. • Words that are spelled the same may have different pronunciations and meanings. • Particular visual formats signal genre or text categories.	• How to quickly and flexibly use information on more content-specific text. • How to work with words that are constructed by putting several meaning units together. • How to decide what roots and bases of words may be when the derivatives are not spelled the same. • That uncommon spellings may be used for dialect variations.

FIGURE 13-1   Learning About Visual Information

that focuses on principles of word knowledge such as order and constancy. Early on, teachers will help children learn that a word is written with specific letters in a left-to-right sequence, and that every time that sequence of letters occurs, the word remains the same. Children can later apply the processes they learned to use on simple words to acquire a reading vocabulary of greater size and complexity.

Learning How to Use Visual Information While Reading

As children are learning about directionality and print conventions as well as developing a reading vocabulary, they are also learning how to find and fix reading errors, figure out or problem solve new words, and read with phrasing and fluency (Clay 1991a). It will be important in shared reading experiences for teachers to help children use visual information in order to note errors and to figure out unfamiliar words. It is always helpful to teach children to use visual information in conjunction with meaning and language with prompts such as, "Check to see if what you read looks right and makes sense." The outcome of this teaching will be children who demonstrate flexible use of meaning, language, and visual information while reading.

For emergent readers, reading is characterized by the use of word-by-word matching and a few known high-frequency words to self-monitor or self-check. At the early stage readers begin to use detailed letter information to monitor, problem solve, and self-correct their reading. In order to figure out new words, they use some letter-sound knowledge and larger units of visual information within the words. With a strong foundation for problem solving using this kind of information, children in transitional, self-extending, and advanced stages work to quickly and efficiently apply their knowledge on more challenging words. While continuously bringing together the information sources, children extend their understandings to include how some units of visual information carry meaning within themselves. Although this occurs more extensively at the self-extending stage, early and transitional readers also encounter words with meaning carried in the visual representation (e.g., *to, too, two*). Moreover, through the reading of increasingly challenging texts, the advanced reader learns about and is able to use morphological information. A child at the advanced level will be able to use affixes as well as root and base words to construct the meaning for unknown words (e.g., *medicinal* from *medicine*).

Making Good Teaching Decisions

When engaging readers in a shared book experience, teachers will want to select a text that will help children use what they already know and help them learn something new. To do this, carefully evaluate the amount of text and its layout on the page so that this aspect of the reading does not create a challenge beyond what the children can reasonably handle. Additionally, consider the following: illustrations, vocabulary, concepts, language structures, and how the author presents the story. With all this information in mind, teachers can select a text that is slightly harder than the readers can read independently. Because the reading is done together, each child is supported within the group context by more capable others. Also consider the format of enlarged print charts, big books, and overhead transparencies.

When planning for shared reading, teachers will need to gather other useful materials such as pointers and masking devices of varying lengths and sizes. It is important to use pointers that allow all the children to see the shared text. Use of pointers changes over time from deliberate word-by-word matching to simply sliding the pointer beneath the text to encourage phrased and fluent reading. Masking devices, as described by Holdaway (1979), are used to clearly demonstrate to children features of letters, words, and other visual information within the quantity of print found on a page. Holdaway suggests that "it is vital that when we choose to talk about some detail of print every eye is observing *that* detail at the same time as the accompanying sounds are uttered. Only then are we teaching that crucial eye-voice-ear link which makes print intelligible in the earliest stages of reading" (76). There are a number of masking devices that teachers may want to try with children during shared reading:

■ A *sliding mask* allows teachers to focus on a particular part of the print, such as a letter, word, or word part. It is an especially useful tool for helping children sequence their visual attention left to right across a word and can also be used for confirming predictions using initial letter sequences.

■ A *window mask* may be used to locate specific visual features, such as letters, letter clusters, words, and punctuation. As teachers and children use window masks to isolate print detail, the readers are able to look more carefully without the distractions of surrounding print.

■ A *hinged mask* is used to look at visual detail displayed on an overhead transparency. Oak tag strips are attached to a frame surrounding the text and are pulled through the hinges to reveal the text as it is read.

Examples of all three types of masks can be found at the end of this chapter.

Teachers will also want to gather tools such as different sizes of Post-it Notes to cover and uncover words and word parts, and various sizes of highlighter tape, a brightly colored transparent tape that can be placed on words or word parts.

Teaching Emergent Readers

For children at the emergent level, teachers should consider the characteristics of the shared reading text in relationship to what the reader controls and what the reader

needs to learn how to do next. Consequently, selections should have limited print per line or page, language that is similar to the natural language of children, and illustrations that closely match the words.

The initial reading of the whole selection is for enjoyment and meaning making. In subsequent readings, story meaning remains at the foundation of the experience, and teachers thoughtfully direct children's attention to useful visual information. Teachers can consider the following as a possible instructional sequence for emergent readers:

■ Read together several times the selection entitled "Good Morning To You" (Figure 13-2). Point deliberately below each word.

■ Ask a child to come up to the chart and point appropriately as the group reads.

■ While rereading "Good Morning To You," substitute different classmates' names. This will allow children to begin to use some visual information since they often come to recognize early on the names that are important to them.

■ When children have greater familiarity with the text, call them to the chart to locate the high-frequency word *to*. Ask children to frame the word using their hands or a masking card. This practice will help them develop the ability to use visual information for monitoring or self-checking purposes. In this manner, the children begin to learn early on that what looks right is checked with what sounds right and makes sense.

Teaching Early Readers

As children move to the early stage, teachers might select slightly longer and more complex texts, keeping in mind that shared reading opportunities at this level will be designed to help children use more letter-sound knowledge for monitoring and problem solving new words. The selected texts will also provide more high-frequency words

FIGURE 13-2   "Good Morning To You"

for the children to locate and use while reading. For example, teachers might want to structure a teaching-learning sequence at the early stage similar to this:

▌ Engage the children in a first reading of "The Fly" (Figure 13-3).

▌ In order to help children learn how to make predictions and check their predictions using the print, cover a few words that can be reasonably anticipated by the group. As they read, the children predict each covered word. Ask, "What letter would you expect to see at the beginning of the word _____?" Each predicted word is then uncovered so the children can check their predictions with the visual information they see in the text.

▌ In subsequent readings, call for the children to locate known high-frequency words and help the children use letter-sound

information to sort out meaningful substitutions they make (e.g., *meat* for *ham*).

As children gain more competence, teachers will want to focus their attention to larger units of visual information they are encountering while reading (e.g., *fl* in *fly*, *gr* in *grocery*, and *n't* in *didn't*).

Teaching Transitional Readers
Moving into the transitional reading stage, children come to know when they need to look more carefully at the print detail and how much visual information they need to attend to in order to monitor the reading or problem solve an unknown word. Not only do the readers demonstrate these competencies, but they also have a variety of ways to work with the visual information. They can sound words letter by letter, look for and use larger units of visual information while reading, and begin to problem solve new words by considering a word they already

The fly made a visit to the grocery store. Didn't even knock — went right in the door.

GROCERY

It took a bite of sugar, and it took a bite of ham, Then it sat down to rest on the grocery man.

FIGURE 13-3   "The Fly"

know and linking that knowledge to a new word. Teachers might consider a teaching-learning sequence like this in the transitional stage:

■ Read the poem entitled "New Shoes" together (Figure 13-4). Slide the pointer under the text to facilitate phrased, fluent, and expressive reading.

■ Within this first reading, ask children to predict a few words that have been carefully selected and covered. As the children share possible predictions, uncover the words so they can attend to whatever visual information they find useful to determine the actual text (e.g., if they say *Mother* for *Mommy* in line four, they will use visual information at the middle and/or end of the word to confirm or discount the prediction). This process of bringing meaning, language, and visual cues together while reading helps children bring together information sources on the run. Alternatively, teachers can stop at a word that will be a challenge to the readers and ask them how they might go about figuring out the word (e.g., *wear*). One child might say, "That word looks like *bear*

so it must say *wear*." Another one might say, "I tried *wear* (pronounced as *we're*) and it didn't sound right, but it was close enough to help me think of *wear*." This will encourage children to try different ways of working with the visual information.

■ On subsequent readings call on children to slide the pointer while they attend to the punctuation as a means for improved understanding of the text.

Teaching Self-Extending Readers

Self-extending readers are using visual information in more flexible ways and on more extended, complex texts. Further, they are reading a wider range of genres, and visual information may be represented in ways not previously encountered. These readers are learning how to monitor, problem solve, and self-correct when the words within the text do not have regular sound or spelling patterns. Because many of the words found in texts for self-extending readers are multisyllabic in nature, children may be called on to figure out words syllable by syllable and by using affixes and roots or bases. Although children may be able to problem solve words

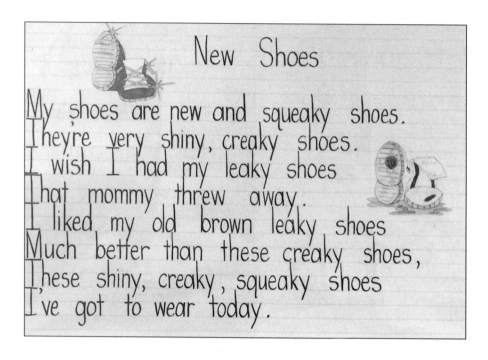

FIGURE 13-4   "New Shoes"

quickly while reading a text, at this level they will need to judge more astutely the meaning of words from the context. They will read words that look the same but are pronounced differently and have different meanings (e.g., "The *wind* is really blowing," and "Don't forget to *wind* the clock"). They will also encounter words that do not look the same and mean different things, but are pronounced the same (e.g., *there, their, they're*). When using shared reading with self-extending readers, teachers will want to help children learn how to decipher visually complex words and to use these words to construct the meaning of text, which will help them extend understandings beyond their present experiences. A teaching-learning sequence for a shared reading experience within this stage could be:

■ Read together the poem entitled "Weather" at the end of this chapter. The poem might be reproduced on an overhead transparency with print that allows all the children to see the enlarged text at the same time. When the reading has been completed, ask the children to discuss what the play on words has been.

After they have identified the author's use of *weather* and *whether*, help them discover that the different spellings, though pronounced the same, signal different meanings. In line five, assist the children to explore how two words with the same spelling carry different meanings (e.g., *weather*).

Teaching Advanced Readers

Advanced readers have to think very little about the letter-sound relationships within words or about visual patterns unique to the English print code. Rather, their new ways of using visual information require them to think about the meaning carried within word parts to figure out unfamiliar words with similar visual patterns, such as using *mort* to problem solve *mortician* or *mortuary*. An advanced reader not only would need to use *mort* to figure out *mortician*, but also would need to bring to the problem solving an understanding of how *-ian* signals a person, while *-ary* signals a place. Advanced readers will be learning much more about morphological information as well as word origins. In the teaching-learning sequence for an advanced reader,

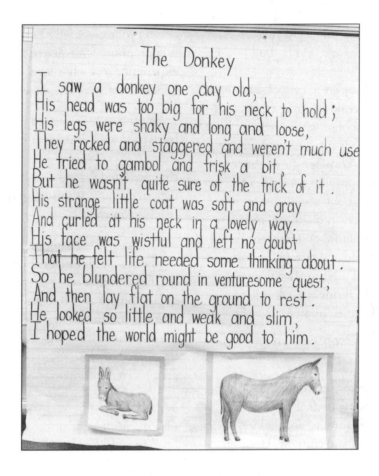

FIGURE 13-5 "The Donkey"

the shared reading experience might consist of the following:

❚ Read and reread "The Donkey" (Figure 13-5) several times for enjoyment and initial understandings.

❚ When the poem is familiar, begin to use it to teach the children more about linking visual information to meaning. Because some sophisticated vocabulary is not made clear through the context of the poem, provide opportunities for children to use resources such as dictionaries to extend their vocabulary. Ask them to find definitions for *gambol* and *quest*.

Also within the poem are several words that include morphemes to study, such as *ly* in *lovely*, *ful* in *wistful*, and *some* in *venturesome*. There are several avenues a word study of this sort may take. In one instruc-

tional technique, teachers could identify the morphemes for the children and have them use the dictionary to search for the meaning of each ending part. Using that information, they could then create lists of words that contain the morphemes. Another approach would be to have children find as many words as possible with each type of morphological ending and then generate the meaning of the morphemes from their lists.

Summary

To ensure positive outcomes from shared reading, teachers must understand the reading process, know how to observe children for the changes they make over time, and know how texts can support or challenge the learning (Clay 1991a). The best teachers of the reading process are the children themselves, who provide evidence of how reading knowledge and skills build over time.

It is essential to sensitively observe and record what each child is doing while reading and to use these observations when planning for and conducting shared reading experiences. Also consider how the children's writing may provide evidence of what they are noticing about visual information. Use this information in planning and in selecting texts that allow children to use all they know how to do and provide opportunities to extend them a bit further through instruction. Your decisions are central to the forward progress of the children.

Suggestions for Professional Development

1. With colleagues in your school, look at several shared reading texts. Discuss the texts with regard to format, vocabulary, language structures, and content. Decide among yourselves whether or not each text is appropriate for a shared reading experience and what level of readers will benefit most from the experience.

2. Select a text for shared reading that you have used with children in your class. With a group of colleagues, share the teaching that occurred during the shared book experience and ask them to discuss the teaching moves.

3. Collect writing samples from your classroom. With one of your colleagues, carefully analyze what the children know about and are able to use regarding visual information in writing. Based on what you see in their writing, discuss how you might use shared reading to help them learn more about visual information.

4. As a follow-up, refer to Chapters 2 and 17 of *Word Matters: Teaching Phonics and Spelling in the Reading/Writing Classroom*.

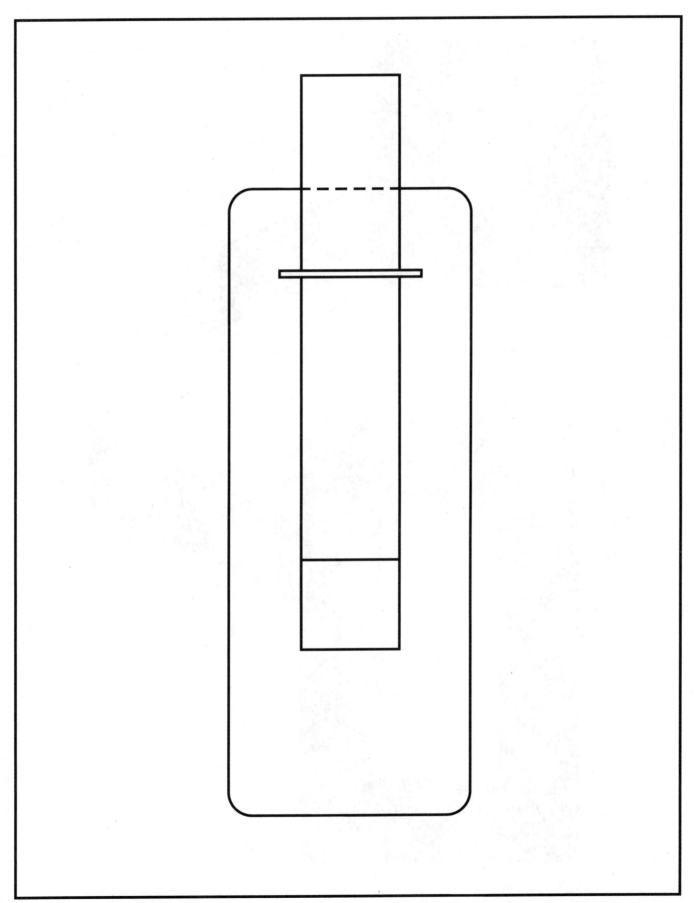

Figure 13-6   Sliding Masks

Figure 13-7a   Window Masks

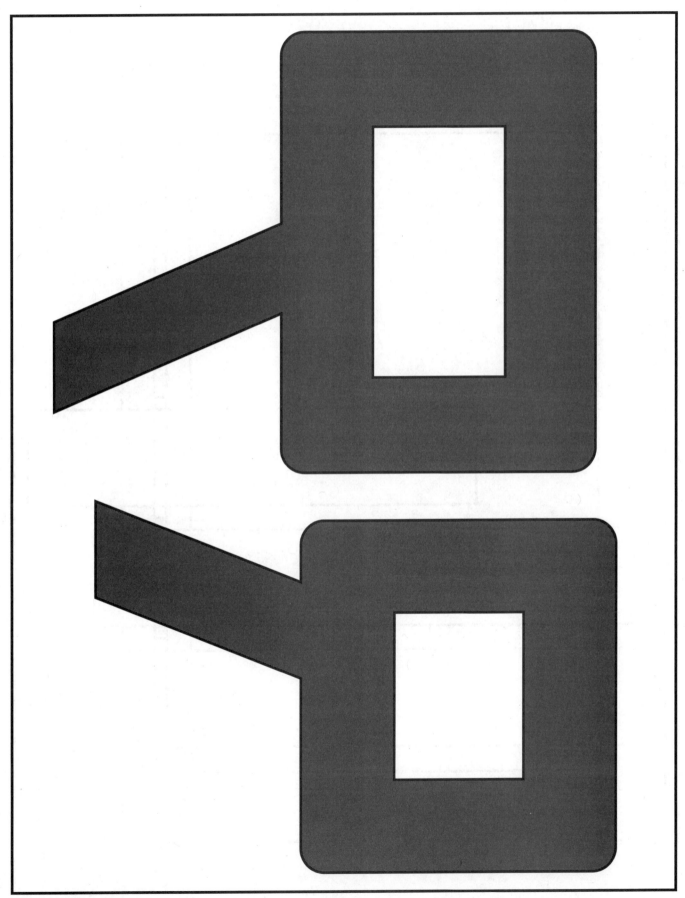

Figure 13-7b   Window Masks

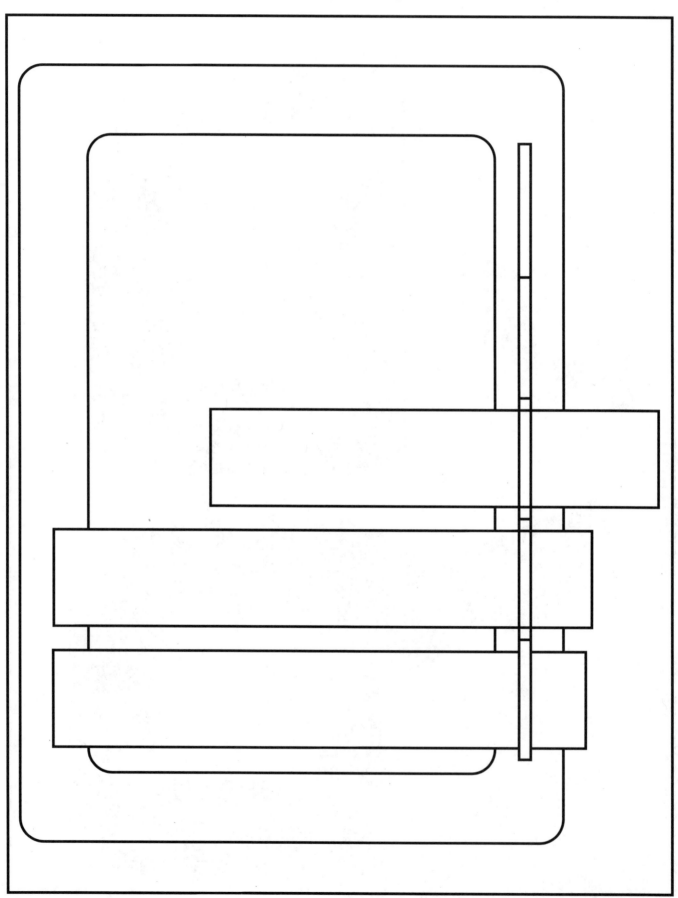

Figure 13-8   Hinged Mask

Weather

Whether the weather be fine
Or whether the weather be not,
Whether the weather be cold
Or whether the weather be hot,
We'll weather the weather
Whatever the weather,
Whether we like it or not.

—Anonymous

Figure 13-9 "Weather"

5

Expert Voices: What Does the Research Say?

In this book we have presented conceptual schema for connecting three curricular strands, each of which includes active teaching and learning of the surrounding skills related to word solving. A literacy curriculum has many facets and many avenues for learning. Each of the instructional contexts that we provide supports learning in a unique way. How can we as teachers sort out the complexities of providing such a range of learning activities and approaches? We run the risk of fragmenting our curriculum and offering piecemeal activities. A classroom program that is built on unconnected activities will not be effective.

In *Word Matters*, the companion volume to this book, we presented ideas for thinking comprehensively about the curriculum for helping children become word solvers. We said that the instructional program must be research-based, coherent, comprehensive, and founded on how children learn over time. And we advocated a shared vision for achievement in word learning, with specific benchmarks to help us in mapping children's progress in learning.

Educators have turned to researchers for assistance in sorting out these complex questions. While sometimes the research has been helpful, often it has been confusing. There are many voices, many perspectives on the role of phonics and spelling in the language arts curriculum. In this section, we strive to understand the cacophony by listening to voices in the field of literacy education that address the controversy. We start with the knowledge that phonics is an essential part of the reading process and spelling is a key aspect of the writing process. We also maintain that reading and writing are language processes and that far more is involved in word solving than the application of a few simple rules. The process is complex, and we must treat it as such.

A thoughtful examination of the research of the last few decades helps us consider reading, writing, and word study as related contexts for learning the role of words in language processes and the principles of how words work. Wilde provides just such a look at the research on how children learn to spell. She synthesizes and analyzes the research on "invented" spelling over the last decades. She explains how the close, detailed descriptions of children's spelling provided researchers, educators, and parents with evidence that children were constructing language for themselves—hearing the sounds in words, making connections to the visual perception of graphic forms, and noticing and using salient features of words. This research helps us realize that children are capable of becoming literate at much earlier ages than had been previously thought. Furthermore, it demonstrated the importance of writing in the development of competent spelling.

Stokes examines the research in reading over the past decades. He recounts conflicting views to help us understand the debates in a constructive light. Stokes proposes reconciling the debate by designing a curriculum based on the multiple facets of children's learning.

Finally, we conclude this book by sharing our own voices on word matters. We summarize the major themes that appear in this book and return to our proposal for an effective curriculum based on how children become word solvers through reading, writing, and word study.

How Children Learn to Spell

Evidence from Decades of Research

Sandra Wilde

Introduction

Over the past decades, researchers have made valuable discoveries about the ways in which children develop their knowledge of the subtle complexities of spelling. From their close observations of children over time, researchers have discovered how children think about words and the task of writing, and how they learn to use even a limited understanding of sounds and letters to begin to represent their ideas in writing. For example, researchers have helped us understand that an important part of learning to spell is trying—taking risks, making attempts, and receiving feedback.

We have also learned from research that a child's early spelling shows us what the child knows at a particular point in time about letter-sound relationships. In this chapter, Wilde helps us understand that these early spellings are not wild or random guesses but systematic attempts to approximate words based on children's current knowledge about how the spelling system works. In other words, invented spellings are systematic and reflect the child's logic. Children's early spellings are partially correct and change over time; they reflect the children's knowledge about words and how they work. There are qualitative differences in children's attempts at spelling,

and we can gauge children's progress by noticing a closer approximation to the conventional spelling (for example, for *sister*, we might see *s*, *sr*, *str*, *sstr*, *sistr*, and *sister*).

Appreciating and encouraging this early process of inventing spelling does not mean neglecting conventional spelling. In fact, the opposite is true. As children work to construct words, they learn important principles that guide them in the direction of standardization, but, in the process, they are also learning to compose and produce text. If children were prevented from becoming writers until they could spell all the words accurately, they would miss valuable experience in composing texts that present their ideas and demonstrate their knowledge. Writing and spelling develop together; learning to spell is a lifetime process.

Consider the following invented spellings, which were the "best" spellings of the word *circus* by 195 first and second graders:

SRCUS (20)
SRKS (10)
SRKUS (8)
CIRCUS (6—second graders only)
CRCUS (5)
SRCKUS (3)
CRKS (2)

(fifty-four other "good" spellings occurred once each, while eighty-seven other children had less satisfactory spellings.)

When I show these spellings to teachers, they see them as a sign that the media are right: kids' spelling is deteriorating. Well, surprise! Ernest Horn collected these spellings in the late 1920s (Horn 1929). Children who are invited to write words that they don't know how to spell—whether in 1929 or 1999—will invent spellings based on their knowledge of language. The big difference between 1929 and now is that children today are encouraged by their teachers to invent spellings in order to express their ideas.

A few decades ago, we assumed that if kids were going to write, they had to know how to spell the words. There's been a truly revolutionary change since then: the use of invented spelling in classroom writing is widespread, and our knowledge about invented spelling has also influenced spelling instruction. Without invented spelling, primary-grade teachers would never have been able to apply the insights about the writing process that emerged from the work of Donald Graves (1983, 1994), Lucy Calkins (1986, 1991), and other pioneers.

Why has there been such a change in how we view the role of spelling in the writing process and, by extension, in how we view helping children learn to spell? Perhaps no other curriculum change has been more subject to misinterpretation by parents and the general public. These changes in our practice have come about not haphazardly but because of a rapidly expanding understanding of how children's knowledge about the spelling of English words develops. In fact, what we know about spelling development hasn't just grown, it's been transformed.

In providing this historical overview about invented spelling, I hope to provide educators with a sense of the theoretical and research underpinnings that inform current classroom practices in spelling. We'll start by

taking a brief look at how spelling was viewed before 1971, the year that began the paradigm shift (Kuhn 1962) of the last quarter century. A discussion of Charles Read's work (1971, 1975) will then provide the foundation for looking at how researchers and practitioners have conceptualized spelling in the 1970s, 1980s, and 1990s. I won't attempt to offer a complete review of the literature on invented spelling (which would be a book in itself). Instead, I'd like to share with teachers several typical and interesting examples of what we've learned about invented spelling once we started trying to see what was going on through children's eyes, with a particular focus on what's been written about instruction.

Prior to 1971, the dominant paradigm for spelling instruction assumed that it was a matter of learning words in a formal program. (That statement is, of course, an oversimplification of a lengthy history—see Hodges 1977—but it represents the heart of the mainstream conventional wisdom.) Fitzsimmons and Loomer (1978) compiled a comprehensive and influential summary of the research in this mold (including references only through 1969). They listed ten practices that were supported by research and ten (many of them the inverse of the first list) that were not.

Seen through today's eyes, the focus of most of this research is clearly quite narrow. For instance:

■ Words to be learned should be presented in list rather than sentence form.
■ High-frequency words should be studied.
■ The test-study method is better than the study-test method.

Virtually all of the practices discussed fall squarely within the paradigm of spelling as the learning of words from lists. There was no discussion of spelling in the writing process, the learning of self-selected words, the role of reading in learning to spell, and so on. (Interestingly, many teachers—although not usually spelling basals—still follow practices that were clearly not supported by even this very conventional vision of research, such as having children write words several times as a memory aid and picking spelling words from the curriculum.)

The typical classroom spelling scene before 1971, therefore (and changing only gradually after that), was one of list-based textbooks, spelling as a separate subject, and the assumption that words should be correctly spelled when children write.

The Beginnings: 1971

Charles Read, who published findings from his dissertation at Harvard (1970) as an article in the *Harvard Educational Review* (1971) and as a longer monograph published by the National Council of Teachers of English (1975), is acknowledged as the "founding father" of the invented spelling revolution because of his understanding that young children produce spellings that are rule-governed and reflect their evolving conceptualizations of how the sound system of English works. Read's focus, interestingly, was not on spelling but on phonology: the first sentence of the 1975 book reads, "The aim of this monograph is to present evidence that young children tacitly categorize the phones [sounds] of English, sometimes in rather surprising ways" (1). Read's innovation was to use the system of spelling that had been spontaneously invented by thirty-two preschool children as a major source of this evidence. (As a follow-up, he also conducted a number of explicit tasks of sound discrimination.)

Read's analysis of young children's invented spellings provided the profound insight of understanding those spellings from their inventors' perspectives: how does the child's conceptualization of this speech sound represent itself in written form? (Previously, examination of spelling errors focused mostly on categorizing them by how they deviated from the standard, such as missing or transposed letters, or by placing them in broad categories, such as phonetic and nonphonetic.) Some of Read's findings were unsurprising. (For instance, children tended to omit the vowel associated with the letters *r, l, m,* and *n* in words like *moth__er, littl__e,* and *op__en*). However, others were less obvious and, while not counterintuitive, hadn't previously been described with Read's attention to linguistic causality. Two of these spelling patterns are fairly simple to understand, but teachers still aren't as widely aware of them as they should be. (In conducting workshops with teachers, I'll sometimes share an invented spelling showing one of these patterns and ask how many first-grade teachers can explain why it occurs. Usually very few, if any, hands are raised.)

First, Read explained why children tend to use CH and J to spell /t/ and /d/ respectively before *r* (e.g., CHRAC for *truck* and JRAGIN for *dragon,* both examples Read's). Taking *tr* for an example, the /r/ phoneme changes the preceding /t/ (technically, affricates it) so that it's similar to /ch/; therefore the /t/ of *truck* is phonetically in between the *t* of *tuck* and the *ch* of *Chuck.* (An indication of this is that if you say "Chruck," it sounds pretty much like "truck," even though "tuck" and "Chuck" are clearly different words.) Similarly, the *d* of *drum* is in between the *d* of *dumb* and the *j* of *jack.* Therefore, when children come up with the spellings CHRAC for *truck* and JRAGIN for *dragon,* they're making just as logical a choice as they would be had they chosen the "correct" consonant. With increasing experience with written language, children will come to spell these sounds more traditionally.

A second spelling pattern Read saw was the omission of nasals (*m* and *n*) before other consonants, as in STAPS for *stamps* and PLAT for *plant.* (These are often referred to as *preconsonantal nasals*). When I ask teachers to hypothesize about why a child would leave out one of these letters, the usual response is "She probably doesn't hear it," implying a deficit on the child's part. But Read illuminated how this pattern is a result of the language itself, not any idiosyncrasy of the child. In normal speech, an /n/ (or /m/ or /ŋ/) before another stop consonant isn't as fully articulated as it would be on its own. There's *something* there, though—a nasalized vowel, which English spelling doesn't represent as such. Children therefore hear the difference between *wet* and *went*, but may not see an obvious way to represent it. (As a second grader once said to me after spelling *went* correctly but then erasing the *n*, "It's sort of like there's an *n* there, but not really.")

To confirm his commonsense assumption that hearing the difference between words with and without preconsonantal nasals wasn't the issue, Read asked kindergartners, "If you have a little piece of paper that you can paste onto something else, is it a *stinker* or a *sticker*?" He noted, "All of the children identified the correct word in each of seven such sentences, and they did not hesitate to tell me what I had already suspected—that the task was easy to the point of silliness" (1975, 57).

Rereading Read's work, I was struck by how he not only explained some of the features of young children's spelling that may seem unusual but also helped us reframe how we think about the issues involved. Thus he helped us see that invented spellings are not only not random, not only rule-governed, but also expressions of children's underlying knowledge base. This insight helps us view children's spellings not in terms of how they deviate from convention but in terms of how the child understands the sounds of English (and, secondarily, their relationship to alphabet letters). Read also provided us with his views on the implications of his work for helping children learn to spell—insights that still sound fresh today and are perhaps still too little practiced. A lengthy quote from Read (1975) serves as a good example of this:

A child who wants to spell *truck* with a *ch-* will not be enlightened by being told that *ch-*

spells "chuh," as in *chicken*. The child already knows that; in fact, the relation between the first segments of *truck* and *chicken* is exactly what he or she wants to represent. Nor will exaggerated (or exasperated) pronunciation of *truck* help much, for monolingual adult speakers of English are usually limited to pronouncing the two possibilities that our phonology allows. We will either insert a false vowel after the [t], which does away with the affrication at the cost of distorting the word [i.e., saying "ta-ruck"], or will exaggerate that very quality which the child wishes to represent [i.e., saying "ttrruck"]. Drill and memorization of words with *tr-* and *dr-* may help the child to learn such cases, but these techniques suggest that spelling is arbitrarily related to speech and can only be memorized. This suggestion is not true of either standard spelling or the child's own invention. Better, it would seem, to say something like, "Yes, *truck* sounds like *chicken* at the beginning, but it is also like the first sound of *toy*, and that's what we show by using a *t*." (77–78)

This quotation illustrates two themes that are as relevant as ever: the importance of the teacher's knowledge about why children produce the spellings they do, and the equal importance of building on what children already know. The central insight provided by Read's work, which has also provided the foundation for much of the research on spelling and insights about practice since then, is that invented spelling reflects knowledge, and that our curriculum should build on that knowledge. Yet the general public for the most part doesn't know this, and still responds as if the percentage of correctly spelled words on a test were the only information that mattered.

Charles Read wasn't the only invented spelling pioneer in 1971. Carol Chomsky, aware of Read's work, used an educator's perspective to make the leap to understanding the role of invented spelling in the writing process. As her title "Write First, Read

Later" (1971, 1972) suggests, she realized that children can write words before they can read them by thinking about the sounds in words and how they relate to the children's knowledge of letters. The crucial insight is that young children can write independently. Such writing is not likely to be correctly spelled, but Chomsky pointed out that there is time for that later; the important idea at this early stage is to encourage the children to construct their own representations of written language. Although Chomsky's focus was to make a case for writing as a precursor of and avenue into reading, her insights about the value of spelling for the young writer continue to be relevant, as seen in the following example.

A child Chomsky was working with chose to start the word *wet* with the letter *r*, since *wet*, for him, began with the same sound as the second syllable of his name, *Harry*, which he knew was spelled with an *r*. Chomsky also pointed out that he didn't know that *w* represents /w/, but only knew its name, "double-u" (usually pronounced /dubayou/). She commented about the importance of accepting Harry's judgments, based on his current knowledge base:

Had I said "No!" when Harry chose the *r* and insisted on *w* (which corresponds to no reality for him), he would have gotten that sad message children so often get in school: "Your judgments are not to be trusted. Do it my way whether it makes sense or not; forget about reality." . . . Far better to let him trust his own accurate judgments and progress according to them than to impose an arbitrariness that at this point would only interfere. (1971, 121)

This insight still sounds important and fresh in its advocacy of tuning in to where the child is and starting there.

Invented Spelling in Classrooms: The 1970s and Early 1980s

Appreciation for children's "invented spelling" did not catch on rapidly after Read's and Chomsky's early work. When I conducted an ERIC search using "invented spelling" as a search term for what had been written in the 1970s, I found only two references to articles, one by Carol Chomsky and one by Rhea Paul. (Marie Clay's 1975 book, *What Did I Write?* also came up in the search, but it includes very little content about spelling.)

Rhea Paul's article, "Invented Spelling in Kindergarten" (1976), described her interest in helping young children express their thoughts more independently than they could by dictating stories. Read's and Chomsky's work, which she cited, gave her a foundation for doing so, and Paul described how her students moved from writing the first letter or sound of a word, to writing the first and last, to representing vowel sounds but without much consistency, to using spelling that became more standardized, thus adding a developmental dimension to Read's mostly synchronic exploration of the phenomenon.[1]

Paul answered handily the concern that children who are encouraged to invent spellings will persist with them: "They seldom invented the same spelling twice! They seemed to attack each word as a new problem, often coming up with a different solution than they had found before" (199). She didn't worry about their often not being able to read back what they'd written, since what clearly mattered to them was the thinking process itself, not its final product.

In 1981 Mary Ellen Giacobbe's article "Who Says That Children Can't Write the First Week of School?" (1981a, 1981b) was published and became quite well known, particularly because of her work with Donald

---

[1]Read did divide his data into two groups—responses from children under six and responses from children six or over—but he didn't particularly focus on development.

Graves. It was around this time that invented spelling began to be encouraged more widely in classrooms, although it was still far from universal. Giacobbe's brief article appeared not in an academic journal but in the magazine *Learning*, which is widely read by classroom teachers.

She made the simple but powerful point that once children know the letters of the alphabet they can express themselves in writing; indeed, by the third day of school, all of her first graders were writing independently. Although from today's perspective this doesn't seem so earth-shattering, Giacobbe pointed out how it differed from the conventional wisdom of the time: "In my education courses, I had been taught that children must first be able to read and when they had a reading vocabulary they could begin to write" (101).

Invented Spelling from Various Perspectives: The 1980s

As invented spelling became more widespread, we began to read about explorations of it from a variety of angles.[2] A sampling of work from the 1980s that I'll discuss includes a comparison of invented and traditional spelling in the classroom, two looks at children's spelling strategies, a consideration of the role of social interaction in spelling, and two articles dealing with special populations: an analysis of children learning to spell in Spanish, and an informed look at dyslexic children's spellings. This represents some of the range of work during that very exciting and productive period.

I begin with the work of Linda Clarke (1988), who conducted an extensive comparison of invented and traditional spelling in first grade, a study that won her a Promising Researcher Award from the National Council of Teachers of English. Clarke

looked at students in four classrooms that had similar curricula. The only difference was each teacher's encouragement of using either invented or traditional spelling in writing. (All four classrooms included regular writing sessions and used basal reader programs with phonics.) Clarke's work is too detailed for me to share all of her findings here, but I'd like to highlight four of them.

First, the invented spelling group outperformed (at a statistically significant level) the traditional spelling group on several formal assessments of spelling and reading. (There were no statistically significant differences that favored the traditional group.) Clarke suggested the following explanation: "The superior spelling and phonic analysis skill of children using invented spelling suggested that they benefited from the practice of matching sound segments of words to letters as they wrote and from using their own sound sequence analysis" (307).

A second finding of Clarke's study is especially interesting since I think she underinterpreted her own data. Consider the table in Figure 14-1 (excerpted from Clarke 1988, 292); the figure refers to a writing sample from May, at the end of the study.

Clarke didn't discuss these particular findings at length, but her abstract says that the invented spelling group's "productions were significantly longer overall and contained significantly more spelling errors" than the other group's.

Have you already realized the important information that Clarke didn't mention? The correctly spelled words from the invented spelling group (rounded to the nearest integer) were 58 percent of 41 words, or 24 words per story; the traditional group's 94 percent of 13 words was only 12 words per story. Therefore, the invented spelling group spelled correctly about *twice* as many words

---

[2]Although I'm focusing on classroom and instructional concerns here, there was also a good deal of important research into spelling development taking place, a large portion of it based at the University of Virginia and summarized in Henderson 1981.

| **Final Writing Sample Results** | | |
Variable	Invented spelling group	Traditional spelling group
Written text length (number of words per child)	40.9	13.2
Percent of words spelled correctly	58.4	94.0

FIGURE 14-1   Final Writing Sample Results (Clarke 1988)

per story as the traditional group! (They also, of course, spelled many more words incorrectly.) The amended table in Figure 14-2 gives a fuller picture than the original one.

Clarke also has figures that help explain why the children in the first group were able to write so much more. The most commonly occurring behavior of the invented spelling group during writing time was unaided writing (31 percent of the time, as opposed to 6 percent of the time for the traditional group). In contrast, the most common activity for the traditional group was waiting for teacher help (18 percent of the time as opposed to 1 percent). Children who are encouraged to use their own spellings are, of course, able to be independent as writers and therefore write appreciably more.

Finally, Clarke also compared low- and high-achieving children from the two groups and found that most of the differences in post-test results could be attributed to the better performance of low-achieving students in the invented spelling group. It is often claimed that less-proficient students need a more structured program and will only be confused by invented spelling. For these children, however, constructing words helped them to acquire knowledge that they weren't getting in other ways. (And remember that both classes used phonics.) It's particularly cruel to deprive low-achieving children of a tool, invented spelling, that enables them not only to express themselves but to acquire information about spelling and phonics.

Another aspect of children's spelling, their strategies as they understood them[3], was explored by Radebaugh (1985). In interviews with children aged seven through ten, she discovered that good spellers especially used a variety of strategies: for easy words they felt their spelling was automatic, and for harder words they thought about the parts of words (e.g., *Dino* plus pterodactyls soaring produced DINO SOAR for *dinosaur*), used mental images, or thought about the sequence of letters or sounds. Weaker spellers, by contrast, had far fewer strategies; if a spelling hadn't been memorized, they typically described themselves as sounding out letter by letter. The importance of this brief but provocative report is the attention it gave not just to looking at children's spellings but to understanding the thought processes behind them.

In my own work in the 1980s (Wilde 1989), I also explored spelling strategies, in

---

[3]I should point out here that the term "spelling strategies" has been used to refer to two different things: the knowledge involved in producing spellings (such as that seen in letter-name spelling or overgeneralization of consonant doubling) or as used here to describe how children go about coming up with a spelling.

Final Writing Sample Results (Amended)

Variable	Invented spelling group	Traditional spelling group
Written text length (number of words per child)	40.9	13.2
Percent of words spelled correctly	58.4	94.0
Number of words spelled correctly*	23.9	12.4
Number of words spelled incorrectly*	16.1	0.8

*The figures in these two rows were not computed by Clarke.

FIGURE 14-2   Final Writing Sample Results (Amended)

this case based on close observations of two children writing in their third- and fourth-grade years. I discovered what I defined as a hierarchy of strategies, ranging from just dashing off a relatively poor spelling as a placeholder through asking others, using dictionaries and other written resources, thinking about the spellings you produce, and finally just knowing how to spell the word. These new kinds of information about spelling strategies are important both in helping us understand the varied spellings that children come up with and in showing us how we can help children expand their repertoire of strategies and their proficiency with them as they use spelling in writing.

Kamii and Randazzo (1985) added another dimension by looking at invented spelling in a social context, and they suggested that children's collaborative construction of spellings is in harmony with a Piagetian view of learning. In encouraging children to work together to figure out how words might be spelled, the authors were following the specifically Piagetian idea that "children construct knowledge by modifying their previous ideas, rather than by accumulating new bits transmitted from the outside, and the exchange of ideas among peers stimulates such modification" (124). These researchers shared a number of specific examples of five- and six-year-olds' constructing spellings as a group. For instance,

children took turns writing soup ingredients on chart paper as their classmates chimed in spelling suggestions, so that KUKABER (cucumber), for instance, was written with some discussion about whether to begin with k or q (understandably, c didn't even occur to them!), and whether or not to put an e before the r.

Although the authors don't present examples from older children, the process is similar; when children are free to converse as they write, they naturally turn to peers to help them remember how to spell a familiar word or figure out a new one. Why is this emphasis on social interaction important? Because it adds another dimension to a task that's typically considered to be either solitary (the child knows the spelling or invents it) or dependent on authority (the teacher, who knows how to spell the word, provides it). Spelling is most commonly seen as merely the memorization of arbitrary (or at best somewhat rule-informed) information, but Kamii and Randazzo point out that such social knowledge (i.e., that which relies on conventions rather than physical reality) still must be constructed by learners as a system of relationships (126). What the social dimension adds is the exploration of alternative hypotheses (about the spelling of particular words such as cucumber as well as the spelling of individual sounds such as the /k/ at cucumber's beginning) in a community of learners who can contribute and assess varied points of view, and without the definitiveness that the teacher can provide. Asking the teacher for a spelling cuts off the thinking process for the child; indeed, Kamii and Randazzo suggest two important pedagogical principles for social interaction with invented spelling: encouraging children to explore spellings together, and reducing "adult power and omniscience as much as possible, in order to encourage the exchange of viewpoints among children" (125).

This Piagetian viewpoint on learning to spell is especially significant for highlighting what learning to spell is all about and how educators should be supporting it. If spelling were merely a matter of transmitting bits of information, then drill and workbooks might seem an appropriate medium. But since the knowledge of a complex system is instead constructed by each learner, the learning process must be an active one. Collaboration with peers promotes an additional level of active thinking: defending one's own views and assessing those of others. Kamii and Randazzo note: "The exchange of ideas is better than an exchange with an adult because children have points of view that are more or less at the same level. The construction of knowledge is facilitated when a child tries to put his knowledge into relationship with ideas that are at a similar level" (125).

Although I'm focusing here on invented spelling in English, it's also important to realize that the phenomenon occurs in other languages; indeed, one would expect that it occurs in all alphabetic languages when learners are invited to construct their own spellings. (Read [1986] compiled findings from a number of studies of invented spelling around the world.) Hudelson (1981–1982), working with Hispanic children in the United States, revealed how the principles that we had come to see as underlying invented spelling were not limited to English. This look at Spanish spelling is valuable for teachers in the United States because so many people speak Spanish, and

also because it disproves the myth that Spanish spelling is completely regular in following the alphabetic principle.

Hudelson's analysis of the spellings of first- and second-grade Spanish speakers showed a variety of forces at work. Her first category of spelling patterns were those that reflected knowledge of letter names and sound-letter relationships, such as ABLAR for *hablar* (since *h* is silent in Spanish) and BAMOS for *vamos* (since *b* and *v* represent the same sound in Spanish). Other spellings reflected a variety of phonetic phenomena. Hudelson's final category, English words that are spelled with Spanish orthography and/or become part of the Spanish of the local community, especially illuminates how actively children use knowledge about language to create spellings. We can tell that first graders writing about something being FANI (*funny*) or about a VAICA (*bike*) are translating their pronunciation of English words into good spellings using Spanish orthographic rules. Another example is the second grader who writes of PENA BARA (*peanut butter*).

The value of adding a cross-linguistic perspective is its confirmation that invented spelling is a complex yet very predictable linguistic exercise that takes different forms with different spelling systems but that follows underlying principles such as relating sounds to letters. Regardless of what language is spoken, invented spelling is both a valuable thinking tool for children and a medium of expressing thought for children who are still too young to know the spellings of many words.

Louisa Moats's 1983 article, "A Comparison of the Spelling Errors of Older Dyslexic and Second-Grade Normal Children," is an important example of how the emerging knowledge base about invented spelling began to influence how we looked at kids who weren't succeeding as spellers. Although much previous research had focused on how dyslexic learners' spellings appeared to be quite deviant, Moats chose to compare dyslexic children's spelling with those of children who were younger but at a comparable level in their spelling development. (Her subjects were second-grade nondyslexic children and dyslexics—defined as students with at least a two-year gap between their normal intelligence and their reading ability—in grades four through eight.[4]) Through an extensive analysis of 810 invented spellings written by 54 children, Moats discovered very few differences between the two groups. In particular, she laid to rest the common notion that dyslexic children have particular problems with phonetic analysis and with letter order (i.e., reversals). Although their spellings may look less phonetically accurate than those of other children their age, this appears to be because of a developmental lag, not any inherent processing problem. As Moats put it:

> If dyslexic children at ages eight to ten . . . have achieved less than a second-grade level of spelling and reading skill, their spelling efforts may appear to be "dysphonetic" in that speech sounds are not well represented. The use of this descriptor, however, may falsely imply that a structural and/or functional deficiency in the auditory analytic aspect of spelling is causally related to the learning disability and is an enduring characteristic of the learner. (131)

Moats was thus critical of earlier researchers who attributed dyslexics' spellings to "underlying process dysfunctions" based not on any positive evidence of such but on an apparent lack of understanding of what normal developmental spelling looks like.

There were a few differences between the two groups. Although the dyslexic children were somewhat better at applying spelling rules and segmenting phonemes, the nondyslexic ones more often remembered high-frequency common words, which certainly suggests that the last instruction dyslexic children need is more work on phonics and spelling rules; they could perhaps be helped (as Moats suggested) to move beyond the single strategy of "sounding out," a strategy which in itself will make one a fairly inaccurate speller. One other difference between the groups was that about 15 percent of the dyslexic children (4 out of 27) had significant problems with letter formation and copying.

The importance of this article (and similarly of Nelson 1980) is that it indicated that our growing knowledge about invented spelling during the 1980s was serving not just to encourage more writing in whole-language classrooms but as an impetus for rethinking how we understood the language development of children often deemed to have underlying (and thus difficult to change) neurological deficits. Approaches to spelling in the field of special education don't appear to have been radically transformed by such insights (and indeed Moats's more recent work [1995] is relatively traditional), but certainly anyone who assesses the writing of struggling students without understanding normal developmental spelling is operating without adequate knowledge.

The 1980s, then, were a period of exploring spelling from a variety of perspectives that gave us a rich understanding of many facets of what had previously been considered a relatively mechanical and superficial aspect of language. Although correct spelling of words that one knows is indeed quite mechanical and superficial, its emergence and development in young learners is complex, fascinating, and amenable to classroom support that promotes active thinking.

---

[4]Note that this definition doesn't assume any particular etiology or process-based definition of dyslexia. Although some educators even question the existence of dyslexia as a clearly defined entity, Moats's article is nonetheless useful in suggesting what might be helpful with children categorized as being dyslexic.

Invented Spelling Today: The 1990s

By the 1990s, invented spelling was familiar to most elementary school teachers and widely encouraged in classrooms as part of the writing process. Also, spelling books—particularly mandated ones—had become far less prevalent, although that situation may be changing. In the place of spelling books, teachers were attempting to help children grow as spellers as part of holistic reading and writing programs. A number of books written for teachers (including my own) explored how spelling curriculum could grow out of what we know about development and how children conceptualize spelling (Laminack and Wood 1996; Wilde 1992, 1997). Some examples of writing informed by knowledge about invented spelling are a study of the effects of invented spelling versus formal study, suggestions for word study, probing first graders' understandings of spelling, and a six-year longitudinal study.

Gettinger's article, "Effects of Invented Spelling and Direct Instruction on Spelling Performance of Second-Grade Boys" (1993), is of special interest because it shows the extent to which even a researcher who seems well within a behaviorist tradition recognizes the importance of looking at invented spelling. Four children, two who were above average ability in language arts and two who were below average, had eight weeks, fifteen minutes a day, of direct instruction in spelling (six words a week) and spent eight weeks with fifteen-minute writing periods in which they were encouraged to come up with their own spellings. (Also during those weeks, six targeted words for the week were posted that they were asked to use in their writing, and the teacher corrected all of their first-draft spelling.)

The results were measured in tests of the targeted words, spelling accuracy in weekly writing samples, and overall quality of writing. Gettinger found that during the invented spelling weeks, the quality of the boys' writing was consistently better, their spelling in the writing samples was somewhat better, and they preferred what they were doing to the direct instruction weeks. The children did perform better on the tests of the targeted words during the weeks of direct instruction. Figure 14-3 shows a table I've extrapolated from Gettinger's data (286).

Interestingly, although the children certainly learned specific words during the weeks they studied them formally, it wasn't that much of an increase over how many they would have known if they hadn't studied them: a little more than two words a week. (With fifteen minutes a day of instructional and testing time, this amounts to thirty-four minutes of instruction for each word learned!) Although Gettinger recognized the many positive outcomes from the invented spelling weeks, she interestingly

---

Spelling Accuracy on Targeted Words

(Based on a weekly list of six words)

	Invented spelling weeks	Direct instruction weeks
High-ability	3.5	5.6
Low-ability	1.5	3.7
All 4	2.5	4.7

FIGURE 14-3   Spelling Accuracy on Targeted Words (Gettinger 1993)

didn't discuss the relationship between better knowledge of the targeted words versus the time it took to learn them (time that was also—as in some other classrooms with formal spelling programs—taken away from writing). This study illuminates how invented spelling has become widespread enough and is taken seriously enough to impact the work of a researcher who is behaviorist enough to refer to positive feedback about writing content and spelling as "reinforcement contingencies."

Invernizzi, Abouzeid, and Gill (1994), who come out of the spelling stages tradition begun by Henderson (1981), wrote about how teacher knowledge of children's spelling development can inform an alternative approach to spelling called *word study*. For instance, a child can sort words ending in /ch/ by the sound that precedes them (the table in Figure 14-4 excerpts the authors'), and then use this to develop some generalizations about spelling. Specifically, when /ch/ is preceded by a short vowel it tends to be spelled *tch*; if preceded by a long vowel or another consonant, it's spelled *ch*.

The authors also show how children's spelling is a rich source of understanding about how language works, as seen in a comparison of historical spellings with children's developmental spellings (Figure 14-5). In this figure, I've shown just two words selected from several in each group. It's striking that children's spellings at different ages explore possibilities that the language itself explored at different historical periods, such as the addition of a final silent *e* to indicate the sound of the previous vowel.

This excellent article not only provides a variety of theoretically sound techniques for teachers to use in bringing spelling more into conscious awareness, it also takes a stand in favor of such instruction. The authors quote Charles Read's comment (1991 in Invernizzi et al. 1994) that he "never imagined that invented spelling, as an activity in and of itself, would become so accepted" (155); neither did he expect (in the words of Invernizzi and her coauthors) that "invented spelling would take the place of an organized approach to spelling instruction" (156). The authors feel that most children need to explore spelling patterns at an appropriate developmental level in order to make spelling knowledge more conscious and systematic. They also make it clear that spelling must be an active thinking process. Teachers cannot tell children spelling rules but must help them extract the rules from their existing knowledge of words.

Weiner (1994), like Radebaugh in 1985, talked to children about their spelling strategies (using a puppet to stimulate writing and conduct a spelling test), but with a greater sophistication that reflected growth in our knowledge base about spelling over those nine years. These first graders' comments about spelling fell into nine categories, many of which clearly related to elements that dominate invented spelling at different developmental levels. For instance, Adam focused on sound-letter relationships when he was asked how he spelled *doll*:

Adam: Doll.

Puppet: Okay. How do you do that?

Word Sort with /ch/ Endings (Invernizzi, Abouzeid, and Gill 1994)

catch	coach	lunch
fetch	peach	belch
ditch	roach	gulch

FIGURE 14-4   Word Sort with /ch/ Endings (Invernizzi, Abouzeid, and Gill 1994)

Historical Spellings (Invernizzi, Abouzeid, and Gill 1994)

Principle of Written English	Historical Spelling	Students' Spellings
Sound	*Anglo-Saxon (1000 AD)* WIF (wife) HEAFONUM (heaven)	*Letter-name (age 6)* WIF HAFAN
Pattern	*Norman French (1440)* YONGE (young) SWETE (sweet)	*Within-Word Pattern (age 8)* YUNGE SWETE
Meaning	*Renaissance (1600)* FOLOWE (follow) MUSIKE (music)	*Syllable Juncture (age 14)* FOLOWE MUSSIC

FIGURE 14-5   Historical Spellings (Invernizzi, Abouzeid, and Gill 1994)

Adam: D.

Puppet: How come?

Adam: 'Cause it makes the D sound.

Puppet: Like how?

Adam: Duh. (322)

Children also talked about relationships between spelling and meaning, even if their knowledge wasn't very highly developed. For instance, Sarah, intending to write *clothes*, wrote CLOSE and commented, "There's two kinds of clothes (close). The clothes they wear and close the door, but [laughs] I don't know if there's a difference how to spell them!" (322).

Weiner also heard pertinent explanations from children who were writing words that they knew how to spell. After Paul wrote *get* on a test, the following dialogue took place:

Puppet: Why did you spell it like that?

Paul: Because I heard it.

Puppet: Heard what?

Paul: Get.

Puppet: Did you hear each sound?

Paul: Nope.

Puppet: What did you do?

Paul: I just wrote it out.

Puppet: You mean you keep that whole word in your head?

Paul: Yep.

Weiner's article is an excellent example of contemporary research on spelling because its consideration of the spellings themselves is grounded in developmental theory, while the developmental information is put in the context of the children's own understanding of their knowledge and strategies.

Finally, we are fortunate to now have available a book-length longitudinal study of children's spelling from kindergarten to sixth grade (Hughes and Searle 1997). This important book is far too rich in its developmental detail to try to summarize, so I'd like to mention just a few interesting findings. First, as children moved beyond early "sound-it-out" spellings, they thought through a variety of information about how words are spelled, belying the common attitude that spelling should make a fairly rapid transition from sounding out to being correct. Children tried to give a phonetic explanation for spelling features that they'd noticed (Saul put two *l*'s in *yellow* because "I sounded out how long the *l* is"), but also remembered the look of words they'd seen in print. (Hana knew that *geese* has five letters and ends in *-ese*, even though she couldn't remember what the first vowel was.) Children also came to understand that there were complex and multiple ways to represent sound; they produced spellings such as REJOYCE ("*re* and then my sister's name") and SIGHN, which Kareem explained by analogy to *sight*.

Hughes and Searle also compared stronger and weaker spellers. One important finding is that all of the good spellers were avid readers, while the weaker spellers' literacy development tended to be slow in general. There were also, however, children they categorized as early readers but "stalled" spellers. Interview excerpts and writing samples from all three groups of children provide a rich picture of how spelling operates for them.

Hughes and Searle's book is well worth reading in its entirety—and indeed every article I've discussed here is also worth reading. If you wish to get a sense of the range of research on spelling since 1970, you get a good start by reading all of these studies, articles, and books—but you should also be aware that they represent only a small sample. The increased interest in spelling in itself reflects our transformed view of it; in some ways, researching spelling is a new field since we have such new tools and perspectives to explore it with.

The Years Ahead

Why is invented spelling so controversial? Is it because our kids' spelling has deteriorated rapidly? The National Assessment of Educational Progress (in Mullis et al. 1994) compared what percentages of words in a writing sample were misspelled in 1984 (when invented spelling was just beginning to be used in classrooms) and 1992 (when it had become quite prevalent). Figure 14-6 shows the findings. None of the differences from 1984 to 1992 were statistically significant, which means that the change from 8 percent to 9 percent at fourth grade likely could have been due to chance.

Yet invented spelling has come under attack from many quarters, and this backlash is perhaps the most significant feature of what is going on today with spelling, since it has affected curriculum and educational expenditures and in some cases limited teacher autonomy. In the classroom, however, the issues are the same as they've always been: How do I help kids become better spellers (particularly as part of the writing process)? and How do I talk to parents about spelling?

Although we have many answers to these questions, there is still more to be learned. I'd like to close by suggesting some possible future questions to explore in research and in classroom practice. There are still issues facing us now that the invented spelling revolution is nearly thirty years old. These questions all assume classrooms in which spelling is incorporated into the writing process.

Percentage of Misspelled Words		
Grade	1984	1992
4th	8	9
8th	4	4
11th	2	2

FIGURE 14-6   Percentage of Misspelled Words (NAEP 1994)

1. When children have been using invented spelling since kindergarten, how can we best support their development as they move into the upper elementary grades? Teachers are finding that children at that age often write very fluently but perhaps don't seem to care very much about whether their spelling is correct, and don't seem to be spelling as well as one would expect given their reading and writing. How can we help to develop more of a spelling consciousness at this age, so that children truly take responsibility for spelling because it's part of being a writer? (This idea differs from holding kids "accountable" for spelling, which is an external control.)

2. What kinds of curriculum are appropriate for kids who aren't succeeding in spelling? In particular, there's a danger of taking time away from free reading to focus on spelling, when reading is crucial. There's also a related question: What should teachers be doing to ensure that all students leave school prepared to function in a world that doesn't find invented spelling appropriate on the job and elsewhere? These concerns have the most impact on working-class students, who will by applying for the kinds of entry-level jobs in which spelling is often used as a screening device.

3. How can we assess spelling in the classroom and beyond? In the classroom, it's easy to know what to do (collect writing samples, analyze spellings, interview kids) but hard to find time. As for large-scale assessments, I believe it's an open question as to what would be most useful. The traditional standardized tests of spelling seem increasingly irrelevant given what we know about developmental spelling; what could we do that's more authentic but still possible on a large scale so that parents and communities can have

feedback about how kids in the aggregate are doing in spelling?

Our whole conceptualization of how to look at spelling has been permanently transformed. Any serious attempt to think about spelling curriculum and instruction has to take into account what we now know about spelling development and the role of spelling in the writing process. Research and practice will continue to expand this knowledge.

Suggestions for Professional Development

Other chapters in this book also provide examples of instruction in spelling based on observation of children. (See also Chapter 13 in *Word Matters*.) With colleagues, discuss Wilde's chapter and make connections to those other chapters. Consider the following:

- ❚ Did you find any surprises in Wilde's summary of the research? For example, in what ways did you modify your definition of "invented spelling"?
- ❚ What are the instructional implications of this body of research? For example, should we encourage "invented spellings"? If so, to what extent?
- ❚ How can we help children move toward standard or conventional spelling?
- ❚ What suggestions do the articles in this section provide for helping children use their own writing to learn about how words work?
- ❚ To what extent do the ideas in this section fit with the research Wilde summarizes?
- ❚ How can the instructional approaches in this section help children move forward in understanding how words work while at the same time encourage them to keep on making good attempts at spelling?

How Do Children Learn to Read?

Evidence from Decades of Research

William Stokes

Introduction

No one system of learning is adequate to support the complex actions related to literacy. The "great debate" is about how children learn to read and write and how we should teach them. Should we emphasize teaching letters and sounds or should we emphasize meaning in first-grade reading instruction? As teachers of young readers and as researchers, we know that our job is to help children learn to recognize and use the elements of words—that is, to become word solvers—while they also are guided by their understanding that reading and writing are meaningful and purposeful.

We know that we can create classroom programs to achieve those twin goals, but we also know that as professional educators we must be knowledgeable about the conflicts in the field and find ways to talk to our colleagues and parents about different instructional approaches. In this chapter Stokes explores the reading debate through a thoughtful examination of the research on teaching children to read. The controversies surrounding reading instruction have been with us a long time. By examining evidence over the past decades, Stokes helps us to understand the instructional choices that are ours today.

How do children learn to read and write? This question is simple and straightforward. And, because it has been studied for generations, we might reasonably expect substantial consensus among theorists, researchers, curriculum specialists, and teachers about how to teach reading, writing, and spelling in the primary grades. Unfortunately, no such consensus exists, and nowhere is this more obvious than in the controversies about the role of phonics instruction. Indeed, the debates have become so fierce and political recently that it is common to hear experienced educators speak of the "reading wars." In my conversations with new teachers and parents of children entering kindergarten and first grade, I have heard their concerns, confusions, even anxiety, about the choice of alternative approaches to literacy instruction. My intention in this chapter is to offer a kind of road map or guide to the current debates by briefly reviewing the essential elements of the debates and their historical context.

Throughout the 1960s, 1970s, and early 1980s, the "great debate" was usually presented as a choice between two methods for teaching reading: *phonics* and *whole word*. Both approaches share the goal of guiding children to learning the relationships between sounds and letters. The difference between these approaches centers on whether the relationships are taught explicitly through sets of phonics rules (e.g., "silent *e*" marks the long vowel in *bite* as distinct from the short vowel in *bit*) or through carefully prepared texts that would enable children to discover the relationships (yielding sentences like "The fat cat sat on the mat" or "Nan can fan Dan").

In the past fifteen years, the debate has usually been presented as the conflict between *whole language* and phonics. *Whole word* should not be confused with whole language, although some participants in these debates do confuse the two. Whole language offers a comprehensive philosophy for teaching; it is not simply an alternative method. I will discuss the essential features of that philosophy in a moment, but it is important to point out immediately that whole language is also concerned with helping children acquire an understanding of the relationships between sounds and letters—the difference lies in how this goal is to be achieved.

Most recently, a new term has entered the debates: *balanced approach*. It is sometimes offered as a compromise between whole language and phonics. Or, it may be understood as an effort to transcend the debates and return a measure of common sense to our understanding of the complexities of literacy and literacy development, including the details of learning to read, write, and spell.

The current debates tend to polarize and oversimplify the differences that do distinguish these alternatives. In the sections that follow, I hope to reverse this tendency and offer a richer context for understanding these controversies and the competing claims made by proponents for each side.

The Fundamental Dilemma

In principle, an alphabet provides a simple visual code for representing an oral language. An ideal alphabet would assign one letter to each sound (or *phoneme*) in the language; thus a spoken language could be written down and read by others who know the code. This requires some knowledge of the sounds of the language and the relationship between sounds and letters. The difficulty with English is that it departs significantly from an ideal alphabetic system. And, the acts of reading and writing are far more complex than merely manipulating a code.

Language is a complex natural and cultural system that relates sounds to meaning. By six years of age typical children will have substantially acquired their native language. This acquisition includes knowledge of sounds (e.g., to produce and perceive the differences between words such as *puzzle*, *puddle*, and *paddle*) and grammar (e.g., to distinguish "the boy hit the ball" and "the boy was hit by the ball"), as well as innumerable subtle features of the meaning and use of language in everyday communication (e.g., recognizing instances of promising, warning, and lying). And, if the children are members of a literate community, they may also appreciate the language of stories and books.

For example, when my daughter was about four years old, her favorite book was *What Do You Do with a Kangaroo* by Mercer Mayer (1973). She had heard the book read aloud many times, she had the entire story memorized, and she could recite the book while looking at the pictures. One day, when I was blocking a doorway she wanted to get through, she put her hands on her hips and said "Get out of my way, you old moose, you!"—a line from the story. I laughed, of course, and let her through.

Yet despite all the knowledge of language and books that this episode suggests, she still could not read the story herself. In fact, she would not become a reader for two more years. The question is, what did she need to learn to become a reader? She knew the letters of the alphabet (she could name all the letters). She could write her own name and that of the family cat and a few other words. She knew *stop* and *exit* signs and many product logos. She understood picture book stories read to her and once dictated her own story, which we made into a book. She understood many of the purposes of writing, including the making of grocery lists and the importance of a letter to Santa Claus. Yet at the age of four, she could not read independently or write anything more than a few words. What did she need to learn? Or, from a developmental perspective, what had to be acquired or achieved, before she could become an independent reader?

If learning to read were simply a matter of learning letter-sound correspondences, and if, for a given language, there were an ideal alphabetic system, then learning to read ought to be a rather easy task of learning a visual code for an already acquired linguistic system. Assuming that a child has substantially acquired the spoken language and has the requisite neurological, cognitive, and perceptual development to acquire the alphabetic code, then it would seem that learning this code might only require a few weeks or months to develop the necessary knowledge and processes to allow quite fluent reading of familiar words, ideas, and stories.

Under these conditions there would be little controversy about the place of phonics in reading instruction. The goal of reading is to construct meanings, and the acquisition of such a simple code would seem to support, rather than delay, access to meanings. Perhaps most children would acquire this code with very little direct instruction, if any. Literacy instruction in school would devote its attention to learning through reading, rather than learning to read.

Unfortunately, English is represented by an alphabet that does not permit an ideal one-to-one correspondence between sounds and letters. To begin with, there are roughly twice as many sounds as letters. Each letter is used to represent several sounds in different contexts (e.g., notice the *t* in *native, nation,* and *nature,* or in *bat, bath,* and *bathe*). Each

sound can be represented by several spellings (e.g., notice the "long *e*" in *be, bee, key, ski, sea,* and *baby*). Moreover, for historical reasons, there are hundreds of exceptions within our complex system of spellings (e.g., *maid* and *said,* or *hear* and *heart*). Experience has shown that many children require at least three years to acquire the written code for English. During this time, learning to read becomes the primary purpose of schooling, while exercising literacy to learn more about the world is largely deferred until mastery of the code is evidenced.

We should not be surprised that there is great controversy concerning how to best support literacy development. First, I'll describe the "phonics" point of view. Some educators, theorists, and researchers search for the most clever and efficient means to organize systematic instruction in honest attempts to speed the process and make it less arduous. Materials and procedures are developed to provide teachers with step-by-step guidelines for phonics instruction. Children who are having greater difficulty are gathered together and provided with even more intensive, systematic instruction to encourage the development of *phonemic awareness.*

Now, I'll describe the "whole language" perspective (see Weaver 1994). Other educators, theorists, and researchers search for ways to support literacy development by subordinating concern for the code to other levels of texts (e.g., words, sentences, whole stories, etc.). Recognizing that children accomplish the tremendously complex task of learning their native language without benefit of formal, systematic instruction, these educators search for means to help children extend those powerful learning systems to the development of literacy. Since language is acquired during use, and since meaning is seldom subordinated to form, the expectation is that literacy too can be acquired most effectively if meaning and communicative purposes are provided more attention. Greatest attention is given to children's gradual, natural emergence of closer approximations of adult competencies and to the role played by parents and teachers as competent models for the authentic uses of literate practices for social purposes.

It should be clear that both models represent sincere efforts to reach many of the same goals. It should also be clear that the differences separating the two views are not likely to be easily resolved. Supporters of the phonics approach tend to view it as scientific and precisely organized and tested, while critics view it as unnecessarily tedious and indeed destructive to authentic literacy. Supporters of whole language tend to view theirs as natural and joyful, leading to greater creativity and love of literature, while their critics tend to view that philosophy as a form of romanticism that will doom many children to poor reading skills and poor spelling.

As I suggested before, recent discussions of a balanced approach may offer a way out of this controversy. At the end of this chapter, I will consider what such an approach might entail. First, however, we should take a closer look at the history of phonics and the controversies about learning to read and write.

Origins of Phonics

When I first became interested in early literacy twenty years ago, a colleague recommended that I read Jeanne Chall's *Learning to Read: The Great Debate* (1967). It introduced me to the dispute between rival approaches to reading instruction, and it left me with the impression that the fundamental choices were phonics ("code emphasis") and whole word ("meaning emphasis"). Although the book clearly draws upon research and opinion dating from the 1910s onward, I got the impression that "the great debate" was a product of the 1950s and 1960s (the updated edition, 1983, adds an additional fifteen years of research and commentary to the debate). (See also Adams 1990.)

A few years later, quite by accident, I encountered Edmund Huey's *The Psychology and Pedagogy of Reading* ([1908] 1968). It quickly established that the debates over reading were by no means of recent origin. That book led me to F. W. Parker (1894) and the startling assertion that phonics dates back to the early sixteenth century. He argued that "the phonic method, as we all know, is over three hundred and fifty years old. It was at the time of its introduction a very profitable departure from the pure alphabetic method, and had its origins in some of the earnest minds that worked contemporaneously with Martin Luther" (196).

As a researcher and educator who was still new to these debates, I was astounded to discover that these issues were not merely recent technical arguments but had occupied educators for more than four hundred years. How did such a controversy arise and what sustains it? There are several replies to these questions, but it may be useful to point out a preliminary and rather surprising fact: there is no unique alphabet for the English language—written English employs the Roman alphabet.

Throughout the middle ages, scholars studied and wrote primarily in Latin, or chose to represent other languages, such as English, using the familiar Roman alphabet. As the English language developed, pronunciations, spellings, and grammatical forms experienced rapid changes, and dialect variations abounded, especially during the period of Middle English. By the beginnings of the emergence of Modern English in the fifteenth century, a highly complex system of written English had evolved (Balmuth 1982). Then, in the period of the Protestant Reformation of the sixteenth and seventeenth centuries, there were widespread efforts to increase literacy rates and to translate, print, and distribute the Latin Bible and other Latin texts in the languages of Europe, including English. The problem confronting the "earnest minds that worked contemporaneously with Martin Luther" was how to help the greatest number of people become literate.

In the case of Latin or related languages, such as Italian and Spanish, an ideal alphabet is closely approximated. For example, the letter *a* has a consistent relationship to a particular phoneme, /a/, as in *agricola*. When adapted to English, the letter *a* can represent a significant number of sounds (e.g., *fat, father, fate, flaw, plaid, beat, bear, said, laugh*). English has approximately forty-four sounds that make meaningful distinctions in the language (dialect variations can extend this number). There are, however, only twenty-six letters, and some of these, such as *c* and *x*, have values that overlap with the letters *s* and *k*. Consequently, English has evolved a very complex system for spellings, and that system has been a challenge to educators since the sixteenth century. This problem of an alphabetic representation of English led to the development of phonics as an effort to specifically teach the complex relation between English sounds and spellings.

New Approaches in the Nineteenth and Early Twentieth Centuries

A careful reading of the historical record for the past two hundred years will reveal that there was a nearly continuous stream of "new" approaches to reading instruction being offered by educators and publishers. The alphabet method is the most ancient approach. It was characterized by an emphasis on learning letter names and spelling words aloud—often in choral drill—until letters, syllables, and, finally, words were memorized. The *New England Primer*, first published around 1680, provided for this form of instruction for more than one hundred years. Webster's *American Spelling Book* continued these practices into the mid-nineteenth century: "students learned the names of letters . . . spelled and pronounced lists of two- and three-letter nonsense syllables, and then spelled and pronounced lists of words of various lengths before they began to read sentences orally" (Shannon 1989, 6).

McGuffey's *Eclectic First Reader for Young Children* introduced a phonics approach during the period from the 1830s to the 1920s. This was also supplemented by what was called a *phonetic* approach (Huey [1908] 1968), in which a modified alphabet was introduced so there might be a greater approximation of a one-to-one correspondence between letters and sounds. Thus, long and short vowels, silent letters, and *digraphs* (e.g., *sh, ch, th*) would all be explicitly marked to aid their recognition. Among these was Leigh's "scientific alphabet" (presented in 1873), which was incorporated into the widely used Funk and Wagnalls reading series.

As early as the 1840s, Horace Mann and other reformers influenced by the work of European educators, especially Pestalozzi and Froebel, advocated for a word method that would omit the drill and recitation associated with spelling and phonic approaches. Instead, emphasis would be placed on learning words with the aid of pictures, objects, sentences, and little stories. From the 1860s to the 1880s, the Oswego Movement fostered the word method, which was typically used in combination with alphabet, phonic, and phonetic methods.

With the gradual rise of the progressive education movement beginning in the 1880s, F. W. Parker advocated for reforms that would entail an even greater emphasis on meaning than the word method. At the core of his proposals was the assertion that "reading is thinking." He proposed a *thought* method through which all efforts were made to keep meaningfulness central to all specific procedures. He advocated that all concerns for reading and writing as skills be subordinated to an integrated curriculum wherein children studied science, history, literature, and other central subjects. Parker argued that reading and writing would be acquired in the context of these subjects. Moreover, he argued that all methods be used in combination provided that meaning remained the foremost concern.

Parker also advocated that writing and

reading be recognized as complementary. Children could be aided in learning letter-sound relationships not only in the context of reading interesting texts, but also in the context of their efforts to create their own texts. Parker boasted of having a library of ten thousand books written by children. In the process of creating these books, the children would of necessity have to attend to letter-by-letter representations of words. John Dewey and others in the progressive education movement carried forward Parker's innovations into the twentieth century, but competing theories and methods continued to coexist.

Recent History of the Phonics Debates

The debates about the teaching of reading became more fierce with the publication of Rudolf Flesch's *Why Johnny Can't Read* (1955), which offered an emotional polemic that tended to vastly oversimplify and polarize the large and complex realms of theory, research, and practice. All reading programs were cast categorically as either phonics or whole word approaches, and the latter was portrayed not only as an utter and absolute failure, but also as a threat to democracy and as evidence of conspiracies between publishers and educators. As Adams (1990) points out, Flesch "developed conspiratorial motives, alluded to communists, and made negative insinuations about the intellectual predispositions and capacities of females and minorities. Thus, not only was the debate politicized, but it was politicized on dimensions that were wholly irrelevant to the question of how best to teach reading" (25).

While the public debates became polarized and while researchers sharply disagreed with one another (see Carbo 1988; Chall 1989; Turner 1989), it is important to note that the differences between approaches were never absolute or categorical, but rather have been matters of emphasis. Competent teachers have always tended to make use of

multiple strategies for fostering children's acquisition of literacy and their development of specific skills. The textbooks themselves have tended to combine approaches.

Moreover, given the nature of local control of schools in the United States, at any given time every alternative approach to reading instruction is being practiced somewhere—and not just in small, isolated pockets. In this context, sweeping historical trends are perhaps little more than sweeping generalizations. In my experience over the past twenty years in eastern Massachusetts, in a region of several million residents distributed throughout more than a hundred communities, it is simply impossible to assert that one approach or another effectively dominated all or nearly all schooling for any period of time.

One community might have just purchased a new basal series, as Boston did in 1988, and be determined to implement a strict, intensive phonics program. Meanwhile, the neighboring city of Cambridge was just beginning to expand a whole language program beyond the confines of the few schools that had been experimenting with it since 1982. Other nearby communities were each following their own local concerns—some shifting in one direction, others in a seemingly opposite direction, and still others in yet another direction. And, of course, each teacher has her or his own history. Teachers certainly develop and change over their careers, but they also tend to reshape or transform their professional competencies rather than utterly replace past practices. It is easy to make too much of grand historical trends unless one also looks very closely at local events.

Chall (1983) suggests that by the 1940s and 1950s, approaches to reading instruction were dominated by the content of the basal reading series issued by publishers, and this content relied principally on the word method. Among these were the "linguistic readers" that sought to restrict the vocabulary in the books so that only words conforming to regular spelling patterns would be encountered in the earliest reading materials. It was proposed that children would naturally analyze the presented patterns, and therefore explicit teaching of basic sound-letter (or *phoneme-grapheme*) correspondences would be unnecessary (Fries 1963; Bloomfield 1933).

In the early 1960s, new versions of older phonetic approaches were offered. In some materials, the alphabet was reformed by adding letters or diacritical markings so that the differences in the sounds associated with the letter combinations (e.g., <u>ea</u> in *bear*, *earth*, *heart*, and *near*) were marked explicitly. Among these were *Distar* and *i.t.a.* or *Initial Teaching Alphabet* (see Chall 1983, 119–125).

Then, "from an almost unanimous preference for meaning-emphasis in the textbooks published before the 1960s," there was a "shift toward code-emphasis in the 1970s" (Chall 1983, 3). Code-emphasis approaches, developed from the 1960s through the 1980s, tended to be referred to collectively as phonics approaches, or even *the* phonics approach—as if there were only one. In fact, however, there were substantial disagreements about the detailed nature of the programs. Readers will notice that it is common today to modify the term *phonics* with any of several other terms: *explicit*, *direct*, *systematic*, *intensive*, and *extensive* are often used. These terms are used in contrast to *indirect*, *inherent*, *implicit*, *analytic*, and *embedded*. Add to this barrage of jargon the tendency of different writers to use the same terms differently, and it is little wonder that new teachers and parents are likely to be anxious about what program their young learners will experience.

Some programs call for beginning with long vowel sounds (because the letter name approximates its sound in a word, as the *a* in *ape*); others call for beginning with short vowel sounds (because these tend to be more regular in short common words, such as *bit*, *fit*, *sit*, etc.). All approaches must introduce the consonants, but there too, there will be disagreements about which and in what order with respect to the vowels.

More recently, there is renewed interest in a very old practice. Some researchers advocate for presenting words as composed of an *onset* and a *rime*. For example, *bake* would be presented as *b* plus *ake*, the advantage being that the child can be introduced to *word families*: *cake*, *fake*, *lake*, *make*, *take* (Adams 1990). Other researchers continue to recommend complete segmentation of words into phonemes (e.g., *s-t-a-n-d*) coupled with teaching *blending* (i.e., *sounding out*, then repeating smoothly as the word would ordinarily be pronounced).

Different publishers of systematic phonics materials may choose among these options, and further differentiate themselves by the extent to which words are presented alone or in sentences or in stories with or without pictures, and so forth. Separate workbooks may be included. And, there will be different emphases given to whole-class lessons, small groups (*ability groupings* or *heterogeneous groupings*), individual one-on-one instruction, and self-guided *seat work* with worksheets.

Another significant difference is whether phonics instruction is separate from or incorporated into instruction for reading comprehension, or indeed, for writing. I have visited many classrooms where separate times are scheduled for reading, for phonics, and for writing—other classrooms join all these together.

Yet another important question is the relationship between reading and writing, or between phonics programs and spelling programs. From the point of view of the learner, especially at the beginning stages, the task of decoding a string of letters is a matter of assigning the correct sounds to a group of letters. For example, consider this nonsense word, *steart*. Should the <u>ear</u> be pronounced as in *bear*, or as in *spear*, or as in *heart*? The writer, however, is presented with the problem of assigning letters to sounds—that is, encoding. Context cannot provide the same help in this instance. The child may wish to spell a word with the final sound *oo*, as in *boo*. Let's assume, for this example, that the child wants to spell a word that begins with *fl-* and ends with the *oo* sound. The child writes *fl*, then pauses to figure out the next letters. Possibilities include *flew*, *flu*, *flue*, or even, from the learners point of view, *floo* or *flo* or *flwo* (as in *too*, *to*, or *two*). Sound-to-letter correspondences are not sufficient. Knowing the intended meaning of the word is required. The question for code emphasis programs is whether to separate or join the teaching of decoding and encoding. Here again, different publishers will offer different options.

While explicit phonics approaches dominated throughout the last thirty years, alternatives also existed. Following the Open Education movement of the early 1970s, there was great interest in the *language experience* approach, which emphasized reliance on the learner's own language and experience, and usually included linking learning to read with writing children's own stories (see Edelsky, Altwerger, and Flores 1991). During this same period, psycholinguistic research in language development and speech perception was yielding new insights about natural language processes. In the language arts journals, the *psycholinguistics of reading* became a common topic throughout the 1970s and 1980s. There was also interest in *sociolinguistic* perspectives. And, during the same period, a few researchers and educators were paying more attention to the relatively neglected "second R," writing. The *writing process* became the center of increased attention by the 1980s.

From about 1980, there was great interest in *emergent literacy*. It was found that when preschool children are immersed in an environment rich in print, they soon discover that writing conveys meaning, has function, and is an aspect of everyday activities. Awareness may begin with product labels (e.g., the logo for a favorite cereal). It soon extends to road signs and other conventional symbols. While recognition of "wholes" clearly precedes the child's appreciation of the details of graphic representations, children soon progress to make finer discriminations (Weaver 1994). In Australia and New Zealand, and to some extent in England and Canada, work had been progressing toward what is known as *natural, developmental literacy learning*. As this work was joined with that of some researchers in this country, the term *whole language* emerged.

By the late 1980s and early 1990s, as whole language became the most talked about "new" approach, a reaction was also forming, sometimes referred to as a "back to basics" movement. Phonics advocates continued to publish research findings that suggested that direct systematic instruction to develop phonemic awareness and to teach letter-sound relationships was especially important for learners who exhibit learning disabilities. In the past few years, the "reading wars" have become ever more fierce, political, and even sometimes apocalyptic. The debates between advocates of whole language and phonics have become explicit features of national political campaigns and have even become elements of positions taken by some conservative religious organizations. The newest medium for these conflicts is the World Wide Web. In a very cursory search for Web sites that address either phonics or whole language, I located more than twenty-five hundred sites. I surveyed more than a hundred of these and found a full range of views including everything from thoughtful, reasonable arguments to utterly uninformed and vicious attacks. Viewing these, I could easily understand the confusion and anxiety many parents and members of the general public may feel concerning these issues.

Toward a Balanced Approach

Most recently, educators have begun speaking of *balanced approaches* in an effort to join the best elements of all the prior programs and perhaps to transcend the seemingly endless reading wars. Properly understood, whole language has always provided for direct instruction intended to guide children to discover the alphabetic principle and letter-sound relationships (see Holdaway 1979 and Weaver 1994). Phonics approaches typically include equal concern for comprehension and fluent reading of meaningful texts. All language arts teachers want children to love reading and to find their voices as writers. At the same time, it is recognized that, at some level, readers and writers of an alphabetic language need guidance to learn the sound system of the language (phonemic awareness) and learn the system of letter-sound correspondences. Newer developments in the field (e.g., *guided reading* and *interactive writing*) offer the greatest promise for establishing programs that explicitly balance concerns for meaning and communication with concerns for accurate and fluent reading and writing (see Fountas and Pinnell 1996). Under the impetus of state "curriculum frameworks" and similar "standards" issued by national professional organizations, school systems and individual teachers are being required to reexamine all their pedagogical practices.

Reading and writing are complex activities; like speech perception and production, they entail the simultaneous processing of information at various levels. Some versions of the phonics vs. whole language debate suggest that one requires a "bottom-up" model of processing, while the other requires a "top-down" model. Fortunately, it is not necessary to choose between these models. Reading and writing require the integration of information from several different levels—it is what cognitive scientists call a parallel processing system. Briefly, there are at least seven levels that must be considered:

1. *Graphic*—visual perception of letters and symbols.

2. *Phonological*—sound system of the language, phonemic awareness, phoneme-grapheme relations.

3. *Lexical*—words, morphophonemic system.

4. *Syntactic*—grammar of sentences and larger units of discourse.

5. *Semantic*—meaning, thematic structures.

6. *Communicative*—intentions, purposes, and pragmatic functions of texts.

7. *Cultural*—shared knowledge and belief that underlies all communications.

All approaches to reading and writing instruction should attend to all levels of processing since each supports the others. In those instances when it is necessary to isolate concerns for one or two levels, attention to other levels should not be long delayed.

Children should be encouraged to use all the resources available to them in their efforts to interpret print or to compose texts. When a child misreads a sentence such as "The car has a big engine" by replacing *motor* for *engine*, then we know that the child is being supported by context, but needs to focus more carefully on the graphic information. If a child should read "The whale could swim" by replacing *cloud* for *could*, then we know that the child is not attending sufficiently to structure and to meaning in context, as well as making a visually based error. As a final example, if a child reads "The pants began to tear" by pronouncing *tear* to rhyme with *fear*, then we know that the child is not attending to word meaning and semantic context. All levels of processing are required for comprehension and fluency.

A balanced approach to literacy instruction offers an opportunity to transcend the endless debates and return a measure of common sense to teaching and learning. Teachers and parents can be supported in the development of effective strategies that recognize the complexity of language and literacy; that connect reading, writing, and oral language; and that promote the development of skills, comprehension, fluency, voice, and appreciation for literature and for the power of written language to shape the world.

Suggestions for Professional Development

1. Stokes encourages us to "take a long view" of the debate over beginning reading instruction. To get perspective on the debate, assemble a group of primary teachers in your school and share the collective historical experiences of the group. Chances are, you will be including teachers who have taught for twenty to thirty years as well as those who are just beginning.

2. Share the controversies that are part of your own history, even if you have been teaching only for a few years.

3. Then, talk about the conflicts and pressures you face in your own classroom today. What do parents expect? What do administrators expect? What do fellow teachers expect? Refer to this chapter to gain a historical perspective on current conflicts.

4. Make an action plan for communicating to the public, parents, and/or administrators about the way you are teaching reading and writing in your classroom. Be sure to include the following:

- How are you helping children attend to word solving?
- How are you helping children know that reading and writing have purpose and meaning?

5. As a follow-up read Chapter 2 in *Word Matters: Teaching Phonics and Spelling in the Reading/Writing Classroom.*

Meeting the Literacy Challenge
The Role of Word Matters

Irene C. Fountas and Gay Su Pinnell

Introduction

In this final chapter we build on the two previous chapters, in which research is synthesized on spelling and reading. We examine five principles of literacy learning and describe a range of word-solving strategies. Our knowledge of the reading and writing processes and the word-solving strategies within them forms the basis for designing a curriculum that supports learners. Rather than swinging with fads and political movements, we need to refine our understanding and build on the evidence of children's learning. That means working over time to develop the theories and sound practice that will accomplish our goals. The authors of this book are educators who are working with teachers and children in classrooms. Their writing is based on research about children's literacy learning as well as their own experiences and observations. Though they have different interests and offer some different perspectives, you will find strong consensus in their view of the role of word solving in successful reading and writing.

Elementary schools that reflect the concepts in this book offer rich oral language and literacy programs for the children they serve. They are places where children talk, where they have conversations with teachers about interesting and important things, where they read and write for real reasons. Children in these schools spend the greatest part of their day talking, reading continuous text, and writing continuous text. Skilled, intensive instruction is provided, but this teaching is based on what children know and need to know at a particular point in time. And in these schools the children have the opportunity to use their own strengths in the learning process. In other words, the school meets children where they are, providing the level of support that is necessary for every child to be successful.

A Comprehensive Framework

At the beginning of this text we suggest a broad, three-pronged framework for conceptualizing a curriculum that helps children learn word-solving strategies across a range of instructional contexts. Children learn about letters, sounds, and words through meaningful encounters with text. Most of the literacy learning that takes place is based in children's experience with continuous text. In good classrooms, children experience a wide variety of high-quality texts. The quality of what they read and write is as important as the amount of time they spend doing so. Classrooms are supplied with books to read aloud and books that are arranged in a gradient for guided reading. There are books that provide information, books to enjoy, and books to take home. This supply of high-quality texts supports the children's own production of the written texts that are evident on the walls and display areas of the classroom and in published collections. Through the generous supply of written text, writing and reading are connected and support each other.

Reading

As children read the enjoyable stories and interesting informational texts that are provided, they are also learning something about how words work. They develop the ability to use phonics skills and other analyses to take words apart while reading for understanding.

Writing

In writing, children also work with authentic texts in formats suited to the messages they are constructing. They write continuous text where appropriate but also explore all other forms of writing, such as lists, planning charts, diagrams, and labels. As children become writers, finding their own voices in written language, they are also learning how to put words together using the rules and patterns of the language. They not only become spellers but they learn a range of strategies for checking on their own written work so that they can take satisfaction in the final product.

Word Study

In a rich language and literacy curriculum, language itself is worthy of study. Through enjoyable experiences in saying rhymes and chants, children develop the phonological awareness that helps them begin to analyze words in the language. They hear parts in words and become sensitive to individual sounds. The experience is extended through hearing stories read aloud and sharing the reading of poems and rhymes, so that chil-

dren connect their ability to detect sounds in words with the orthography or spelling of the language. Orthographic awareness is built through direct experiences with their own names and with group writing experiences that help them make oral-written connections. Word study involves children in the active investigation of words so that they can learn basic principles of how words are constructed.

Principles of Literacy Learning

This section of *Voices on Word Matters* summarizes a large body of research on how children learn to read and write. Over the last decades, we have learned much about these complex processes. We present five principles of literacy learning drawn from the writers of this book (see Figure 16-1). For each of these principles, we will focus on the development of word-solving strategies—that is, how children learn about letters, sounds, and words and how they use what they know as readers and writers. We believe that designing programs based on these principles will take us beyond the debate to a coherent vision of how children learn and what we need to do to ensure their literacy learning.

Reading and writing are complex language processes constructed by individuals.

Although common patterns in learning to read and write are evident, an individual's development is unique. Especially in early literacy learning, children make personal connections between oral and written language. They attend to what is meaningful to them. Their school experiences are important in helping them direct their attention and gradually generalize their literacy knowledge. We cannot simplify and compartmentalize literacy learning any more than we can isolate other kinds of complex learning. As Clay (1998) has stated, we need to create a literacy curriculum that supports many paths to the common outcomes that we desire.

Five Principles of Literacy Learning

∎ Reading and writing are complex language processes constructed by individuals.

∎ Readers and writers work at several levels of the language hierarchy.

∎ Readers and writers acquire and use a variety of flexible strategies to construct meaning.

∎ Reading and writing are different, but complementary, processes.

∎ Readers and writers develop self-extending systems that enable them to expand their literacy expertise while they are reading and writing.

FIGURE 16–1   Five Principles of Literacy Learning

Readers and writers work at several levels of the language hierarchy.

When we talk about reading, we mean that the individual is processing the written language of continuous text. In writing, also, the skill to be developed is the production of coherent, cohesive continuous text. Children may learn about letters, sounds, and words in the active, focused experiences that we have described as "word study," but the real goal of a literacy curriculum is to teach students to use word-solving strategies while reading and writing. That means that readers or writers are constantly shifting from the

meaning level to lower levels such as the particular word they want to write or read and the visual features of the letters in sequence back to the meaning level. Clay (1991a) calls this process "shifting gears."

Competent readers and writers shift gears easily, fluently, and without conscious attention. Literacy learners need constant experiences in reading continuous text so they can practice these cognitive actions. Their purpose, of course, is not to "practice" shifting. None of us reads or writes to "practice" simply so we'll get better. Even young readers are focused on the meaning and enjoyment of the written text; nevertheless, they are engaging in the kind of internal actions that are building a self-extending system or self-improving system.

Readers and writers acquire and use a variety of flexible strategies to construct meaning.

Strategies are the in-the-head processes that learners use to integrate what they already know with new information they are acquiring through their experiences. Strategies are not directly observable, but we can make hypotheses about these cognitive actions by carefully observing behavior. Readers and writers have a range of strategies that access information from every level of the hierarchy of language. They simultaneously use several sources of information, including meaning, language syntax, and visual aspects of words. The strategies are the actions by which they access and use all kinds of information to search and check while reading and writing. Within that process, word solving takes place.

Competent readers and writers are solving words all of the time. Sometimes word solving means analyzing or taking a word apart in order to read it; sometimes it means spelling it. It also means simply checking on what one has read or written. Even when we are reading and writing with high accuracy, a monitoring system, built through our knowledge of words and the language system, is constantly on the alert to detect and correct error.

Many words in reading do not have to be taken apart; they are solved simply because they are known. Readers continually expand their repertoire of words. We have emphasized the importance and usefulness of known words from the beginning. Even kindergartners who know the words *the* and *I* can begin to monitor and check on their own reading because there are some certainties within the text. In writing, known words assist greatly in the construction of the text. When words are not known, competent readers and writers solve them. Let's look

specifically at word-solving strategies in five useful categories.

Sound

Readers and writers use their knowledge of letter-sound connections, from simple to complex relationships, in the solving of words. They learn that you can read or write some words by thinking about the sounds (for example, *sad* and *cat*). At first, they learn some of the simple letter-sound relationships, such as relating one letter to one sound. In reading they may use the first letter of a word or one of the letters as a tool for solving the word in connection with meaning. Soon, they begin to see that there are patterns of letters that represent sounds. Children's early writing reveals stages of development in which they use letter names and letter-sound relationships to represent words or parts of words even before they know conventional spelling.

It is important for children to learn to hear the individual sounds in words as well as the parts of words and connect them to the graphic symbols. In writing, you can prompt children to say the word slowly; listen for the sounds; and write the sounds in order, with each sound represented by one or more letters. When a reader is attempting an unfamiliar word, you might prompt the child to think of the letter-to-sound relationships that provide a key to the word or to check on the reading to be sure that it "looks right."

Look

Readers and writers are pattern detectors and pattern users. Children learn to notice that there are common spelling patterns. They learn that you can read or write some words by thinking about the way they look (for example, *the* and *night*). They use this knowledge to visually analyze words in reading because they have internalized some basic patterns. For example, a reader does not need to "sound out" *ing* but simply recognizes the letter cluster any time it's added to the end of a word. Connecting words or word parts through common spelling patterns helps in generating new words. Spelling principles are complex, but they can be discovered through examining and sorting words into categories. To help children use the way words look, you can encourage them to try several patterns and think of other words with that pattern.

Mean

Readers and writers learn to recognize and use morphemic elements of words. They learn that you can read or write some words by thinking about what they mean (for example, *two*, *walkway*, or *sidewalk*). These basic meaning units of language form words, and word parts can be used both to figure out unfamiliar words and to build words. The building blocks include single words as well as morphemic units that add meaning (*man + ly = manly*). Prompting students to think about what the word means will help them discover the underlying patterns that will unlock the word. They can also try to find meaningful parts of known words that can be put together to form new words. The spelling of words is actually connected to the meaning in very logical ways, as children will discover when they have opportunities to work with words across time.

Connect

Readers and writers learn to make connections between words in many ways. They learn that you can use what you know about how a word sounds, how it looks, or what it means to figure out a new word (for example, if you know *stop* and *day*, you will be better able to figure out *stay*). The goal in connecting words is to develop a way of thinking about words. Encourage children to think of other words that are like this one in some way and use those connections to analyze the word.

Inquire

Readers and writers learn that they can use references and resources to learn more about words. The word study curriculum supports children in learning strategies that help them solve words in active ways. Some of these word-solving strategies are techniques that help them think about how words sound, how they look, and what they mean. Some techniques involve connecting words. Inquiry is a key process in word solving, so we want to be sure that children develop curiosity about words and constantly search for ways to connect them.

We want students to learn all of the skills that, ultimately, will make them independent. Young children quickly learn to use the wall charts that they make with the teacher and continue to add to over time; they use word walls and other references that are easily accessible. Ultimately, they will use the sophisticated support materials that adult readers and writers use, such as a thesaurus, dictionary, computer, and the Internet.

Reading and writing are different, but complementary, processes.

Even for adults, the process of reading contributes to writing and vice versa. Many of us have had the experience of reading something exciting and being inspired to write. At a deeper level, the meanings and language patterns that we internalize from wide reading become available to us as writers. Through writing, even as adults, we learn more about reading. For example, writing a mystery, a research report, or a poem helps the writer know much more about how the text is structured to convey meaning to the reader and promotes appreciation and a sharper noticing of the writer's craft. In a sense, writers write with reading in mind and readers read with writing in mind.

There seems to be reciprocity in terms of reading vocabulary and writing vocabulary, and learning reading and writing involve developing many of the same understandings, including knowledge of:

■ How letters look.
■ The printer's code—the conventions of written language.
■ How letters and sounds are related.

- ▮ The way words are constructed using meaning, sound patterns, and word parts.
- ▮ The way the text is organized.
- ▮ How to work at several levels of a language hierarchy.

Readers and writers develop self-extending systems that enable them to expand their literacy expertise while they are reading and writing.

Readers and writers are not simply accumulating a collection of known words and a set of disparate skills. They are building a network of smoothly coordinated strategies. The system is making sense to them; one understanding is connected to another in a way that gives learning momentum. Readers and writers develop generative abilities that enable them to learn a great deal more. In other words, they are not just learning to read or write particular words. They are learning *how* to read and write. They are learning *how* to learn words because they are learning how words work.

No user of the language would be able to read or write very much if every word had to be learned in isolation. There are just too many words, and the learning would be inefficient. In fact, we never teach children all the words; they never learn all the words. They just learn ways of getting to them. The repertoire of words a reader or writer knows and uses is continually expanding because it is based on deeply held, active knowledge of how the structure of words is connected to meaning.

What Does a Balanced Approach to Literacy Education Mean?

In concluding his review of the research on learning to read, Stokes (Chapter 15) urges educators to transcend the debates of phonics and other approaches by working for a "balanced approach" to literacy education. We do not believe that creating a balanced approach means starting with a literature-based program and *putting in* some systematic phonics instruction; nor do we believe that

it involves adding some experiences with literature to a curriculum that is essentially composed of lessons on decoding in a classroom where the primary materials are controlled texts. Instead, we think of "balance" not as the *literal answer* but as a word that will *help us begin to think* about what the curriculum should be like.

We believe the key to excellent literacy education is not in combining approaches; it is based on our understanding—as teachers—of how children learn oral and written language and how language systems are structured. Thinking about the curriculum as "eclectic"—a little of this and that sprinkled into the school day—will fragment our efforts and lead to inefficient and ineffective teaching.

An excellent language and literacy curriculum provides for varied reading and writing activities, all of which engage children in meaningful literacy (Routman 1991, 1993). Just as it is for adults, language for children must be connected. In this book, we have turned our attention to the design of a curriculum to support children's becoming effective word solvers in reading (phonics) and writing (spelling), but we have not limited our view to the focused types of activities that comprise word study, no matter how powerful or interesting they may be. Children are word solvers throughout the school day as they use language in many ways. The conceptual model prompts us to think about word solving in reading, writing, and more focused experiences (see Fountas, Chapter 2).

There is a need for clarity in thinking and language as we consider our work in classrooms. For example, we are not teaching books or word study activities; we are teaching children to be word solvers. When people say that we need to teach phonics, they really mean that we need to teach children to read, using all strategies—including word solving—effectively. When they say that we need to teach spelling, they really mean that children must learn to use the conventions that are necessary to communicate effectively.

Those are very important goals for the literacy curriculum.

Refining Our Understandings

Meeting the literacy challenge means ensuring that all children have access to literacy through participation in an organized, high-quality, instructional program. Good teaching for every child, every year, is essential. The literacy opportunities for any child depend on the teaching decisions made every day related to the child's learning.

We can achieve our goals if we carefully consider decisions, refining our understandings through the acts of teaching. This act of reflection has more promise for effective literacy education than purchasing programs or swinging from one political position to another.

We support children's learning because what we say and what we do is consistent with what we have learned from the children we teach. Because we have listened carefully to them as learners, observing their behavior closely over time and using that information to inform our teaching day by day and moment by moment, we establish our theory on a solid base.

Instead of relying on a collection of "do's and don'ts" that we have been taught or read, we are constantly testing every approach and interaction against the evidence of learning on the part of the children we teach. In talking with colleagues, we reflect on our teaching decisions and evaluate them in terms of children's learning. When we share our insights and the data from our teaching, we are able to engage in dialogue that refines our beliefs and builds new understandings. We are able to challenge ourselves as learners.

The goal of literacy improvement in our schools offers a great challenge. Meeting that challenge means listening to many voices, including those of children. In the conversation will be the ongoing development of new understandings about word matters.

Bibliography

Professional Books and Resources

Adams, M. J. 1990. *Beginning to Read: Thinking and Learning About Print.* Cambridge, MA: MIT Press.

Askew, B. J., & I. C. Fountas. 1998. "Building an Early Reading Process: Active from the Start!" *The Reading Teacher* 52: 2–10.

Askew, B. J., & D. F. Frasier. Unpublished manuscript. Early Writing: An Exploration of Literacy Opportunities.

Bachman, J. 1983. "The Role of Psycholinguistic Skills in Reading Acquisition: A Look at Early Readers." *Reading Research Quarterly* 18: 466–479.

Balmuth, M. 1982. *The Roots of Phonics: A Historical Introduction.* New York: Teachers College Press.

Baron, J. 1977. "Mechanisms for Pronouncing Printed Words: Use and Acquisition." In *Basic Processes in Reading: Perception and Comprehension*, eds. D. LaBerge and S. J. Samuels, 176–216. Hillsdale, NJ: Lawrence Erlbaum.

Bear, D. R., & D. Barone. 1989. "Using Children's Spellings to Group for Word Study and Directed Reading in the Primary Classroom." *Reading Psychology* 10: 275–292.

Bear, D., M. Invernizzi, S. Templeton, & F. Johnston. 1996. *Words Their Way: Word Study for Phonics, Vocabulary, and Spelling.* Columbus, OH: Merrill.

Bissex, G. 1980. *GNYS AT WRK: A Child Learns to Write and Read.* Cambridge, MA: Harvard University Press.

Bloomfield, L. 1933. *Language.* New York: Holt, Rinehart and Winston.

Bodrova, E., & D. L. Leong. 1996. *Tools of the Mind: The Vygotskian Approach to Early Childhood Education.* Columbus, OH: Merrill.

Booth, D. 1994. *Spelling Links.* Markham, ONT: Pembroke.

———. 1997. *Literacy Techniques.* Markham, ONT: Pembroke.

Bredekamp, S., & C. Copple, eds. 1997. *Developmentally Appropriate Practice in Early Childhood Programs.* Washington, DC: National Association for the Education of Young Children.

Bruck, M., & R. Treiman. 1992. "Learning to Pronounce Words: The Limitations of Analogies." *Reading Research Quarterly* 27: 374–388.

Bruner, J. S. 1983. *Beyond the Information Given: Studies in the Psychology of Knowing.* New York: Norton.

Buchanan, E. 1989. *Spelling for Whole Language Classrooms.* Winnepeg, Manitoba: Whole Language Consultants.

Button, K., M. Johnson, and P. Furgerson. 1996. "Interactive Writing in a Primary Classroom." *The Reading Teacher* 49 (6): 446–454.

Calkins, L. M. 1986. *The Art of Teaching Writing.* 2d ed. Portsmouth, NH: Heinemann.

———. 1991. *Living Between the Lines.* Portsmouth, NH: Heinemann.

Carbo, M. 1988. "Debunking the Great Phonics Myth." *Phi Delta Kappan* 70 (3): 226–240.

Cazden, C. B. 1988. *Classroom Discourse: The*

Language and Teaching of Learning. Portsmouth, NH: Heinemann.

———. 1992. "How Knowledge About Language Helps the Classroom Teacher—Or Does It? A Personal Account." In *Whole Language Plus: Essays on Literacy in the United States and New Zealand*, ed. C. Cazden. New York: Teachers College Press.

Center, Y., K. Wheldall, L. Freeman, L. Outhred, & M. McNaught. 1995. "An Evaluation of Reading Recovery." *Reading Research Quarterly* 30 (2): 240–263.

Chall, J. S. 1967. *Learning to Read: The Great Debate.* New York: McGraw-Hill.

———. 1983. *Learning to Read: The Great Debate.* Updated ed. New York: McGraw-Hill.

———. 1989. "Learning to Read: The Great Debate Twenty Years Later: A Response to 'Debunking the Great Phonics Myth.'" *Phi Delta Kappan* 70 (7): 521–538.

Chomsky, C. 1971. "Write First, Read Later." *Childhood Education* 47: 296–299.

———. 1972. "Write Now, Read Later." In *Language in Early Childhood Education*, ed. Courtney B. Cazden. Washington, DC: Association for Education of Young Children.

Chomsky, N., & M. Halle. 1968. *The Sound Patterns of English.* New York: Harper & Row.

Chukovsky, K. 1927/1963. *From Two to Five.* Berkeley: University of California Press.

Clarke, L. K. 1988. "Invented Versus Traditional Spelling in First Graders' Writings: Effects on Learning to Spell and Read." *Research in the Teaching of English* 22: 281–309.

Clay, M. M. 1966. Emergent Reading Behaviour. Ph.D. Diss., University of Auckland, New Zealand.

———. 1975. *What Did I Write?* Portsmouth, NH: Heinemann.

———. 1979. *The Early Detection of Reading Difficulties.* 3d ed. Portsmouth, NH: Heinemann.

———. 1982. *Observing Young Readers.* Portsmouth, NH: Heinemann.

———. 1991a. *Becoming Literate: The Construction of Inner Control.* Portsmouth, NH: Heinemann.

———. 1991b. "Introducing a New Storybook to Young Readers." *The Reading Teacher.* 45: 264–273.

———. 1991c. "Developmental Learning Puzzles Me." *Australian Journal of Reading* 14 (4): 263–275.

———. 1993a. *An Observation Survey of Early Literacy Achievement.* Portsmouth, NH: Heinemann.

———. 1993b. *Reading Recovery: A Guidebook for Teachers in Training.* Portsmouth, NH: Heinemann.

———. 1998. *By Different Paths to Common Outcomes.* York, ME: Stenhouse.

Cooper, R. P., & R. N. Aslin. 1989. "The Language Environment of the Young Infant: Implications for Early Perceptual Development." *Canadian Journal of Psychology* 43 (2): 247–265.

Cramer, R. L. 1993. Spelling. Paper presented at the George Graham Lectures in Reading, University of Virginia, Charlottesville, Virginia.

Cummings, D. 1988. *American English Spelling: An Informal Description.* Baltimore, MD: Johns Hopkins Univeristy Press.

Cunningham, P. M. 1995. *Phonics They Use: Words for Reading and Writing.* 2d ed. New York: HarperCollins.

Cunningham, P. M., & R. L. Allington. 1999. *Classrooms That Work: They Can All Read and Write.* 2d ed. New York: HarperCollins.

Cunningham, P. M., & J. W. Cunningham. 1992. "Making Words: Enhancing the Invented Spelling-Decoding Connection." *The Reading Teacher* 46: 106–115.

Cunningham, P. M., & D. P. Hall. 1994a *Making Words.* Carthage, IL: Good Apple.

———. 1994b. *Making Big Words.* Carthage, IL: Good Apple.

———. 1997a. *Making More Words.* Carthage, IL: Good Apple.

———. 1997b. *Making More Big Words.* Carthage, IL: Good Apple.

———. 1997c. *Month by Month Phonics for First Grade: Systematic, Multilevel Instruction.* Greensboro, NC: Carson-Dellosa.

———. 1998a. *Month by Month Phonics for the Upper Grades: A Second Chance for Struggling Readers and Students Learning English.* Greensboro, NC: Carson-Dellosa.

———. 1998b. *Month by Month Phonics for Third Grade: Systematic, Multilevel Instruction.* Greensboro, NC: Carson-Dellosa.

DeCasper, A. J., & W. P. Fifer. 1980. "Of Human Bonding: Newborns Prefer Their Mothers' Voices." *Science* 208: 1174–1176.

DeCasper, A. J., & M. Spense. 1986. "Prenatal Maternal Speech Influences Newborns' Perception of Speech Sounds." *Infant Behavior and Development* 9: 133–150.

Dunn, S. 1987. *Butterscotch Dreams.* Markham, ONT: Pembroke.

Durkin, D. 1966. *Children Who Read Early.* New York: Teachers College Press.

Edelsky, C., B. Altwerger, & B. Flores. 1991. *Whole Language: What's the Difference?* Portsmouth, NH: Heinemann.

Ehri, L. C., & C. Robbins. 1992. "Beginners Need Some Decoding Skill to Read by Analogy." *Reading Research Quarterly* 22: 12–26.

Fitzsimmons, R. J., & B. M. Loomer. 1978. *Spelling: Learning and Instruction.* Des Moines: Iowa State Department of Public Instruction. ERIC ED 176 285.

Flesch, R. 1955. *Why Johnny Can't Read and What You Can Do About It.* New York: Harper & Bros.

Fodor, J. A., T. G. Bever, & M. F. Garrett. 1974. *The Psychology of Language.* New York: Mc-Graw-Hill.

Fountas, I. C., & G. S. Pinnell. 1996. *Guided Reading: Good First Teaching for All Children.* Portsmouth, NH: Heinemann.

Fries, C. 1963. *Linguistics and Reading.* New York: Holt, Rinehart and Winston.

Frith, U. 1980. *Cognitive Processes in Spelling.* London: Academic Press.

Gentry, J. R., & J. W. Gillet. 1993. *Teaching Kids to Spell.* Portsmouth, NH: Heinemann.

Gettinger, M. 1993. "Effects of Invented Spelling and Direct Instruction on Spelling Performance of Second-Grade Boys." *Journal of Applied Behavior Analysis* 26: 281–291.

Giacobbe, M. E. 1981a. "Kids *Can* Write the First Week of School." *Learning* 10: 130–132.

———. 1981b. "Who Says That Children Can't Write the First Week of School?" In *Donald Graves in Australia,* ed. R. D. Walshe. Rozelle, NSW: Primary English Teachers Association. Distributed in the U.S. by Heinemann.

Goswami, U., & P. E. Bryant. 1990. *Phonological Skills and Learning to Read.* Hillsdale, NJ: Lawrence Erlbaum.

Graves, D. H. 1983. *Writing: Teachers and Children at Work.* Portsmouth, NH: Heinemann.

———. 1994. *A Fresh Look at Writing.* Portsmouth, NH: Heinemann.

Hall, D. P., & P. M. Cunningham. 1997. *Reading and Writing for Kindergarten: Systematic, Multilevel Instruction.* Greensboro, NC: Carson-Dellosa.

———. 1998. *Month by Month Phonics for Second Grade: Systematic, Multilevel Instruction.* Greensboro, NC: Carson-Dellosa.

Hall, D. P., P. M. Cunningham, & J. W. Cunningham. 1995. "Multilevel Spelling Instruction in Third Grade Classrooms." In *Perspectives on Literacy Research and Practice,* eds. K. A. Hinchman, D. J. Leu, & C. K. Kinzer. Forty-fourth Yearbook of the National Reading Conference. Chicago: National Reading Conference.

Hall, M. 1981. *Teaching Reading as a Language Experience.* 3d ed. Columbus, OH: Merrill.

Hanna, P., R. Hodges, & J. Hanna. 1971. *Spelling: Structure and Strategies.* Boston: Houghton Mifflin.

Henderson, E. H. 1981. *Learn to Read and Spell: The Child's Knowledge of Words.* DeKalb: Northern Illinois University Press.

———. 1990. *Teaching Spelling.* 2d ed. Boston: Houghton Mifflin.

Henderson, E., T. Estes, & S. Stonecash. 1972. "An Exploratory Study of Word Acquisition Among First Graders at Midyear in a Language Experience Approach." *Journal of Reading Behavior* 4: 21–30.

Henry, J., & B. J. Wiley. 1996. *Interactive Writing for the Very First Time: Helpful Hints.* Columbus: The Ohio State University Early Literacy Learning Initiative.

Hodges, R. E. 1977. "In Adam's Fall: A Brief History of Spelling Instruction in the United States." In *Reading and Writing Instruction in the United States: Historical Trends,* ed. H. Alan Robinson. Newark, DE: International Reading Association.

Holdaway, D. 1979. *The Foundations of Literacy.* Sydney: Ashton Scholastic.

Horn, E. 1929. "The Influence of Past Experiences upon Spelling." *Journal of Education Research* 19: 283–288.

Hudelson, S. 1981–1982. "An Introductory Examination of Children's Invented Spelling in Spanish." *NABE Journal* 6 (2–3): 53–67.

Huey, E. B. 1908/1968. *The Psychology and Pedagogy of Reading.* Cambridge, MA: MIT Press.

Hughes, M., & D. Searle. 1997. *The Violent E and Other Tricky Sounds.* York, ME: Stenhouse.

Invernizzi, M., M. Abouzeid, & J. T. Gill. 1994. "Using Students' Invented Spellings as a Guide for Spelling Instruction That Emphasizes Word Study." *The Elementary School Journal* 95 (2): 155–167.

Jenkins, C. 1996. *Inside the Writing Portfolio: What We Need to Know to Assess Children's Writing.* Portsmouth, NH: Heinemann.

Johnston, P. 1992. *Constructive Evaluation of Literate Activity.* New York: Longman.

———. 1997. *Knowing Literacy: Constructive Literacy Assessment.* York, ME: Stenhouse.

Kamii, C., & M. Randazzo. 1985. "Social Interaction and Invention Spelling." *Language Arts* 62: 124–133.

Kudlinski, K. V. 1991. *Helen Keller: A Light for the Blind*. New York: Puffin Books.

Kuhn, T. 1962. *The Structure of Scientific Revolutions*. Chicago: University of Chicago Press.

Laminack, L., & K. Wood. 1996. *Spelling in Use: Looking Closely at Spelling in Whole Language Classrooms*. Urbana, IL: National Council of Teachers of English.

Lee, D., & R. Van Allen. 1963. *Learning to Read Through Experience*. New York: Appleton-Century-Crofts.

Luria, A. R. 1973. *The Working Brain: An Introduction to Neuropsychology*. New York: Basic Books.

———. 1980. *Higher Cortical Functions in Man*. New York: Consultants Bureau.

Manolakes, G. 1975. "The Teaching of Spelling: A Pilot Study." *Elementary English* 52: 243–247.

Martin, B., Jr. 1972. *Instant Readers Teachers' Manual*. New York: Henry Holt.

McCarrier, A., & I. Patacca. 1994. "Children's Literature: The Focal Point of an Early Literacy Learning Program." In *Extending Charlotte's Web*, eds. B. Cullinan and J. Hickman. Norwood, MA: Christopher-Gordon.

McKenzie, M. G. 1985. "Shared Writing: Apprenticeship in Writing." *Literacy Matters (1 & 2)*. England: Ilea Center for Language in Primary Education.

Mehler, J., P. W. Jusczyk, G. Lambertz, N. Halsted, J. Bertoncini, & C. Amiel-Tison. 1988. "A Precursor of Language Acquisition in Young Infants." *Cognition* 29: 143–178.

Moats, L. C. 1983. "A Comparison of the Spelling Errors of Older Dyslexic and Second-Grade Normal Children." *Annals of Dyslexia* 33: 121–140.

———. 1995. *Spelling: Development, Disability, and Instruction*. Baltimore: York Press.

Moffett, J. & B. J. Wagner. 1993. "What Works in Play." *Language Arts* 70 (January).

Moore, B. 1985. *Words That Taste Good*. Markham, Ontario: Pembroke.

Morris, D. 1992. Learning to Spell in Third-Grade Classrooms. Paper presented at the National Reading Conference, December, San Antonio, Texas.

Mudre, L. 1994. *Checklist for Interactive Writing*. Columbus: The Ohio State University Early Literacy Learning Initiative.

Mullis, I., et al. 1994. *NAEP 1992 Trends in Academic Progress*. Princeton, NJ: Educational Testing Service. ERIC ED 378 237.

Nelson, H. E. 1980. "Analysis of Spelling Errors in Normal and Dyslexic Children." In *Cognitive Processes in Spelling*, ed. U. Frith. New York: Academic Press.

Parker, F. W. 1894. *Talks on Pedagogics*. New York: E. L. Kellogg.

Paul, R. 1976. "Invented Spelling in Kindergarten." *Young Children* 31: 195–200.

Peterson, R., & M. Eeds. 1990. *Grand Conversations: Literature Groups in Action*. New York: Scholastic.

Pinnell, G. S., & A. McCarrier. 1994. "Interactive Writing: A Transition Tool for Assisting Children in Learning to Read and Write." In *Getting Reading Right from the Start: Effective Early Literacy Interventions*, eds. E. Hiebert and B. Taylor. Needham Heights, MA: Allyn & Bacon.

Pinnell, G. S., & I. C. Fountas. 1997. *Help America Read: A Handbook for Volunteers*. Portsmouth, NH: Heinemann.

———. 1998. *Word Matters: Teaching Phonics and Spelling in the Reading/Writing Classroom*. Portsmouth, NH: Heinemann.

Powell, D., & D. Hornsby. 1993. *Learning Phonics and Spelling in a Whole Language Classroom*. New York: Scholastic.

Radebaugh, M. R. 1985. "Children's Perceptions of Their Spelling Strategies." *Reading Teacher* 38: 532–536.

Read, C. 1970. Children's Perceptions of the Sounds of English: Phonology from Three to Six. Ph.D. diss., Harvard University.

———. 1971. "Pre-School Children's Knowledge of English Phonology." *Harvard Educational Review* 41 (1): 1–34.

———. 1975. *Children's Categorizations of Speech Sounds in English*. Research Report No. 17. Urbana, IL: National Council of Teachers of English.

———. 1986. *Children's Creative Spelling*. Boston: Routledge & Kegan Paul.

———. 1991. Literacy and Language Variations. Address delivered at the George Graham Lecture in Reading. Williamsburg, Virginia, February.

Rogoff, B. 1990. *Apprenticeship in Thinking: Cognitive Development in Social Context*. New York: Oxford University Press.

Rosenshine, B., & R. Stevens. 1984. "Classroom Instruction in Reading." In *The Handbook of Reading Research*, eds. P. D. Pearson, R. Barr, M. L. Kamil, and P. Mosenthal, 745–799. New York: Longman.

Routman, R. 1991. *Invitations: Changing as Teachers and Learners K–12*. Portsmouth, NH: Heinemann.

———. 1993. "The Uses and Abuses of Invented Spelling." *Instructor* 102: 36–40.

Schickedanz, J. A. 1990. *Adam's Righting Revolutions: One Child's Literacy Development from Infancy Through Grade One*. Portsmouth, NH: Heinemann.

Shannon, P. 1989. *Broken Promises: Reading Instruction in Twentieth-Century America*. New York: Bergin and Garvey.

Smith, F. 1982. *Writing and the Writer*. New York: Holt, Rinehart, and Winston.

———. 1994. *Understanding Reading*. Hillsdale, NJ: Lawrence Erlbaum.

Stauffer, R. 1980. *The Language Experience Approach to the Teaching of Reading*. 2d ed. New York: Harper & Row.

Swartz, L. 1994. "Spelling Games." In *Spelling Links* by D. Booth. Markham, ONT: Pembroke.

Teale, W. H., & E. Sulzby. 1986. *Emergent Literacy: Writing and Reading*. Norwood, NJ: Ablex.

Templeton, S., & D. Bear, eds. 1992. *Development of Orthographic Knowledge and the Foundations of Literacy: Memorial Festschrift for Edmund H. Henderson*. New York: Lawrence Erlbaum.

Tierney, R. J., & T. Shanahan. 1991. "Research on the Reading-Writing Relationship: Interactions, Transactions, and Outcomes." In *The Handbook of Reading Research*, 2d ed., eds. P. D. Pearson, R. Barr, M. Kamil, and P. Mosenthal. New York: Longman.

Tierney, R., M. Carter, & L. Desai. 1991. *Portfolio Assessment in the Reading-Writing Classroom*. Norwood, MA: Christopher-Gordon.

Treiman, R. 1992. "The Role of Intrasyllabic Units in Learning to Read and Spell." In *Reading Acquistion*, eds. P. B. Gough, L. C. Ehri, and R. Treiman, 65–106. Hillsdale, NJ: Lawrence Erlbaum.

———. 1993. *Beginning to Spell: A Study of First-Grade Children*. New York: Oxford University Press.

Turner, R. 1989. "The 'Great' Debate: Can Both Carbo and Chall Be Right?" *Phi Delta Kappan* 71 (4): 276–283.

Venezky, R. 1970. *The Structure of English Orthography*. The Hague: Mouton.

Vygotsky, L. S. 1978. *Mind in Society: The Development of Higher Psychological Processes*, eds. M. Cole, V. John-Steiner, S. Scribner, and E. Souberman. Cambridge, MA: Harvard University Press.

———. 1986. *Thought and Language*. Cambridge, MA: MIT Press.

Weaver, C. 1994. *Reading Process and Practice: From Socio-Psycholinguistics to Whole Language*. 2d ed. Portsmouth, NH: Heinemann.

Weiner, S. 1994. "Four First Graders' Descriptions of How They Spell." *The Elementary School Journal* 94: 315–330.

Wilde, S. 1989. "Understanding Spelling Strategies: A Kid-Watcher's Guide to Spelling, Part 2." In *The Whole Language Evaluation Book*, eds. K. Goodman, Y. Goodman, & W. Hood. Portsmouth, NH: Heinemann.

———. 1992. *You Kan Red This! Spelling and Punctuation for Whole Language Classrooms, K–6*. Portsmouth, NH: Heinemann.

———. 1997. *What's a Schwa Sound Anyway? A Holistic Guide to Phonetics, Phonics, and Spelling*. Portsmouth, NH: Heinemann.

Wiley, B. J. 1994. The Construction of Curriculum and the Culture of Literacy in Three Kindergartens. Unpublished doctoral dissertation. The Ohio State University, Columbus, OH.

Wood, D. 1988. *How Children Think and Learn*. Oxford: Basil Blackwell.

Wood, D., J. Bruner, & G. Ross. 1976. "The Role of Tutoring in Problem Solving." *Journal of Child Psychology and Psychiatry* 17: 89–100.

Yolen, J. 1991. "The Route to Story." *The New Advocate* 4: 143–149.

Zutell, J. 1996. "The Direct Spelling Thinking Activity (DSTA): Providing an Effective Balance in Word Study Instruction." *The Reading Teacher* 50 (2): 98–108.

———. 1998. "Word Sorting: A Developmental Spelling Approach to Word Study for Delayed Readers." *Reading and Writing Quarterly* 14 (2): 219–238.

Children's Books

Agee, J. 1991. *Go Hang a Salami! I'm a Lasagna Hog! and Other Palindromes*. New York: HarperCollins.

Ahlberg, A., & J. Ahlberg. 1980. *Funnybones*. London: William Heinemann.

Base, G. 1987. *Animalia*. Toronto: Irwin.

Bloksberg, R. 1995. *The Hole in Harry's Pocket*. Boston: Houghton Mifflin.

Booth, D. 1993. *Dr. Knickerbocker and Other Rhymes*. Illus. M. Kovalski. Toronto: Kids Can Press.

Brown, M. W. 1977. *Goodnight Moon*. New York: HarperCollins.

Brown, M. 1983. *What Do You Call a Dumb Bunny? And Other Rabbit Riddles, Games,*

Jokes, and Cartoons. New York: Little, Brown.

Brown, R. 1981. *A Dark Tale.* New York: Scholastic.

Cleary, B. 1970. *Runaway Ralph.* New York: Morrow Junior Books.

Dahl, R. 1988. *Matilda.* New York: Viking.

Degen, B. 1983. *Jamberry.* New York: Harper & Row.

DePaola, T. 1981. *Fin M'Coul: The Giant of Knockmany Hill.* New York: Holiday House.

Domanska, J. 1969. *The Great Big Enormous Turnip.* New York: Macmillan.

Elting, M., & J. Folsom. 1980. *Q Is for Duck: An Alphabet Guessing Game.* New York: Clarion.

Fitch, S. 1992. *There Were Monkeys in My Kitchen.* Toronto: Doubleday Canada.

Folsom, M., and M. Folsom. 1985. *Easy as Pie: A Guessing Game of Sayings.* New York: Clarion.

Funk, C. E. 1948. *A Hog on Ice and Other Curious Expressions.* New York: Harper & Row.

Galdone, P. 1979. *The Three Little Pigs.* New York: Houghton Mifflin.

Gwynne, F. 1970. *The King Who Rained.* New York: Dutton.

———. 1976. *Chocolate Moose for Dinner.* New York: Dutton.

———. 1980. *The Sixteen Hand Horse.* New York: Prentice Hall.

———. 1984. *A Little Pigeon Toad.* New York: Simon & Schuster.

Hawkins, C., & J. Hawkins. 1990. *Knock! Knock!* London: Walker.

Heller, R. 1987. *A Cache of Jewels and Other Collective Nouns.* New York: Putnam.

———. 1988. *Kites Sail High: A Book About Verbs.* New York: Putnam.

———. 1989. *Many Luscious Lollipops: A Book About Adjectives.* New York: Putnam.

———. 1990. *Merry-Go-Round: A Book About Nouns.* New York: Putnam.

Hennessy, G. G. 1990. *Jake Baked the Cake.* New York: Viking Penguin.

Keller, C. 1991. *Daffynitions.* New York: Simon & Schuster.

Koch, M. 1989. *Just One More.* New York: Greenwillow.

———. 1991. *Hoot Howl Hiss.* New York: Greenwillow.

Kovalski, M. 1987. *The Wheels on the Bus.* Toronto: Kids Can Press.

Lear, E. 1994. *There Was an Old Man . . . A Collection of Limericks.* Toronto: Kids Can Press.

Lee, D. 1970. *Garbage Delight.* New York: Macmillan.

———. 1977. *Nicholas Knock & Other Rhymes.* New York: Macmillan.

———. 1983. *Jelly Belly.* New York: Macmillan.

———. 1987. *Alligator Pie.* New York: Macmillan.

LeSieg, T. 1972. *In a People House.* New York: Random House.

Lester, A. 1989. *Rosie Sips Spiders.* New York: Houghton Mifflin.

Limburg, P. R. 1989. *Weird! The Complete Book of Halloween.* New York: Macmillan.

Lottridge, C. 1986. *One Watermelon Seed.* Toronto: Oxford University Press.

McPhail, D. 1993. *Pigs Aplenty, Pigs Galore!* New York: Dutton.

———. 1995. *Pigs Ahoy!* New York: Dutton.

———. 1996. *Those Can-Do Pigs.* New York: Dutton.

Maestro, G. 1986. *What's Mite Might? Homophone Riddles to Boost Your Word Power!* New York: Clarion.

———. 1984. *What's a Frank Frank? Tasty Homograph Riddles.* New York: Clarion.

Mahurin, T. 1995. *Jeremy Kooloo.* New York: Dutton.

Maizels, J. 1996. *The Amazing Pop-up Grammar Book.* New York: Dutton.

Martin, B. Jr. 1970. *Brown Bear, Brown Bear.* New York: Holt, Rinehart and Winston.

Marshall, J. 1989. *The Three Little Pigs.* New York: E. P. Dutton.

Mayer, M. 1973. *What Do You Do with a Kangaroo.* New York: Four Winds Press.

Moore, B. 1985. *Words That Taste Good.* Markham, ONT: Pembroke.

Most, B. 1990a. *The Cow that Went Oink.* New York: Harcourt Brace.

———. 1990b. *There's an Ant in Anthony and Pets in Trumpets.* New York: William Morrow.

———. 1991. *Pets in Trumpets and Other Word Play Riddles.* Orlando: Harcourt Brace Jovanovich.

———. 1992. *Zoodles.* Orlando: Harcourt Brace Jovanovich.

O'Connor, J. 1986. *The Teeny Tiny Woman.* Illus. R. W. Alley. New York: Random House.

Pilkey, D. 1997. *The Dumb Bunnies Go to the Zoo.* New York: Scholastic.

Polacco, P. 1995. *Babushka's Mother Goose.* New York: Philomel.

Prelutsky, J. 1996. *A Pizza the Size of the Sun.* New York: Greenwillow.

Rankin, L. 1991. *The Handmade Alphabet.* New York: Dial.

Roop, P. 1984. *Go Hog Wild!* New York: Lerner.

Rylant, C. 1987. *Henry & Mudge.* New York: Simon & Schuster.

Schwartz, A. 1973. *Tomfoolery: Trickery and Foolery with Words.* New York: J. B. Lippincott.

———. 1979. *Chin Music: Tall Talk and Other Talk.* New York: J. B. Lippincott.

———. 1982. *The Cat's Elbow and Other Secret Languages.* New York: Farrar, Straus & Giroux.

———. 1990. *Flapdoodle.* New York: HarperCollins.

———. 1992. *Busy Buzzing Bumblebees and Other Tongue Twisters.* New York: HarperCollins.

Seeger, P. 1986. *Abiyoyo: Based on a South African Lullaby and Folk Tale.* New York: Macmillan.

Seuss, Dr. 1957. *The Cat in the Hat.* New York: Beginner Books.

———. 1960a. *Green Eggs and Ham.* New York: Beginner Books.

———. 1960b. *One Fish Two Fish Red Fish Blue Fish.* New York: Beginner Books.

———. 1970. *Mr. Brown Can Moo, Can You?* New York: Beginner Books.

Shannon, G. 1996. *Tomorrow's Alphabet.* Illus. D. Crews. New York: Greenwillow.

Shaw, N. 1989. *Sheep on a Ship.* New York: Houghton Mifflin.

Spier, P. 1972. *Crash! Bang! Boom!* New York: Dutton.

———. 1988. *Gobble Growl Grunt.* New York: Doubleday.

Steig, W. 1968. *CDB.* New York: Windmill.

———. 1971. *Amos and Boris.* New York: Farrar, Straus & Giroux.

———. 1984. *CDC.* New York: Farrar, Straus & Giroux.

Sterne, N. 1979. *Tyrannosaurs Wrecks: A Book of Dinosaur Riddles.* New York: Crowell.

Terban, M. 1982. *Eight Ate: A Feast of Homonym Riddles.* New York: Clarion.

———. 1983. *In a Pickle and Other Funny Idioms.* New York: Clarion.

———. 1984. *I Think I Thought and Other Tricky Verbs.* New York: Clarion.

———. 1985. *Too Hot to Hoot: A Collection of Funny Palindrome Riddles.* New York: Clarion.

———. 1986. *Your Foot's on My Feet and Other Tricky Nouns.* New York: Clarion.

———. 1988. *The Dove Dove: Funny Homograph Riddles.* New York: Clarion.

———. 1989. *Superdupers!* New York: Clarion.

———. 1992. *Funny You Should Ask.* New York: Clarion.

Thaler, M. 1986. *King Kong's Underwear.* New York: Avon.

Van Allsburg, C. 1985. *The Polar Express.* Boston: Houghton Mifflin.

Wood, A. 1984. *The Napping House.* New York: Harcourt Brace.

———. 1992. *Silly Sally.* San Diego: Harcourt Brace.

Wood, J. 1992. *Moo Moo Brown Cow.* San Diego: Harcourt Brace.

Contributors

Billie J. Askew is a Professor of Reading in the Department of Reading and Bilingual Education at Texas Woman's University. Her professional interests include early literacy and the prevention of reading difficulties, and specific research interests include exploration of comprehending processes and writing behaviors of young readers and writers.

David Booth is a Professor of Education at The Ontario Institute for Studies in Education of the University of Toronto where he teaches both preservice and graduate courses in the arts in education, drama, literacy, and children's literature. He is also the Coordinator of the Elementary Program at OISE/UT. He is the author of *Literacy Techniques* and *Guiding the Reading Process*, both published by Stenhouse.

Patricia M. Cunningham is a Professor at Wake Forest University in Winston-Salem, North Carolina. She received her B.A. from the University of Rhode Island, her M.A. from Florida State University, and her Ph.D. from the University of Georgia. In addition to university teaching, she worked for ten years in public school positions, including teaching first grade, fourth grade, and remedial reading, and serving as curriculum coor-

dinator and director of reading. Dr. Cunningham has published numerous articles, coauthored several reading textbooks, and with Richard Allington coauthored *Classrooms That Work: They Can ALL Read and Write* and *Schools That Work: Where All Children Read and Write*. Her major interest is in finding alternative teaching strategies for students commonly classified as "at risk."

Diane E. DeFord is a Professor in the School of Teaching and Learning at The Ohio State University. She is a classroom teacher and also tutors children in the Reading Recovery program. She is the author/editor of *Bridges to Literacy: Learning from Reading Recovery* and *Partners in Learning: Teachers and Children in Reading Recovery*. She has also authored numerous articles that appear in professional journals as well as several children's books, including *The Day Miss Francie Got Skunked*. She has worked to develop comprehensive assessment systems for improving school practice and also directs the AmeriCorps for Literacy and Math, a service project of The Ohio State University.

Irene C. Fountas is a Professor in the School of Education at Lesley College in Cambridge, Massachusetts. She has been a classroom teacher, a language arts specialist, and a consultant in school districts across the nation and abroad. She directs the Early Literacy Project and other field-based projects.

Dorothy P. Hall graduated from Worcester State College in Massachusetts with a B.S. in Elementary Education, and received her M.Ed., C.A.S., and Ed.D. from the University of North Carolina, Greensboro. She has taught first, second, third, and fourth grades and also at the college level. Dottie is currently a curriculum coordinator in the Winston-Salem/Forsyth County Schools. She has written journal articles and chapters for edited collections, and has coauthored ten books with Patricia Cunningham. Dottie works with teachers, schools, and school systems around the country to implement the strategies she write and talks about.

Justina Henry earned a Ph.D. at Kent State University, Kent, Ohio. She has been a Head Start, kindergarten, and first grade teacher, worked as a Title I reading teacher, and later was a Reading Recovery teacher leader. Justina served as an associate editor for *The Reading Teacher*, a journal of the International Reading Association (IRA), and received the Literacy Award of the Ohio Council of the IRA in 1993. Currently, Justina is a program coordinator and trainer for Literacy Collaborative at The Ohio State University.

Susan Hundley is an Assistant Professor at Lesley College in Cambridge, Massachusetts. She has taught primary grade children for many years and has worked extensively with children experiencing literacy difficulties. Her current work centers on collaborating with schools to provide effective comprehensive literacy instruction.

Carol Brennan Jenkins has worked in the field of literacy for twenty-five years as a classroom teacher, reading specialist, and teacher educator. She currently teaches courses in literacy at Boston University and coordinates the Elementary Education pro-

gram. She also works side-by-side with teachers in classrooms, tapping their expertise and supporting their efforts. She is the recipient of the Massachusetts Reading Association and the International Reading Association's Celebrate Literacy Award. She is the author of *Inside the Writing Portfolio: What We Need to Know to Assess Children's Writing*, published by Heinemann.

Carol A. Lyons is a Professor of Education at The Ohio State University. She has been teaching graduate courses and conducting research on literacy learning and teacher development for more than twenty years. For the last fifteen years, Dr. Lyons has been teaching Reading Recovery students and examining teachers' thinking, decision making, curriculum development, and practice. She has published numerous articles in the field of reading disability, teacher and student learning, and literacy instruction, and is the coauthor of *Partners in Learning: Teachers and Children in Reading Recovery* and *Bridges to Literacy*.

Andrea McCarrier received her Ph.D. from The Ohio State University. Presently she is the director of the Literacy Collaborative at The Ohio State University. The Literacy Collaborative is a project that trains a building teacher to provide long-term staff development for the building staff.

Ida Patacca teaches kindergarten in the Columbus, Ohio, public schools. For the past ten years she has collaborated with the Literacy Collaborative staff in the development of training materials for that project.

Gay Su Pinnell is a Professor in the School of Teaching and Learning at The Ohio State University. She has extensive experience in classroom teaching and field-based research, and in developing comprehensive approaches to literacy education.

Diane Powell is both an experienced primary grade teacher and a teacher who has provided specialized literacy instruction to children who experience difficulty learning to read and write. She is currently an Assistant Professor at Lesley College in Cambridge, Massachusetts, where she works with teachers and schools to provide effective literacy instruction for all children.

William Stokes, Ed.D., is a Professor at Lesley College, Director of the Hood Children's Literacy Project, and Co-Director of the Literacy Institute. Emergent literacy is his principal area of interest, and he has undertaken research on language development and literacy for more than twenty years. Current areas of exploration include the ability of children to become literate in social contexts of home and school, as well as the conditions of second language acquisition and consequences for literacy (and bi-literacy) for linguistic minority children.

Sandra Wilde is Professor of Curriculum and Instruction at Portland State University in Oregon. She is the author, co-author, or editor of seven books, including two about spelling and phonics: *What's a Schwa Sound Anyway?: A Holistic Guide to Phonetics, Phonics, and Spelling* and *You Kan Red This! Spelling and Punctuation for Whole Language Classrooms, K–6*. Both are published by Heinemann.

Barbara Joan Wiley is a program coordinator for the Literacy Collaborative at The Ohio State University, where she works with teachers as they train to become literacy coordinators in their schools. She has been a classroom teacher and reading specialist in school districts across the nation and abroad.

Jerry Zutell is a Professor at The Ohio State University, where he teaches courses on literacy learning and teaching. He is most interested in the development, assessment, and instruction of children's word knowledge. Dr. Zutell is the developer of the Directed Thinking Spelling Activity (DSTA) and one of the senior authors on the Zaner-Bloser Spell It—Write! spelling series.

Index